Unleashed

A storyteller's odyssey

Roger Van Noord

To Jessica,
who failed to teach Mac
basic elements of banking

CONTENTS

Preface

Al MacLeese was a remarkable storyteller.

The greatest story he never told, except in bits and pieces, was about his life. He could deftly organize his newspaper column from beginning to end but was intimidated by writing anything more substantial.

On numerous occasions over more than 40 years of friendship, I pressed Mac to write his biography. I wasn't alone. Others who heard his unforgettable stories about the Navy and the hard-drinking era of journalism told him he had to write a book.

A year before he died in Maine, I began reading "The Guernsey Literary and Potato Peel Pie Society," a novel composed of a series of letters about life on that Channel Island during the German occupation in World War II. The exchange of letters creates a compelling narrative of war stories.

MacLeese had his own "war stories" – his escapades, often related to his ongoing battle with alcoholism and his life on the edge. In his distinctive manner, he wrote about many of those experiences in our correspondence.

That gave me the idea, which I broached to him, to use that correspondence as a way to tell some of those stories and illustrate his "unique personality." I told him: "We could write a section of your biography, with flashbacks, through our actual email exchange." He seemed receptive.

When he died after a fall in 2012, I wondered if he had started a life history. Alas, he left no diary, no journal, and apparently no fragments of an autobiography.

In a variation of my "Potato Peel Pie" idea, I decided to write his biography with him providing much of the narrative himself through his often biographical columns and through our correspondence, including 250 emails and letters from him after he left Michigan and moved to Hallowell, Maine, a decade before he died.

Although some of the emails and letters are short, many could stand alone as columns about incidents in his life, before and during his years in Hallowell. Recognizing their quality, one could view them as an extension of a columnist's career cut too short.

Through that correspondence and his columns, he is involved in telling his life story, in his own words, with his own flair, his own delicious detail. In the manner of "Potato Peel Pie," his correspondence helps create something more personal, more earthy and less filtered than a column written with an eye toward public consumption.

In general, I found him to be an honest broker when dealing with his history, especially in describing his frailties. Like many storytellers, though, in order to tell a more captivating story, he took license to romanticize certain anecdotes or make them more humorous.

It's hard to imagine his grittier episodes, or his repetitively self-destructive behavior, being funny to a wife, or a friend, at the time.

He was a complex man, and much of his complexity could be traced to alcoholism. He was self-centered (often saying: "It's all about me") and also generous; he could be seen as unlikeable and as "the most charming human being ... and such good company."

The correspondence begins with an email he wrote on Christmas Eve, 2002, setting the scene in Hallowell, where he moved from Bridgeport, Michigan, a year and a half after his fourth wife died. It continues in sequence, ending with a letter written nearly 10 years later, three weeks before his death.

Not all of our correspondence during that period still exists. I didn't begin saving his emails and letters until I realized how much effort he put into them and how much I enjoyed re-reading them.

He took care with his writing and occasionally pointed out nuggets that he feared had been missed. He was irritated by a typo or a missing word that he noticed after sending an email.

I corrected punctuation and other obvious mistakes, typos and misspellings, which seemed to occur more often when he had too much to drink. For the most part, his email "copy" was clean, as we said in the newspaper business, befitting the best of copy editors.

His vocabulary was prodigious, and I found myself going to the dictionary often. Several "typos" turned out to be words. His language could be brutal, poetic and coarse; he sprinkled in numerous variations of the F-word, salt suitable for the drunken sailor he once was.

The existing correspondence is not presented in its entirety. Much of the editing was done because of privacy concerns, repetitive or mundane issues, and matters that were considered too "inside baseball" or confusing, such as an investigation that obsessed him.

The locations of any cuts are indicated with an ellipsis, and with a fourth dot for the end of a sentence. [Square brackets indicate where information is added for context or identification purposes.]

Except where indicated, the correspondence is an email. Subject lines or headers for the emails and letters are those we put on them at the time.

To highlight his side of the conversation, I have edited out most of the portions of my correspondence that he did not comment on or that aren't necessary to understand his. Occasionally, there are jumps in the conversational flow because of phone calls between us that answered questions raised or initiated avenues of discussion.

His on-again, off-again relationships with his three sisters are painted with a broad brush. Developing his sibling issues, real and imagined, while being fair and balanced, would take a book as long as this. He could be both cutting and kind with them, depending on his mood and whether they were reconciled or a "former sister," as he put it.

In his later years, his sibling relationships were often ambivalent at best, but he realized he wasn't blameless. He once said: "I have no brothers; sometimes I wonder whether my sisters do."

MacLeese had one child, a son born in Miami to his third wife and later adopted by her next husband. By his own admission, Mac was never much of a father to Doug and their relationship was conflicted.

Aided by his fourth wife, Connie, who was the love of his life and who wore almost all of the couple's functionary hats, including social secretary, MacLeese and his son reconnected when Doug turned 18. Later, on his own, MacLeese designated Doug as the sole beneficiary of his retirement fund.

As presented, the correspondence omits details of his investigation of someone who he insisted had insulted his cats.

MacLeese was passionate about exacting retribution, and he was hot on a trail that led him down the rabbit hole into a labyrinth of online interconnections and even into conspiratorial theories about why members of the DuPont family spelled their last name differently.

Because he was so consumed by it, his investigation was cause for concern about his mental state. Yet he showed enough real-world awareness to perceive that others were thinking he might be going off the rails in his ire at his alleged axis of evil-doers.

In the early 1970s, Mac and I took a trip to Toronto with Connie and my first wife, Sharon. He believed he was primarily a Scot then, and Sharon and I gave him an anatomically correct Scottish doll on that trip. In Hallowell, the red-bearded Scot was still with him, sitting next to a row of books on his desk. The doll moved with him to Jonesport, Maine, where he died.

We shared events, some deeply personal, in each other's lives. That continued in the correspondence.

When I took an early retirement as managing editor of the Flint Journal in May of 1997, Mac was there, slurping Jack Daniels and making a slurring attempt at a speech.

In writing a roast for my "Retirement Page," he played off our heritage debates by reporting the discovery that my branch of the Van Noord clan "sprang from a Timothy South and a Bridget West, both of Irish-English stock. The pair wed in 1634 in Cripplegate, a one-pub jerkwater outside London.

"Records revealed that in 1640 the Souths were in Old Bailey, each drawing 5- to 10-year jolts in Newgate Prison for crimes in St. Giles-in-the-Field. After the Souths did their time, a concerned magistrate deported them to Hollow Land, known to outlanders as Holland....

"The Souths became Noords through a truly hilarious (in retrospect) incident involving a waggish Rotterdam customs official. Thirty years after the former Souths settled in Utrecht, one of their 12 children stuck a Van in front of the Noord. It was excusable social climbing, and common enough among second generations of the immigrant classes."

Sharon died from metastatic melanoma on Christmas Day of that same year, and he and Connie were there to offer support, with Mac writing in a guest book that he would remember "her laughter & her ready way with a rejoinder – and how she always suspected I was a little crazy. I'll miss her."

Nearly two years later, I had been dating Jessica for a couple of months when I wanted to introduce her to Connie and Himself, as Connie referred to Mac, over breakfast on Dec. 19, 1999. They canceled because he was ill. Four days later, Connie had a heart attack and a seizure or a stroke. Jessica never did meet Connie, who died Dec. 29, almost exactly two years after Sharon.

While I was down south that winter, Jessica introduced herself to MacLeese and met him for breakfast several times. They had something in common: Jessica had lost her spouse a year earlier.

Jessica and I married in September of 2000, and we invited him to Christmas dinner that year. The next June, he moved to Hallowell, Maine.

Within weeks, he was involved with a woman and planning to marry her that fall in Maine. I was to be the best man. Jessica and I planned a trip to New Brunswick before the wedding.

The wedding, however, was called off. "My apologies for the false-alarm nuptials alert," he wrote. "Incompatability rules."

We still took the trip to New Brunswick, stopping off in Maine to see him. We met for breakfast, memorable because of his eating habits.

He ordered two fried eggs, sunny side up, with hash browns, all arriving neatly arranged on his plate. His first order of business was to thoroughly stir all of it up with a spoon into a yolky melange. Then he began eating. The process didn't surprise me but then I had spent a few years working for him on the copy desk, where it seemed to be a work rule that he spill a huge Styrofoam cupful of coffee a day.

Jessica, a banker before we got married, was horrified by his financial indiscretions, and he rather enjoyed horrifying her by telling her he was accepting every credit card offer he could and planning to spend to their limits. In his view, there was no risk; by the time the credit card companies caught up with him, he would be dead. After having had a good time in the meanwhile.

Well, any thoughts of an imminent demise were exaggerated. The next winter, he was still breathing and still charging on his credit cards when he drove down to Gulf Shores, Alabama, where we were spending the winter in our condo.

We rarely saw him during the 10 days he was there. He wanted to stay in a motel; I think he thought it would cramp his style to stay with us. Which suited us just fine. Visions of cigarette burns and spilled coffee were dancing in our heads.

He went off bar hopping, where he met a millionaire, and they hit it off. Two kindred souls, trolling for women or whatever. We did join them for late breakfasts at a place called L.A. Dawg House.

That was the last time we would see him. In the next 10 years, our view of him would come through his descriptive emails and letters.

"... besides the protestations of each of us, it really is all about me, and I think my me is a good little guy valiantly struggling to get out and play without fear or favor.... and if I win some praise or attention or admiration, why I think I could stand a little of that...."

Al MacLeese
Oct. 21, 2005

Part 1: Mac vs. Michael Moore

The days of drinking his way out of more than three-dozen newspaper jobs and three marriages behind him, Al MacLeese was in his prime – thanks largely to the stabilizing influence of his fourth wife. He was writing four columns a week for the Flint Journal when Peter C. Cavanaugh became a regular reader.

Cavanaugh, the general manager of a Flint radio station, called the columns "brilliant stuff." He sent MacLeese a note on how impressed he was, and they met for lunch at the Red Rooster, an upscale Flint restaurant.

When MacLeese launched into an anecdote about feeding his driver's license to a hamster in Florida, Cavanaugh realized Al not only could write, he had the gift of gab. He should be in radio, talk radio.

As the new general manager of WWCK-FM, a Flint rock station, Cavanaugh brought with him an hour of talk radio called "Radio Free Flint," hosted by a young Flint gadfly named Michael Moore, who nine years later, with "Roger & Me," would become a critically acclaimed filmmaker.

This was not your usual Sunday morning public-affairs broadcasting. It was live, everything was on the table for discussion, with an open bank of phone lines.

Within weeks, Cavanaugh proposed slotting a radio version of MacLeese's column, "MacLeese Unleashed," in the 9 o'clock hour immediately after Moore's hour-long show. He talked to the Journal editor, who agreed to let Al do it.

Moore was already controversial in Flint. He was the editor of an alternative newspaper, the Flint Voice, with a print run of about 15,000, and he was not shy about chiding the local establishment press, namely the Journal, for its coverage and non-coverage of certain stories.

1

Two years earlier, in 1978, MacLeese had met Moore for the first time. In a column, he gave a prescient analysis in answering his own question about what Moore was like.

"Aggressive, intelligent, abrasive, creative, overbearing, a tough adversary, childishly aloof toward society's restrictions, analytical, manipulative, dedicated, charming, offensive, obsessed with going his own way but equally dedicated and sincere in his stated desire to help people feel better about themselves.

"A tough nut to crack, the Moore Conundrum," MacLeese wrote. "One would hope he can find the flexibility to be more effective at things he wishes to do. But one can forget that hope. Moore will continue to march to the beat of that different drummer."

In 1980, there was a decided strain between the Journal and Moore. MacLeese ratcheted up the tension with a column that reviewed the "Radio Free Flint" show on WWCK, six weeks before MacLeese made his radio debut.

The show, MacLeese said, is "an extension of the Voice, the newspaper that offers an alternative (read correct) outlook. *Where people really care.* As contrasted to the Journal, routinely referred to by the Voice as the Urinal."

Radio Free Flint's style "was to unquestioningly entertain all assaults upon the 'Establishment,' no matter how ill-founded, ill-stated or one-sided." Using words and phrases like biased and on-air distortions, MacLeese declared the show a washout "aside from the misleading generalizations and shaky conclusions."

Moore, he said, "derides the 'objective' approach to journalism – the attempt by most reporters to give both sides of events. He says 'Establishment' journalists aren't truly objective and points to his own (well-meaning) 'subjectivity.'

"It's hard to be objective, but that doesn't stop most reporters from trying. And we goof now and then in all the ways you can, and everybody who is watching closely gets on us and contends occasional error represents calculated policy. Well, that's the territory.

"I had been among those willing to accept Moore, self-appointed leader of baffled or perturbed youth, as generally being on the side of the angels in his sometimes admirable efforts to free youngsters from some of the shackles society imposes in its zeal to keep things from flying apart.

"Now I think Mike may wish to be on the side of the angels but just doesn't know where they're camped. For sure, they haven't been Mikeside the past two Sundays."

The reaction from a Moore supporter was fierce. In a letter to the editor, he called MacLeese's column a "vicious hatchet job," a "shoddy piece of so-called journalism," a smear, character assassination, and a "terrible abuse of the enormous power MacLeese has as a featured columnist" in a daily newspaper.

"It's one thing for MacLeese to have his opinions, but it's quite another to express them as maliciously and unfairly as he did in this case. To distort and misrepresent any feeling, caring human being the way he did Moore leaves serious doubt about MacLeese's professional integrity."

With that background, Cavanaugh prepped Moore to be on his best behavior for MacLeese's first show of "The Dread Media and You" on Aug. 31, 1980.

"Al went on Michael Moore's show at 8:45," Cavanaugh said, "and Michael was really good to Al, then Michael stayed on for the first part of Al's show." Soon after MacLeese was in charge of the debate, on his own show, he interjected: "You're an asshole." There was no delay to wipe it out. "Michael laughed and laughed."

The two shows ran without commercials, and the hosts had free rein. They could talk about anything they wanted. "The phone lines would light up," Cavanaugh said, and the shows "got unheard-of ratings" for their time slots.

At one point, Cavanaugh wrote MacLeese that he would defy any Flint radio station to "match our Sunday morning 9-to-10 slot for true controversy and naked truth at its most spontaneous levels."

Moore and MacLeese tolerated each other as they passed the torch between shows, Cavanaugh said, and both would talk about each other on the air.

MacLeese's show lasted less than four months. He was the one who ended it. Cavanaugh said it was taking a toll on MacLeese, having to get up early after a Saturday night of what Cavanaugh suspected was heavy drinking.

Cavanaugh called MacLeese the last of the old-time newspaper rogues.

"Al was a unique guy," Cavanaugh said, "naturally gifted, equally as talented" as Michael Moore. "If someone would have asked me then to bet who would go on to fame and fortune, I would have put my money on Al MacLeese."

In his column, MacLeese was known for being funny and fearless, although in the correspondence that follows from his Maine years, he did admit to a weak moment where he had second thoughts about writing about a stockade experience involving masturbation

3

and the Bible. His correspondence also allowed him the freedom to be profane.

Within a year after he ended his radio show, MacLeese's career was taking on water.

A sea change in editors at the Flint Journal swamped him personally and professionally. He performed spectacular falls off the wagon as anger and depression turned him into a grumpy old man. He began smoking more pot as a way to stay off booze.

And in the unkindest cut of all, his "MacLeese Unleashed"column was emasculated before it died under suspicious circumstances.

During a period of purgatory as a copy editor, which he termed "the best of all so-so worlds," he made a fateful decision to enlist in a Michael Moore endeavor, a national journalism article criticizing the Flint Journal leadership for being too cozy with community groups. MacLeese allowed Moore to quote him making unflinchingly critical comments in the article.

Within months, he took an early retirement and became a house husband for Connie, a fellow newsperson and the most important woman in his life. At that point he had been married to her for almost two decades, far outstripping the longevity of his first three marriages combined.

Except when it came to Connie, his relationships with the other sex seemed the epitome of the old saying: "Women – can't live with them, can't live without them." Women seemed to be attracted to him, too, and he ventured into extramarital affairs at various points in his life. In his correspondence, he also refers to consorting with prostitutes.

Continuing to fast forward toward when his correspondence begins in Hallowell, Maine, he eventually unretired to work part time as a copy editor, at first under Connie, who was then the news editor at the Saginaw News. A cancer survivor, Connie was suffering from congestive heart failure when she had a heart attack and a seizure or a stroke. She died days later.

MacLeese retired again a year after her death. Rudderless without her, he debated what to do next. His oldest sister, Joan, stepped in and persuaded him to move to Maine. She bought a walk-up condo to rent him in Hallowell, near Augusta, and he took three cats east with him. Once again, he said he hoped to work on a book he had in mind. That had been his early retirement plan, too.

Shortly after his arrival in Maine, he met a woman and they put their relationship on the fast track. They planned to marry that fall in

Allagash, a town in northernmost Maine. The location was portentous because Mac had served on a ship called the USS Allagash, albeit in an uncommonly undistinguished manner, while in the Navy.

A few weeks before the wedding, they became disengaged after their "fourth major dispute in a 9-week relationship." The break-up, he said, was "relatively civil with both disputants wishing each other best of luck."

MacLeese rarely had expectations of good fortune, except during a few years in Maine, where manna eventually dropped into his lap. That was two years after he was introduced to the "second Christ" because of his connections with Michael Moore, but that's getting ahead of the story.

At the time of his disengagement, he had developed the theory, akin to a scam, that he would die before credit card companies badgered him for payment on amounts due. He could max out all of his cards without penalty. No day of reckoning. He'd be dead.

He did roll up huge debts, totaling in excess of $30,000, mainly on four credit cards. His annual income from Social Security, pension and an annuity was less than that. It didn't take a math wizard to figure out he was in financial trouble. And, what was more inconvenient, he was still alive.

MacLeese began to explore bankruptcy, which is where the correspondence begins.

[Hallowell ME; Dec. 24, 2002]

R and J:

Here's a joke for you, probably one you've heard: "How can you pick out an Irishman in a topless bar?" Answer: "He's the one that's there to drink."

This is early morn of day before Christmas, and I can hear (and see) salt trucks swooshing down Water Street in Hallowell anticipation of snow for everybody and overtime for those who work for the city. Here is a glimpse of how Maine, to this outlander, seems so attractively different: Yesterday I was in a group driving to a Christmas house party outside Augusta. As we passed the Capitol building, a guy named Josh said, "There's the governor."

The governor is a new one, John Baldacci. I looked over and there was the guv and two other guys standing all alone, talking and gesturing in a walkway, the only people in sight. No entourage, no ragamuffins from press, no buxom interns, eccentric hangers-on.

I have been in Maine for just 18 months and already have seen two governors in flesh; elsewhere I have gone years and years without seeing hardly any in-person governors.

Baldacci's predecessor, Angus King [now a U.S. senator from Maine], is in and out of the Hallowell haunts, all by his lonesome, and draws only mild interest or comment. "Yeah, we are impressed that you are the governor, but let's not go on and on about that."

Some folks are "cool" without a bit of the excruciating awareness of how cool they are.

At the house party we attended, the more adventurous guests repaired to garage and engaged in "shotgunning." A few contestants in middle of circle of observers. Each contestant has cold can of beer at mouth and, simultaneously punches holes in the cans with nail or some such thing, gulps down beer that comes shooting out. Idea is to empty can quicker than competitors do, but no fair if most is dribbling down chin. Judges are on hand to name winner.

This is a barbaric practice, drawing crowds similar to those that attended bear-baitings and dog fights and the burning of cats in cages during coronations.

I did not compete. Some woman won, to chagrin of several males.

Happy Holidays, Almac

[Gulf Shores AL; Feb. 9, 2003]

Hey Mac —

Yes, Virginia, we are alive and well in Alabama. And baby makes three. We are three down here, have been three since Christmas, when Jessica got back her baby, a six-year-old Welsh terrier. She had given her up when her husband died. She was working then, and away too much of the day, so her brother took her. We tried out Pumpkin over Christmas, and she adjusted well....

UNLEASHED

There was an article in the Mobile paper today.... Seems the area along the beach is being flooded with these illegal aliens, [many from] the Czech Republic....

Jessica says hi.... She wonders if you have a new babe hanging on your arm.

RJ

[Hallowell; Feb. 10]

Howdy Friends and Neighbors:

It is good to know you-all are alive and well in the many-Czechered outpost on the balmy 'Bama shores. And am happy to re-confirm that the only use for a Czech is to provide wordplays for us superannuated newspaper guys as well as plays on the Czech word for hed writers....

It is cold here but upside is that weather is often sleety and snowy with a lot of gales and two noreasters this winter so far. The streets are a sea of crusted or melting mud, dirt beats salt in these here parts, and you have to walk in the streets downtown because the sidewalks are either mounded with snow or glazed with ice. Or there are 15-foot long icicles hanging from the eaves of the tall buildings.

I have fallen down several times and, miraculously, not broken the right elbow although that would allow for a certain sense of symmetry opposite the left elbow....

I am doing a lot of productive things.... After a false start in August, I am actually going through with the process of declaring bankruptcy, having hired [an attorney] to ramrod the thing through....

"Do I still have to make payments on the $33,000 owed to one bank and four credit card companies?"

"No," the counselor counseled.

"What if they start harassing me?"

"Just tell them to call me, they can harass me," [she] said.

"I can live with that," I said....

Then, as if not sated with good works and direct actions, I also set about filing my income taxes for last year. It skipped my mind last year, and so I am now filing for both last year and this year all in one fell swoop with a CPA from Augusta....

(You may notice now and in the future that all my contacts with professionals — the feared suits — are with those of the female persuasion. I have found they are more sensitive, more nurturing....)

Speaking of females, I am now sort of keeping company with a woman who is not only my age but older by six months. I was 72 last month.... She's closer to emphysema than me....

(By the way, filing for bankruptcy may sound like I am in dire straits but the net effect will be, I trust, that I will now have enough to live on without the curse of the credit cards hanging over my head because I have no more credit cards, at least ones that I can use. F. Scott claimed — famously — that there were "no second acts in American lives." Quotation sounds good but is or can be bullshit....

Later, Mac

[Gulf Shores; Feb. 12]

Hey Mac —

... Didn't Congress just pass something making it harder to declare bankruptcy? ...

The only news I forgot to impart last time was that I am actually working on a novel.... Have a general outline done, characters drawn and about 80 pages or so of a rough draft. Hope your editing skills haven't dulled if I ever get this baby finished. I've been thinking about putting someone named Bud in it, but haven't yet. It's a newspapering novel....

RJ

[Hallowell; Feb, 13]

Hi:

... I had just assumed you folks knew about [a certain] book, but, as George Bush would say, I "misunderestimated" the awareness of snowbirds, who

8

apparently spend half the year preparing to go south and the other half preparing to go north. Why can't you folks settle down like normal people?

... I was just looking around the place to find the book to give you the title and publisher ... but, naturally, I can't locate the godamned thing and my patience for such enterprises ranges from slim to none and slim is out of town. This may be a small place but I am entirely capable of misplacing the ice box. And the fact that I use the term ice box should tip you off to the nature of the problem.

You are right, there were news stories last year about a move to get Congress to make it tougher for weasels like me to declare, aver and attest and avow that we are bankrupt. Movement was sponsored (duh!) by banks and credit card companies, but it never got very far owing to parlous state of the economy and resultant public opinion.... So folks like me still have a window of opportunity, as we say, though the credit card wolverines are still in there pitching....

It's good to hear that you are working on writing something.... I keep "writing" stuff in my head, the ongoing interior monologue, but lack motivation and have lost any semblance of confidence that I will ever do anything along those lines. Perhaps once I get through this patch of bad road, my latest mid-life crisis, maybe something will change.

As it is, I count it a major triumph when I make it down to the market to buy the necessaries and get back to the house without getting trampled by a moose. (I have a major, major cold, nose running like a faucet, and that makes the freeze more binding.)

Congratulations on hooking up with Pumpkin. Fogarty, Faraday and Finley [his cats] can be pains in the ass, particularly when I am overwrought, but if it weren't for their company I would be saying more than just hello to the walls.

Worse thing about the cold these past few weeks is that there is no relief by talking a walk through the woods or along the Kennebec ... the newspapers and radio worrywarts are telling us not to go outside unless we have a darn good reason. So I am holed up and reading everything but cereal boxes. And I do not need to hear, by return email, that the temps are approaching 50, 60 or 70.

Mac

[Feb. 16]

Roger:

Am so painfully jealous of somebody I know writing a book — another book! — that I lacked the good grace before now to ask what this book is about. What is this book about? And how in the name of sweet Christ from East Jodhpurs in the Thumb can you possibly work somebody named "Bud" into it? What's the matter with somebody named "Mac"?

Does Bud [refers to his longtime boozing partner, LeRoy E. Tripp, who died in 1987] have more charisma, more cachet, more character flaws, more star power than me? Can I help it if I was never in a stalag? More to the point, is Bud the guy that drove down the Hank Williams Lonesome Highway to expose the Czechs in chicanery right in your backyard?

Is Bud the one that took you on the tour of that French-type fort, explained what the complex defensive structures, gun emplacements and steep stairs portended? Did Bud introduce you and Jessica to the [millionaire] and another Dutcher to boot? Did Bud leave big tips at the Dawg? Why not have a character who's an amalgam of Bud and Mac, one with my good points and Bud's bad points?

… So is this a book about a newspaper person? Write what you know, so I guess you're not writing about a Jewish transvestite CPA from the Bronx.

I am willing to help edit. I'm thinking I could come down with Faraday, Fogarty and Finley and set up camp in your guest room. We could put the litter box in there and all four of us would use it, save wear and tear on your bathroom; we would not smoke or claw furniture except in the guest room and only after 6 p.m.

I won't drink anything except Bushmills. I think Jessica would go along, knowing her guests were sparking your muse and drinking only good stuff from the Irish distilleries…. (Faraday, Fogarty and Finley have grown accustomed to Fancy Feast in the small gourmet cans, nine

10

a day, and Jessica could lay in a store of them if that's not too much trouble.)

You still have the balcony overlooking the Caddies and customized SUVs, right? If I run into [the millionaire] and one of his hotties, they could stay out there on the balcony, couldn't they? I'd guess we'd all need passes to get past the ex-Seal and Special Forces guards downstairs?

Did you know, by the way, that I wrote a letter to [that waitress] in the open-air bar where all the bikers cavorted? And that she never responded? Could you and Jessica go down there and see if she's still there — she could, if agreeable, stay with me ... in the guest room.

These are just some of the things I am mulling if I decide to collaborate on this book. M comes before V in the dictionary and I was thinking it could be bylined by Al MacLeese and "RVN." Sixty-forty, I'm thinking.

These are thoughts going through my mind in the predawn hours, as I develop bronchitis with copious sputum and irritating hacks as I read "The Magic Mountain" by Thomas Mann. Mann's Hans Castorp is, if you'll remember, in a TB sanitarium in the Alps; Hans has become euphoric, doubtless due to the exhilaration one feels in high altitudes knowing that the asylum keepers will take care of him. Mann explains in an afterword to his magnum opus that "Magic Mountain" is a "quester" novel a la Goethe and Wagner and Spenser, sort of an effete Gawain Does the Alps. Perhaps we could make Bud-Mac tubercular and naive as hell in the bargain.

Think about it.

Mac

[Feb. 20]

Well, Mac, I don't know how to break this to you gently but although Jessica laughed several times while reading your latest, she didn't make an immediate invitation to the F-Troopites and their patron saint. Mumbled something about not having a guest room, new/old dog chasing cats, lots of nitpicking and hemhawing. So the waitress at the Barefoot Bar or wherever might have to wait for another year.

11

Maybe I could add Fogarty MacBud to my novel, which, yes, is about newspapering. Write about that which you have a modicum of familiarity, as Radar was wont to say while taking a writing course in Korea….

RJ

[Feb. 21]

R and J:

I knew in my heart of hearts that my offer to grace your place with cats, [the millionaire], his doxie of the moment, the sweetie from the Barefoot Bar, and cases of Bushmills and Benson & Hedges, and boxes of blue pencils was doomed from the start. So I take my rejection in good humor, which is my charming and affable way.

Someday, though, literary historians will write that "while Van Dutch garnered Pulitzer and Nobel prizes from "Ink-Stained Wretch," along with a MacArthur genius grant of $3 million, critics noted he would have done even better if he (and his wife Jessica) had had the good sense to take up the generous offer of copy editor Al MacLeese and allowed MacLeese to visit Gulf Shores to edit his magnum opus and offer invaluable insights and guidance. But it was not to be owing to the intransigence of...."

Finally got around to visiting doctor's office next door and was given medication to combat persistent hacking, coughing, wheezing and leakage from eyes. Am now reviling self for not visiting doc two weeks ago; am weak but reviving. This aging sucks. The sawbones gave me a liquid with codeine in it after asking if I "minded" codeine. I said I did not as long as it was for medicinal purposes and everything was aboveboard.

Temps actually got up into the thirties here yesterday and I heard words like "tropical" and "balmy" at the market on Water Street.

I get all my news from the Internet these days, having canceled cable and nixed an antenna for telly…. Thought I might miss TV quite a bit, but, after a couple of days of weaning I found change was relatively painless. And heaps cheaper. I do have a little Sony radio, but it doesn't get stations beyond Boston and I can't get Imus, who I confess I miss.

Later, Mac

[March 1]

Dear RJs:

... Received your latest email and, though vastly amused at the humor therein, do not count it as a legitimate response to my laboriously crafted ... communication.

Speaking of emails, I have been getting a lot of spam lately and, curiously enough, subjects range from breast enlargement opportunities to Viagra offerings to queries about debt management.

But I do not need to have my breasts enlarged.

I am invited to spaghetti and meatball dinner tomorrow at the apartment of my friend Maisie, and friend Heather will also be there. Maisie and Heather are waitresses at the Liberal Cup, and they are my chief contacts with Cup chums. Have not been to Cup in more than three weeks.... Indeed, have not been into a bar in almost a month as I am practicing "living within my means."

Tell me more about the work in progress, Roger. Yes, I know it is about newspapering, but am presuming there is a plot with a beginning, middle and end. Where is the locale, who is the protagonist, and what quest is involved? Will there be any sex or is it a realistic work?

Mac

[March 4]

Hey Mac —

... About my novel. What's it about? So far about 160 pages or so. An example of the humor within. It's about newspapering, but then I told you that. More specifically about the trials and tribulations and assorted affairs of one city hall reporter. Recognize anyone? There are various plots and subplots, some may be a bit obscure to someone who has never worked on a paper....

A storyteller's odyssey

The locale so far is Riverside, a Flint-Saginaw-ish town. What do you think of fictional settings in the novels you read? ... I did it to avoid a lot of research on city and state law. By making the setting generic, I can make the laws generic. Some points of the novel get a little technical. I didn't want to feel bogged down by getting it exactly right.

You asked about sex. There is some hanky-panky going on, so therefore it is an unrealistic work. I think that's how I describe it. Hanky-panky. Didn't want to get bogged down by getting it exactly right. That's the working title: Not getting it exactly right.

RJ

[March 7]

R and J:

... I'm not drinking or smoking these days, haven't been downtown hardly at all for a month.... The weather is so harsh I do not feel too deprived, but am developing a touch of cabin fever.

I feel a lot better about my situation now that I am dry and smoke-free, and the bankruptcy thing seems to be going well.... Have gotten a lot of mail from the five involved debtors, but this has caused me no anguish because I simply do not open the letters. This was my own idea, but one endorsed by my attorney. I am through paying them, and legally to boot, so why read this distressing stuff?

Regarding the setting for novel: Have you read Ed McBain's novels on the 87th Precinct? This series is tops in police procedurals; McBain's given name is Evan Hunter, he wrote "The Blackboard Jungle."

McBain calls his city Isola, and it has several boroughs, a stock market, tall buildings, hard-bitten cops, and it is on the Atlantic Ocean and, well, it is New York City. But a city sans the hassles to which you refer: the getting all that dreary mundane shit about streets and towns and buildings and east and west and so forth. If McBain can invent a city the size of New York, you can do even better with a Saginaw-Flint. I believe McBain drew up a map at the start of his 87th Precinct series, and went on from there in his

14

very own town, brooking no carping from editors and readers. Forget the fact-checking! ...

Later, Mac

[March 29]

Hi Folks:

You'll find this hard to believe but I did something stupid in regard to my most recent email to y'all snowbirds. I wrote a long and penetrating analysis of American literature.... I cannot recall all the gems in this cluster of wisdom, but ... I wrote this email before logging on, and duly dispatched it to the area known to the in-crowd as mail waiting to be sent. And forgot about it and there, alas, it waited for about two weeks. All this while I thought it had reached sunny Gulf Shores, and was beginning to be irritated at the lack of response by the snowbirds, albeit I knew they are laggard and lax like most would-be Dixie cuppers, stunned by too much sun.

About three days ago I chanced to be in mail waiting to be sent and saw the letter but, incredibly, further compounded my initial error of omission by deleting it, figuring it was a mere pale copy of the original and that I should clean up my queues. Then, upon receipt of your most recent email, I realized that Senior Moment 5,327 and 5,328 had been racked up, filed and forgotten as I wandered off to stand by the window wondering what had impelled me to stand by the window. So I apologize for being mentally enfeebled and probably a prime candidate for assisted living or, in a worst-case scenario, a return to some state hospital.

... Last three months the heating bill, which includes electricity and propane gas, was more than $300 for each of those months. So I have been paying more for heat and electricity than I have been paying [sister] Joan for rent. The prices of propane and electricity are outrageous in Maine and when you have a war and a particularly harsh winter, it is easy to be driven to the poorhouse.

Speaking of the poorhouse, my bankruptcy hearing is April 21.... The hearing, I am told, is pro forma, just a ritual, so by April 22 I believe I will be able to proudly aver that I have weaseled out of $33,000 (and change) in debts....

(Jessica, I know you realize I am abashed to have had to include a bank in my bankruptcy, but, hey, you can't have a war without killing some [innocents]. Just ask Herr Warlordobermeisterstrum Rumsfeld.)

Am well into my second month of not drinking booze, not smoking weed, and not smoking cigarettes. I seem to have regained my sense of touch and taste, and am beginning to feel like what I suppose normal humans feel. And I can now think in a fairly rational manner, which helps a great deal. And incredibly enough, I am cooking bacon and eggs, steaks and hamburgers in the frying pan, and eating canned fruit, canned vegetables and nuts.

Yesterday my friend Maisie and I walked the rail trail along the Kennebec for the first time in months. The ice jam at Augusta was breaking up and big chunks of ice were flowing down the river, but the temps were more than 50 and songbirds were sweetening the air.

This last nugget of news will be quite startling, so I hope da bot of youse are sitting down: I have attended three Buddhist meditation sessions over the past three weeks. I go to the sessions with Maisie's mother, Janet.... You sit in a darkened room for an hour, not moving, facing the wall amid the flickering candlelight amid a few bongs and chimes. Nobody says anything and there is no dogma to kick around. Some sit in the lotus position but they let me sit in a chair.

Buddhists are just seeking enlightenment or so they say. I go to find a way to clear my mind of the recriminations and remorseful thoughts it has grown accustomed to.

For a long time I have had a hard time sleeping or doing anything because I was always brooding about past errors, present errors, and even getting into future errors. Having conversations about that slight in 1950 by the bartender in Norfolk. That kind of dreck.

So the meditation sessions are helping me to push away the repetitive garbage and try to live in the now. To not think so damned much.

Worth a try, and there's no collection plate. We have the sessions in a house of an Augusta Buddhist and even get free tea after the sitdowns. Beats these barbaric Western spiritual stabs all hollow....

Later, Mac

[April 26]

Hi vandutches:

All the snow is gone here and now we find the granite hills are mainly mud. Frost wrote a poem about two tramps in mudtime in northern New England; I had thought he was being poetic about the muck, but no, springtime is mudtime. Maine has three seasons: mudtime, blackfly time and winter.

Maisie and I walked trail yesterday, the four miles to Augusta and back, just our second outing this year. But I intend to walk three or four times a week from here on out. What with yoga once a week and the weekly mental strain of trying to bully the mind into attaining something near nirvana (sitting in a chair and staring at a wall requires energy), I suspect I will be getting enough exercise.

At the zendo in home of Buddhist in Augusta, each meeting ends with the Buddhist honcho reciting, in tones reminiscent of James Earl Jones, a homily which ends with the phrase, "Do not squander your life." I always think, "Jesus, now they tell me."

Roger, we did not, in our phone talk, discuss ... title for work in progress that is steeping over there in the corner? ...

Later, Mac

[Grand Blanc MI; April 27]

Mac —

We are packing up to head south again ... to stalk the wild asparagus in the Smokies... [I need] some photos of lady-slippers....

Working title [of work in progress] is "Whores and Hounds," a reference to attributes of journalists....

A storyteller's odyssey

Michael Moore was being castigated on Fox last week, and a while later I asked [Jessica] to guess who had a radio show in Flint on Sunday mornings. I had to provide the answer, Michael Moore. Then I asked her to guess [whose show followed Moore's]. She fell off the chair when I said Al MacLeese. Getting up, she said: "He's got to write a book."

RJ

[May 3]

Hi Snowbirds:

... on the local newspaper front, a guy I know ... came up to me at the market and whispered in my ear that the Kennebec Journal had just terminated 18 employees for economic reasons.... I therefore concluded that even if they hadn't fired me last fall [from a copy editing job for an inability to comprehend their computer system], I probably would have gotten the ax last week.

More news later on, I have to go down to market and get the papers, perhaps read about how the robust Rummy slapped three reporters silly over having the temerity to ask a two-part question.

Mac

[May 15]

Hi Reynoldses [A corruption of his RJ greeting, referring to R.J. Reynolds Tobacco Co.]:

... We have lady-slippers in Maine, too, along with feral asparagus; Maisie said during our 4-mile morning walk today that she recently saw some in the Vaughan Woods.... I go to meditation at the zendo in Augusta with Maisie's mother, Janet, who is a painter in her spare time. And occasionally have coffee at the Higher Grounds on Water Street with Maisie's father, Baron Wormser, who is the Maine poet laureate, and a nice guy....

The Wormsers are one of the few Jewish families living hereabouts and they seem to have sort of adopted this Scot-Irish waif. The Scots, so I've heard, are called "the

Jews of the British Isles," so it seems like a good fit (as we former members of the corporate world often say).

My first month as a bankrupter, free and clear of the costs of declaring bankruptcy and getting right with Uncle Sam, is this month, Roger. Which means I now live creditcardless and within my means with the bonus of not having to pay monthly on the 33 big ones now legally off the books. So I have enough to live on and am better off financially thanks to this "second chance."

[The bank] and four credit-card companies seem to be still nipping along without my foolish help. And the dirty secret about filing for bankruptcy is that it is easy as falling off a log and I have fallen off a few in my time and know whereof I speak. It is a particularly good ploy if you are a doddering septuagenarian and a Korean War veteran to boot because who wishes to hound one of these poor bastards into the poorhouse?

Finley just jumped up in my lap, making it difficult to type, so will sign off now, musing over my status as a war veteran whose most hazardous duty was in sundry brigs, saloons and fleabags along the dangerous East Coast.

Mac

[June 2]

Hi Reynoldses:

... Jessica, what do your Catholic henchpersons say about Buddhists? I certainly don't want to join an outfit that's in bad odor with the pope! On the other, these Budheads appeal to me: No dogma, no higher power ready to chuck a thunderbolt down at you while He or She is protecting lousy swallows.

Also, I am doing my Budhead thing at home: no collections and no need to mingle with the common herd; I just sit in my chair meditating, chasing vagrant thoughts in search of an approach to enlightenment, which is kind of fun but busy work because most human thoughts are akin to the activity of wiener dogs running after thrown sticks and then, after catching the sticks, drooling on them, fetching them again and again even though sticks are not good to eat.

19

Well, enough religious talk. It's spring in Hallowell and I am walking four miles or more a day; yesterday I saw a woodchuck and a fox on the trail and, being a sort of Budhead, felt no desire to kill them, which if I did would have been very bad karma and I would pay for it dearly next time I come back, reincarnated as a beetle or Shirley Macwhatever.

Later, Almac

[June 20]

Greetings:

Just observed my 120th day without ingesting harmful substances and expect at least a card or, at worst, a nod of recognition from Michigan, where the garden spot of Benton Harbor gets so much good ink. Connie was born there, oddly enough, but her parents had the good sense to quickly move to Jackson....

Am still meditating up a storm, thrice daily, sometimes in the woods, where fellow walkers (and runners) approach with a certain amount of trepidation; I think they think meditators might be mentally unbalanced cranks that could be dangerous if disturbed. Fortunately, most of the runners and walkers have dogs to protect them....

Weather getting summery here, making my four-mile daily treks a bit sweatier and pace somewhat reduced. Have three venues for walks: Vaughn Woods, where I saw a truly huge woodpecker (pileated?) yesterday; the rail trail along Kennebec, where I spotted a yearling deer last week, a rarity along the river; and the streets of Hallowell, which are steep, gradients that would daunt manfolks younger than me, and where I spotted a cannon ... looking down on the Kennebec.

How is the book doing? Well, enough about you people, I must go ... to grocery store to get Times for Friday puzzle, which is a tough one, thence to spend half-hour or more on sitting chair, then to woods where, if I choose, I can meditate while walking, which is more than Jerry Ford could or can do.

In the house, I meditate sitting in a straight-backed chair facing a wall. On the wall I have tacked a picture of the Buddha, and stuck a red thumbtack on his nose, focusing on that while counting breaths and trying to stave off or only briefly entertain vagrant thoughts, which keep popping up, as vagrants do. I can ponder Buddha's "Four Noble Truths" and "[Noble] Eightfold Path."

Now is the time, of course, for bot of youse to rush to your reference book to satisfy for yourselves the burning question: What are the Four Noble Truths, the Eightfold Path?

Later, Almac

[June 28]

Dear Van Dutchers,

Roger, it is a shame and a crime that no-necks from lowlands that once were nolands get to go to bonnie Scotland while those of true Scots heritage must stay behind, sitting around meditating amidst the uncaring stumpjumpers of central Maine. Jessica at least has creds for visiting the British Isles, but you, Roger, are merely going there to steal more images of innocent birds (thereby also taking their very souls) and returning ghoulishly to the USA, there to profit at art fairs from crass and ignoble exploitation.

But have a good time anyhow.

Meantime I managed to stay clean and sober here in Hallowell despite the utmost provocations of the past week — a fairly horrendous time during which history once again repeated itself.

I had thrown a load of filthy clothes into the washing machine last week, and retired to the bedroom to do a "challenger" crossword puzzle from a book of true testers, and about an hour and a half later came back to the living room area to find water spewing every whichway from the washer. I managed to cut water off to the machine and proceeded to mop up water, and was congratulating myself over how the damage seemed minimal, but the other shoe dropped about a half-hour later when the guy that lives downstairs came home to find the real damage down there.

He called and it wasn't long before we were lugging a huge soaked antique braided rug out onto the lawn. Suffice to say there was ceiling damage, damage to his floor, one wall and so on. Cause of this mess was that a water rubber hose had burst in my antiquated Thin Twin Whirlpool washer-dryer.

How much all this is going to cost, I do not yet know. I do not have any insurance ... but guy downstairs does have insurance. Joan says it is only money and "we" will pay it off.... This proved a severe test to my sobriety but through meditation I have managed to keep a good thought and stave off ideas of drinking, smoking and howling at the moon.

... Oh, just yesterday I got the final papers on my bankruptcy. My debts to the four credit-card people and [the bank] have been "discharged." I managed to keep my car during all this, having changed from lease to buy and having "reaffirmed" my intention to pay for the car, which will take three more years, I think.

Earlier in this message you may have noticed a reference to history repeating itself. It did, and in this manner: In 1951, on the naval base at Norfolk, another PAL (prisoner at large) and myself were arrested by SPs after a brawl at the PX beer place, and tossed into a minibrig on the base, along with several other miscreants. I had a top bunk and, after passing out from all the beer, proceeded to micturate in my already disreputable white uniform.

A large seaman occupied the lower bunk and it did not escape his notice, upon awakening, to find that he had been pissed upon. There was a great hue and cry, more scuffling, and the SPs rushed in and shipped the whole lot of us off to Camp Allen, where Marines just returned from Korea were waiting, eager to start torturing Navy wimps.

Fortunately, the guy who lives downstairs is a nice fellow, not fresh from the Korean wastelands, and already three times this week he has said to me, "These things happen...." That should be my line, but, hey, I will take any break coming....

Later, Almac....

22

[Aug. 26]

No stone unturned

Hi Reynoldses:

Couldn't resist that half-assed header [referring to Roger's problems relating to laser surgery to remove kidney stones], especially since it can, in Roger's case (as a known molester and harasser of shore birds) be turned around to "no tern unstoned" as the Dutchperson goes about taking pictures of inoffensive puffins amid lesser birds and the odd raggedy-assed Shetland pony. You had quite a siege there, Roger....

... my little problems jousting with depression — the "black dog" of Churchill's designation and aka the noonday demon — fade to puniness and I can only tip my hat to Roger (and Jessica) as I clutch close to my lesser woes.

(As the Indian chief said after surviving the Trail of Tears, "I have suffered somewhat." Which I guess is the only way to handle the downsides inherent in the quaintly labeled golden years. I bet the person who dreamed that phrase up was a thirty-something ad writer.)

... Meantime, am trying to get back on track with meditation.... had found it almost impossible to do successful meditation in aftermath of The Day the Washing Machine Broke....

Cats are doing OK, though Fogie is restricted in movements ... took him to the vet and Fogie apparently has arthritis and a buckling hindleg on the port side. He is, after all, in his 21st year.

Finley and Faraday are more cheerful since I started letting them go outside during the day. Had feared they might run off and join Action Hero Georgie-Porgie on that aircraft carrier but no, they stick close and come when called, which is fairly amazing ... you folks have heard the line about the hardest job in America — herding cats.

This email [represents] the first time I have accessed the computer in two weeks or more as I continue to haunt the library, and read about eight or nine books a week — during those periods, of course, when I am not reading magazines and the disinformation on cereal boxes....

Friend Mac

[Oct. 9]

Hi Reynoldses:

Was sitting outside the bakery downtown this morning and a farmer was selling apples out of his van. He tried to sell me some, but I told him I had false teeth and stuck to bananas. He opened his mouth wide and had no teeth at all. Said he still eats apples; so I had to fall back on the fact that I don't even like apples. He accepted that with good grace.

Good to hear that you got back from Scotland sojourn safe and sound and that you had another good trip. I'm going as soon after I win the lotto as I can....

We are all excited here along the Kennebec about the leak in Washington [outing undercover CIA agent Valerie Plame] but reassured now that Bush has opined that leaks are bad and he certainly wants to get to the bottom of this one....

Not that I give a rat's ass about any of this save for the fact that the newsy months have given me lots of pleasure in my golden years, lightening up the days as the news flows in. As Don Imus, who grows to be a bore, put it: "You can't make this stuff up."

... But now for the trivia: My team has won two trivia contests in past month; both pots more than $200. I suspect we're winning because of our team name: "Al's Coholics." (You can't make this stuff up.) ...

Later, Mac

[Nov. 10]

Hey Mac —

... By the way, I still have to flesh out one character [in novel], and one facet is that she likes "Rockford Files." I tossed in that she also likes John D. MacDonald.... He's dead now, isn't he? Maybe I could make some snide comment

UNLEASHED

about her liking dead [detective] series and dead detective
novelists....

RJ

[Nov. 11]

Hi Reynoldses:

... [she] likes MacDonald probably because he wrote 21
books, all with a color in the title, and all starring Travis
McGee, a Florida guy who made his living by going after the
sharks that victimized the good folks.

I used to have all the McGee series and, while he is not
quite like Rockford, I am sure that someone who likes
Rockford would probably like McGee ... both are unofficial
crime fighters who do saintlike feats in helping out folks in
distress. McGee is a more serious fellow than Rockford, but
he grows on you and MacDonald was a great writer in his
genre....

I once wrote him including a mention of McGee in a column
and he was nice enough to write back. [A colleague, Don]
Dahlstrom, on getting wind that I had a letter from THE
MacDonald, quickly put it on a copying machine.... Oh, and
one other similarity: both McGee (Marines) and Rockford, a
dogface, did battle against the evil enemy in Korea....

Friday I am flying to Vegas with five friends.... I am going
out sans credit cards and with only 250 scoots to lose so
probably will be dealt out of the blackjack action before our
72 hours are up. But then, that's why you go to Lost Wages
with friends — so's you can borrow money from them when
you go broke.... [All] are of the age where their mommies
and daddies are younger than I.

Later, Mac....

[Nov. 19]

Vandutchers:

I know you-all are dying to hear what happened in Las
Vegas after the Hallowell Six went Continental last Saturday
and alighted at sunset at McCarran International for a 72-

hour evasion of our off-season Maine ennui ... yrs trly wearing fedora over an Abe-Lincolnish beard. Five lost money, one didn't ... the most cautious of the low-rollers, gaming mere pittances....

My highlight: Playing the quarter slots, I was stabbing away at the stupid machine, not knowing what the symbols I saw on the payline meant when all of the sudden the machine starting pinging and bonging and a thousand quarters tinnily spewed out, drawing a small audience. It was a jackpot but no big whoop, a mere $250. Which I managed to lose at blackjack before many more hours had passed.

Another highlight: Within an hour two strangers commented on my fedora and beard. First guy said I looked like a leprechaun and when I said I was Irish but not small enough to be a leprechaun, he said he didn't give a shit, I looked like a leprechaun, period. I got away from him but next ran into a security guard who said, "And otherwise Mr. Lincoln, how didja like the play?"

... Reynoldses, go to Vegas during journeys around globe, Scotland can do without you very well for a spell, and there is a lot more to do in Vegas nowadays than gamble and goggle at Wayne Newton. A lightshow downtown near Binion's casino would knock your socks off ... awesome, and I do not use "awesome" cheaply like increasing numbers of English speakers do. People were gawking like rubes who'd just fallen off the sugar beet truck. And there are theme-park attractions, and two truly hardcore rollercoaster rides high above city.

Of course, my bankroll is teeny and the bank account hovers near zero and there are two weeks to go till the eagle defecates once more at the first of any month ... but in meantime I can fall back on the kindness of my Hallowell friends....

Mac

[Nov. 29]

Hi Reynoldses:

Was invited to family dinner for Thanksgiving yesterday and met a woman in late sixties.... She lives in Vermont and I am going to send her a letter, a snail mail no less, and see what occurs. I believe she could very well be looking for an amiable oldster to bop around with and I just happen to know one....

There were about ten people and six kids and five dogs at this turkey dinner and it was a pleasant couple of hours. We beheaded no lobsters. I have made some good friends here and herewith an extreme example:

Went truly bust in Vegas and, on return, told an inquiring friend that not only was I flat broke but my bank account was minus forty-four dollars. The next morning [one of my Vegas companions] stopped by my condo with a gift certificate worth $180 for the nearby Boynton's Market. Fellow trekkers knew I had almost two weeks to go before the defecations by the eagle and his other fine-feathered chums....

Later, Mac

[Dec. 9]

Hey Roger:

... I have been invited to spend Christmas at son Doug's home [with him, his wife and their two sons].... I always feel uncomfortable around Doug, even though he has always acted OK around me. But I know that my not attempting to get in touch with him during his formative years has not been, never could be, forgotten....

Under my regime of the past four months I go out for the night on just one day — Tuesday — which happens to be today. That's the night of Trivia at the Liberal Cup ... and did you know that "Moose" was the very last word of the dying Henry David Thoreau? ...

Later, Almac

[Dec. 21]

Dear Reynoldses:

... the big news in Maine is tidings about me....

A storyteller's odyssey

On return from Christmas [at son's home], I will travel through Vermont, where a gay guy can marry another gay guy but they must adopt Howard Dean. (I just made that joke up and I think it is pretty good. Hereby claim credit and if you hear it on Leno or Letterman, that's not exactly plagiarism but they should at least give credit where it's due.)

A Vermont woman ... invited me to stay over at her place while on return to my beloved condo in Maine. If Ronald Reagan can have a beloved ranch, I can have a beloved condo in my equally beloved state of Maine. This Vermont person has a very nice house of her own in a very nice town and is a single woman of a certain age, which happens to match mine.

As you both well know, I am now a single man on an income fixed by an idiot, which would be me. A piteous man who pays rent and has committed bankruptcy within the very last year; a man who has cast out 87.3 per cent of his family, one who has gotten fired from a third-rate newspaper and busted up his elbow as he walked while drunk. Poor man's personal belongings, his estate, could be taken away on a Flexible Flyer. When he goes on the road he doesn't stop in a Motel Six, he stops in a Motel 4.

There's a possibility here, Reynoldses: I could, with no evil intent whatsoever, marry "up" as they say. Greatly improve my situation, my financial ratings would soar; I could thrive in a state which will soon see its former governor become leader of the free world as opposed to being the governor of a jerkwater place....

If certain writhings and wrenchings of fate occurred in (admittedly) unusual ways, why I could in January become President Dean's press secretary/butt boy. In any case, some of my Hallowell chums, both male and female, have suggested that it would be prudent of me to lay in a supply of Viagra for the Vermont layover, if you'll excuse that term. And no need for septuagenarians concerning themselves over birth control issues.

My luck may point me to what, in such situations, is often called the spare room or, worse, the attic. There is a good chance that she is almost as smart as myself. (I know that's egotistical and am now wondering if it is ungrammatical as

28

well.) Anyhow, I got your yule card and it joins the one from Doug and family as the only two cards that have reached my door this year....

In any case, Happy Holidays.

Mac

Part 2: Bullied beginning

A child of the Depression, MacLeese wrote that his first memory was of his father coming home and announcing he had been laid off.

"I seem to remember him lasering a scowl in my direction and I have convinced myself that I remember thinking: 'My God, he's been laid off and it's my fault. I must have caused this Depression by getting borned!' Naturally, when I grew up, I turned to drink. Any human with that crushing burden who DID NOT turn to drink would have been a superior creation indeed."

In describing other early memories, his tongue was planted more firmly in cheek. He recalled an uncle who forced him to learn how to tie his shoelaces and also tossed him off a Long Island Sound dock to impress on him how to swim. "I'm going to get even with that uncle, because I am still scared of shoelaces."

Alan Noone MacLeese was "borned" on Jan. 5, 1931, to Alfred and Helen McLeese. A year earlier, in the 1930 census, his father was listed as a cigar store clerk, and his mother as a dental hygienist. After Alan arrived, his mother became a housewife.

Alan was born 15 months after his sister Joan, and for more than 13 years, they were the only children in the family. Helen, Joan said, thought Alfred was movie-star handsome, that he looked like Lew Ayres. Alan inherited much of his father's looks but not his baldness.

In Joan's first memory, Alan was sitting diagonally from her in their crib in New York City. He was about 9 months old and raising a stink. She recalled that a woman, perhaps a babysitter, was upset because Alan had made a mess with a bowel movement.

When Alan was 2, the family moved from their northern Manhattan apartment near the Cloisters to a rented home on Clover Street near the center of Ansonia, Connecticut.

Those who knew Alan's mother during his formative years, in the midst of the Depression, did not remember her for warmth or laughter. A friend of Joan's said: "She didn't show much emotion and didn't invest in people."

Unlike with his father, about whom he dredged up experiences that were mainly unpleasant, such as being ordered to kill litters of kittens, Alan didn't recall his mother in any deep impactful way.

One of his memories of her was from the period in Ansonia, where the mothers on their block had different ways to call their kids home from play.

"Some mothers would yodel, others yipped, one rang a bell, one used a pig call – 'Sou-eee, sou-eeee, soueeeeah!' Another contented herself with hoarse screams," MacLeese wrote.

"Mother would whistle, and she was good, too. And sister Joan and I would have to come trotting home, usually interrupted while committing some pleasurable childish felony."

He said he didn't inherit that whistling talent. "I could not whistle worth a hoot, and only gained a small ability after getting false teeth."

Joan and Alan were being raised by their mother. While the family was in Ansonia, their father was usually gone, apparently looking for work or taking odd jobs where work was available.

Alan was 8 when they moved again, to a cottage in the "exceedingly rural" outskirts of Oxford, Connecticut. That home was on a hill east of Six Mile Brook. Later, they would move part way down the hill, into a house a half mile from the Housatonic River.

In their first years in Oxford, Alan and Joan slept in the same room, beds diagonally opposite each other. They told each other stories across the room before going to sleep.

To get to school, they walked a mile and a half down Route 34. Oxford's Riverside School, a one-room wooden schoolhouse with a wood stove, had one teacher for the dozen or so pupils in eight grades. Alan was one of two in his grade.

Irene was one of two Penders sisters in the school. She was a friend of Joan's and was a grade behind Alan at Riverside. She described Joan as gregarious and Alan as a loner.

"During recess, he would go into the woods [adjacent to the school] and whittle. He was a quiet, withdrawn kid. He didn't seek people out and his self-confidence was low."

Irene's older sister, Jeanne, said Alan, like many of the boys, had high-top leather boots with a pocket on the side that closed with a snap. "They kept a knife in there."

Jeanne remembered Alan as a "nice, polite boy, with a soft voice." Although he was "very bright, very smart, a thinker," he didn't volunteer to answer questions in class.

One of Irene's early memories of Alan is from a visit to see Joan. Alan was in a flannel shirt and dungarees, carrying a fishing pole and a book, and walking with a dog. Spunky, a predominantly white mutt the size of a terrier, followed him everywhere, to fish in the brook or the river and even to school, where Spunky waited until Alan was ready to head home.

On another visit, Irene saw Alan reading while eating a raw potato.

Alan's fourth-grade teacher saw something in him that would hold true throughout his life.

In his report card, she described "a keen interest in reading ... he does this well, gaining much from what he reads. His interests are wide.... He enjoys reporting to the group bits of news which others have missed...."

Irene said Joan and Alan were close. "She was the one he leaned on." Joan said they never argued.

Both Irene and Joan said Alan was teased and bullied in grade school, probably because he was small and didn't mix with most other boys. "Two bullies lived close to him," Irene said, "and he tried to avoid them. Alan was never treated like one of the boys."

"In truth," MacLeese wrote later, "I think I blanked out a lot of the early years at Riverside."

Walking was a way of life for him then, and his enjoyment of it would continue into his Hallowell years.

"We used to walk five or six miles just to get to some place where we could do a little walking.... I marvel at the discipline I have used to force myself to walk all my life. Since I was a toddler, I have walked off-and-on from the time I got up in the morning to the time I crawled into bed. I walked to school, to the woods, to the river, to the bathroom. I have even sleepwalked."

32

As he grew older, he took up hunting with a .22-caliber rifle for rabbits and squirrels, which they ate. He also hunted pheasants, or, as a friend called them, fazzinks. The friend, the son of a White Russian couple, would ask: "Wanna go for fazzinks?" Off they went.

His father told him never to walk along Route 34 with his gun. Joan said that one day their father saw Alan breaking that rule and he slapped him.

Joan said Alan resented their father, who wanted him to be a regular guy. Alan was more of a reader. Irene said Alfred McLeese was outgoing and sociable but she seldom saw him with Alan. Joan said father never hunted or fished with son.

When it came to drinking, there is a range of opinion about the parent. Joan said their father drank occasionally but was not a problem drinker. Irene said Alfred, like her own father, was one of that area's many weekend or "Irish alcoholics," who would get together and begin drinking hard on Friday night and sober up for work on Monday.

In MacLeese's view, his father was an alcoholic, without qualification. That's what he told his niece Pamela when they talked in depth about him.

He told her, and Joan mentioned this, too, about the times his father would take him along to the bar but force him to stay in the car while he went inside and drank until after dark, another example of their arm's-length relationship.

"Alan said he would be alone in the car and freezing," Pamela said. "As he got older, maybe 13 or 14, Alan was able to join his father in the bar. He would just sit there while the men would talk and drink."

To Pamela, there was an antipathy between Alan and his father, and she found it telling that his father "never called Alan by his first name. Never."

As far as alcohol and Alan were concerned, he did not drink until he was in the Navy. "He never touched the stuff," Joan said.

There was one trait father and son shared. Both were restless and neither could relax easily, Joan said. Alan himself said: "I am seldom at ease. Perhaps this is normal. Which makes me uneasy."

MacLeese did have one fond memory related to his father, and that involved the house his father built and the family's first Christmas in it.

He was almost 12 years old, and his family "had lived through the Depression – renting homes, apartments, and, eventually, a shack in rural Connecticut – complete with kerosene lamps, no running water and plenty of running mice."

A factory job as a machinist before and during the start of World War II paid a good wage and allowed his father to save enough to buy a piece of land near the rented cottage and build a house for the family of four. It was a wooden house with a round-stone front and a flagstone terrace.

"Our own house, three bedrooms, a bath and a real fireplace with mantel," he said. "The first house of our own for all of us, and the first Christmas with it around us was the most memorable. Stockings over a fireplace built by a wordless and patient Swede stonemason. Even chestnuts, roasting on an open fire.... Joan said it was nice to settle back in a house built, than one a-building."

The new house also meant that Joan and Alan each had a bedroom.

After the house was finished, the family soon grew. Sharon was born in 1944 and Deborah in 1947.

While growing up during the war, Alan imitated war heroes by practicing jungle fighting. "Hid behind trees a lot, lobbed imaginary grenades, briskly crawled forward."

And he admired Jack London and Joe DiMaggio.

"Frank Sinatra? He was skinny and black-haired and sang, creating an unseemly stir amongst young women.... I was skinny and black-haired and unpopular with girls and did not appreciate Frank worth a hoot."

DiMaggio and Alan had their first encounter on a bright autumn day in 1939, when Alan was 8, and DiMaggio was patrolling centerfield.

"On the bus to Yankee Stadium I had hoped that DiMag would do good in our first 'meeting.' Maybe go 3 for 4, throw out a couple of those stupid Red Sox at the plate. He did go 3 for 4; I don't know what I was worrying about."

He ended up seeing the Yankee Clipper play several times, and then they "got together" again, after DiMag's baseball career ended, in a bar they both frequented in San Francisco. "You did not intrude on Joe's privacy, you respected it. Most did anyway...."

In 1944, Alan started high school in Derby, Connecticut, an industrial town 15 miles away, and his years there were unremarkable.

Although his fourth-grade teacher had him pegged in his report card, MacLeese would write this decades later: "I do not fondly recall any schoolteacher...."

He did remember a high school English teacher who hit him on the head with a book after he imprudently corrected a misspelling the teacher had made on the blackboard. Another teacher "kicked me in the rear end because I was not doing pushups enthusiastically enough during my football career, which ended after four hours of practice."

MacLeese took part of the blame for this lack of student-teacher rapport. "I was an introverted little shaver and preferred killing squirrels and trapping muskrats to going to school." Or maybe it was because of a certain grade-school teacher. "I gave an apple to [her] once, and she gave the damn thing to another kid the next day. It'll be a long time before I get over that."

No mentor was apparent in his formative years, or in his career. He couldn't say a teacher had helped shape his life. Likewise, there was no friend, no coworker, and no relative, including either of his parents, that he credited with crucial guidance.

He had no religious moorings, unless you count the dabbling in Buddhist meditation early in his Hallowell years. He was largely left to his own devices, for better or for worse, mostly the latter after he joined the Navy, until he married Connie.

Alan did have that early bond with his sister, though, and he followed her lead on changing his name. Joan had been told the family had dropped the A in their last name generations back, and when they were in high school, she put the A back in McLeese, changing her last name to MacLeese. Unfortunately, she put the A in the wrong spot. It had been McAleese for ancestors in Ulster.

As for a job, his main one during high school was as a pin setter in a bowling alley. Joan said he always was a hard worker growing up. But not on his studies.

"In my final year of high school I was failing two subjects, slightly below my yearly average. The science teacher, who functioned as adviser to those paddling backwards in dire straits, told me that in a class of 90, I was thrashing about with The Bottom Five."

Several days later, the science teacher "sat down with me to say that the last time they had graduated someone with a record like mine, the fellow had left and gotten run over by a parked car. But he noted that the school would graduate a fellow who promised to join the Navy, where people were always 'finding' themselves."

So MacLeese faced a choice: Not graduate or enlist immediately and graduate with the class of 1948. He chose to join the Navy and see the world. But he said he never did "find" himself during the four years he served.

Hours after graduating, he lit his "first Lucky Strike Red (Green had gone to war, never to return) outside a restaurant in Derby, Conn. Irrationally, wonderfully, I felt as suave as George Raft, as debonair as Fred Astaire, as tough as John Garfield."

Although his tastes changed – Camel, Chesterfield, Phillip Morris and Benson & Hedges among them – he smoked two cartons a week for decades except when he was locked up, broke, or both.

He once wrote that he smoked "for the most piddling of reasons. It allows me to function."

His proclivity for falling asleep while smoking, or while dropping a lit Zippo, would leave several wounds over the two decades after high school. An "angry, puckered scar" above his knee aspired to become purple-heart worthy during one beachside conversation he related:

A fellow at the beach in Miami, noticing the scar, which looks rather like a bullet wound, said this, cryptically: "Looks like you stood up when you should have shut up."

Wry, self-deprecating, I said: "Well, friend, that little argument was going on long before I headed west."

"Korea," he said, still cryptic.

"It wasn't Naples," I said, jutting my jaw a bit and still looking keenly out at the ocean with my chilling-grey eyes fixed on a tough-looking gull that looked like it might get up to some nastiness.

"I was in the Big One," he said, diffidently.

"They all were big," I said.

MacLeese concluded: "It was wonderful. I hadn't told a single lie and yet had conveyed the impression of myself fiercely charging those unspeakable Koreans and protecting all the Ma & Pa stores that ever were. My friend obviously respected me the more for my untold acts of heroism and we got along famously.

"It would have been depressing for him to hear the truth – that I had fallen asleep in the lobby of a skid-row hotel in Boston while smoking. Who wants to hear such sordid little tales?"

[Jan 5, 2004]

Part two of what went before

RJs:

Godamned machine caused premature ejaculation.
Sometimes I hit a key way over to the lower left of the
keyboard and it sends stuff hither and yon. Do not know

what key it is, but it does this every once in a while and I apologize for whatever inconvenience this might have caused down to the Redneck Riviera.

What was I saying? Oh, yes, I was supposed to see the Vermont woman after Christmas after I was supposed to see son and family.... I weaseled out of trip to [visit son], and also scotched layover in Vermont on way back to Maine. Could hardly be expected to venture down the East Coast during a Code Orange alert in the dead of winter, could I?

So now I leave for [Vermont] Wednesday a.m. and even got MapQuest to give me the routes. It is not known at this point how long I will be there and whether I will be consigned to a spare room....

Later, Almac

[Jan. 6]

RJs:

... Once I wrote a column about my love affair with Hershey when not drinking. I would take the chocolates to bed, eat them while half asleep. Confessed in column that Connie used to awaken me while I had chocolate dribbling down my jowls. [One colleague] buttonholed me and wondered aloud and disgustedly how anyone would think that this kind of behavior was worthy of print in his beloved Journal. [He] disliked me with a passion, and I am very sorry to note that he is dead and I am not....

[Jan. 6, part two]

I am distraught and at loss for words. I sent a message and it got returned, because I had put a k on the end of [email address]. Why can't these AOL motherhumpers figure out these minor errors instead of sending them back two days later with some garbled and accusatory explanation?

I hate this and am not going to put up with it much longer. I had written a highly entertaining email, practically a column ... and for all I know it wound up in an accountant's file in Omaha. Or maybe it went to ... where Christ lost his underwear, sitting there unread in some Basque shepherd's misbegotten and drafty yurt....

A storyteller's odyssey

All these pearls of mine cast in the direction of … some ex-jai alai player's shack in deepest Idaho, while he is outside making ewes turn. And there is naught I can do about it except to fume and stamp my feet. And, since there is no longer any feeling in my left foot, this is not all that satisfying.

Well, yes, I am now 73, despite your unawareness of this vital event, and have received no gifts and congrats and kudos from either the Flint Urinal or the Saginaw News. So be it, they never promised me a rose garden.

I am still on track to leave tomorrow for Vermont and probably will be stopped at the N.H.-Vt. border once they find out I think Mr. Dean is even a bigger schmuck than the current resident of the oval office. And that is going some…. I bet he, if elected, will get us in several more wars just through shooting from the lip as well as the hip and saying stupid provocative things that George W. doesn't say merely because no one told him to say them.

… I am the kind of guy who couldn't get laid in a French whorehouse with a thousand-dollar bill. Still, even a blind pig can occasionally find a truffle. I will write if and when I return from Vermont [which] has the longest covered bridge in the world, or did I already tell you-all or did you know anyhow. I have to be careful with anecdotes, because I find I have started telling the same jokes to the same people, which, they tell me, is a red flag for Irish Alzheimers (in which the micks forget everything but their grudges).

Later, Almac

[Jan. 21]

Enlarge penis, breasts, cut debts, get fantastic sex w/dwarfs

Hi Reynoldses,

… Have been holed up in Hallowell for ten days recovering from cold or flu or somesuch. Felt so bad I was afraid I wouldn't die. Tottered out only to get orange juice, milk and NYT [New York Times]. Too sick even to do crossword puzzles…. But am beginning to sit up and take nourishment — and even trying some solid food. And cheered up

38

yesterday to hear about the Michael Jackson law enacted in La-la Land: three tykes and you're out.

Have quit smoking and drinking booze (again) and, like Mark Twain said about quitting smoking, "it's the easiest thing in the world to do, I've done it a thousand times."

... Last week, noticing I had only $5 in the bank ... I cut loose house cleaner and canceled cable TV.... The silence around the shotgun is golden in more ways than one. Have no radio, so computer is now my sole source of news, and it does job handily and I don't have to listen to Imus' ... mumblings....

Almac

[Jan. 28]

Hey Mac —

By the way, try to avoid putting such salacious headers on your emails! I just now discovered your latest (aging for a week) in some spam-blocker file, along with a bunch of Viagra ads and suspected computer virus-causing agents....

... Speaking of Viagra, did you ever make it to Vermont or did you get snowed in whilst still in Maine? Since we didn't hear from you (or find your latest, see above graf), we had visions of your car being found in some Vermont snowbank with a Dean sticker on the back bumper....

RJ

[Jan. 29]

Squeaky clean header

RJs:

Hardly think that having fantastic sex with dwarfs comes under the heading of spam, but what do I know?

... Yes, I did make it down to Vermont, and stayed three days (separate bedrooms but on same floor) ... in her lovely and well-appointed home.... [We] get along pretty good and are corresponding via the emails.... She has more money than me (doesn't everyone?) and is now cavorting about the

... Sunshine State, whilst I am still recovering from severe respiratory ailment ... have had cough and allied miseries for almost a month now....

[She] has invited me back to Vermont come spring, and we shall see what we shall see. She has plans to relocate in Florida permanently and perhaps, if I can ingratiate myself with her, she might bring me along as male companion and walker.

Am taking nothing ... nothing ... pillwise for this cold problem and, indeed, have weaned myself off anti-anxiety pills and Prozac and even aspirin and am completely drug free, even to point of not smoking for past month and avoiding alcohol, too. This clean-living is not all virtue, was too sick to smoke or drink and flat broke for past three weeks and even forced to go on the tab at local market.

(These Mainahs are cautious, though; they will put seemingly trustworthy local denizens on the tab at market, but not for smokes and beer or wine.) But now the first of the month looms and the checks have begun to flow two days early, and I may go out and get pie-eyed for the sheer hell of it, just to put an end to the ennui of living in single-digit temp Maine with multiple frozen digits....

Mac

[Jan. 29]

Mac — ... Thought you might be interested in two cutlines I saw in the Mobile Register's suburban edition this week. The Register's a pretty good paper, but these cutlines were a first for me. They ran a picture of four people, then ran the names, but added this phrase "in no particular order." So I guess it's like a contest to put the people in left to right order. They also did this with another picture of six people on the same page.

Just reporting on changes in journalism since we left.

RJ

[Feb. 4]

Caption action

UNLEASHED

Hi Rjs:

I have given some thought to Mobile Register cutlines and, unaccustomed as I am to being charitable, pose this query: Could it be that an admirable smartass on the copy desk slipped "no particular order" past a particularly obnoxious slotperson....

Time will tell, and if more "in no particular order" cutlines appear, then the RJs should seize opportunity to make a hundred scoots or so from the New Yorker by shipping that caption for consideration in its bottom-of-the-page feature on newspaper gaffes....

Later, Mac

[Feb. 14]

RJs:

I hope you folks are in a position, being in Alabama, to pass this recollection of mine along to proper authorities. When I was down in Gulf Shores a couple of years ago I visited the VFW bar several times and talked to a helicopter pilot at length about one of his personal recollections while he served in Alabama in the 1970s. This pilot, who seemed the soul of rectitude, told me he was driving along a road near Dannelly AFB one day and slewed to a stop when he saw a National Guard officer assisting an elderly black lesbian woman whose car had broken down....

My informant said it was George W. Bush, who had just left the base after breaking the sonic barrier three times in one afternoon and conducting top secret meetings concerning his clandestine long-distance sorties to Vietnam while under the pretense of being a non-flyer.

(He said Mr. Bush had worked with the Seals, the Rangers, and the Green Berets in the Middle East, the Pacific Rim, and in several hotspots near the Horn of Africa. Also, he said, George W. Bush provided air cover for John Kerry's river boat in the Mekong Delta, saving Kerry's crew and fourteen French nuns.)

Anyhow, George Bush helped the elderly lesbian and provided aid and comfort to several puppies and kittens that had been in the car before the breakdown. Bush, my

41

informant said, specifically asked that he not mention this incident because he (Bush) "was undercover and flying under the radar while on detached duty."

Later, Almac

[Feb. 14]

Mac —

... there have been a spate of cockfighting stories on TV and in the Mobile (no particular order) Register lately. That is not news, but a follow-up or related story was of interest. This story told of betting on dogs fighting pigs. Which I guess is not that unusual down here. One official said the practice is a gray area in the law that they might need to look into....

RJ

[Feb. 17]

Hey Mac —

Since we can't seem to get your Mac to play nice with my PC, I'm sending you a package today so you can play nicely with pencil or pen. This will be the first two "books" of my latest draft, less than half of the MS.... Consider the MS an Alabama pig about to enter the pit for some Alabama sport with a dog....

R(J)

[Feb. 17]

Thanks for the confidence

Roger and Jessica,

It will be great to get rogered via an actual script rather than one of his laconic emails. Appreciate sending copy of Roger's work along. Am very glad you folks value whatever contribution I might make.

(Surely, I will find something amiss in text. And ... snippily point out how disappointingly stupid no-neck of a Dutchman you are....)

So it was good to get this "assignment." I have dwelt in the "Existence Period" lately, a state described by Pulitzer winner Richard Ford in "Independence Day." Not living, existing in a kind of cocoon, a limbo. Feeling in some kind of control, only there's not that much to control. So it will be good to put my mind to a writing problem.

And, better yet, I have just recently formed an idea, finalllly, on how I can do something I have long wanted to do: write about my life, pulling very few punches. It's often lowdown sordid stuff, but has a taint of the universal.

Won't bore you-all with this incipient scheme, save that till later.... Meantime, can't wait to catch him out — maybe nail oxymorons like Greater Hoboken ... or refute a claim that lowlanders are almost as good as highlanders.

Later, Mac

[Feb. 28]

Not gone, no forwarding

Hi Reynoldses,

Joe Gores wrote several classics about a San Francisco skiptracing agency, a repo outfit, and one of his most notable works, entitled, "Gone, No Forwarding," played on the post office stamps regarding runners who had left some address: "Gone, no forwarding."

Well, I am not gone from current address ... and the joys of living in a condo amid the nubile stews, the kidney-shaped pool, the table tennis room, the shuffleboarding facility, and the nine-hole Bobby Jones golf course.

The stewardesses — flight attendants, sorry — give me no rest and are always leaving their thongs and Miraclebras around the place, and I am always mistaking them for scarves or bandannas or handkerchiefs.

... Joan volunteered to help me pay crushing winter heating bills and cut rent $50 per month. So it would now be more expensive to leave than stay, an exact reversal of situation....

... I have unpacked all my worldly possessions. Do I feel like an idiot, all this ... packing and unpacking? The short answer is, yes, but I talk to myself a lot and that takes the edge off, though it does make Finley, Faraday and Fogarty wince and hunch their shoulders.

Under my new decor, the well-hung redheaded Scot from Toronto, in his kilt, now hangs on the wall to your right as you enter condo, his cudgel and tie close to his left hand.

Got your package of prose and haven't opened it yet because I am going to visit friends in Bar Harbor for a couple of days ... and will take it to pore over in a room of my own in a great, almost majestic rented house my chums have on a bluff overlooking Bar Harbor — and looking up at its (relatively) impressive little mountains where, they tell me, clouds scud by looking like dirty white buffalo....

Oh, and I hear through the Net and newspapers that the people who manage my annuity may come under investigation.... (You may recall that ... after Connie died, a broker in Saginaw Township persuaded me to put our IRAs, $95,000 worth, into a variable deferred annuity tied to the market. [MacLeese said he did so because he was afraid to be in control of that much money while still drinking or thinking about drinking and was worried about blowing it.]

(The annuity, of course, has been paying off at a much smaller monthly rate than predicted since the market started its nosedive about 30 seconds after I signed the contract.... I can't touch this money, so they keep alleging, and this, I guess, is what I get for uncharacteristic prudence....)

Later, Mac

[Feb. 29]

Hi Mac —

... I don't think Jessica has seen the well-hung Scot, but I am sure she would be grateful he has survived various packings and unpackings. We are a tad jealous that you have been to Vegas and now on way to Bah Hahbah, whilst we are literally stuck in the coolish sand down here in L.A. [Lower Alabama]....

Reynolds....

[March 13]

Roger:

That ain't no Alabama pig, that's more like a top coon dog in good voice and his prime....

Started reading draft and stayed right with it till I ran out of pages. This from an inveterate reader who goes through six or seven novels a week, and tosses at least two early on....

I really like the developing characters, the density of the writing, the seldom-wasted words, the newspaper inside stuff, the linear drive, the understated humor, but most of all like the thing that could separate this work from most others of the stripe. That is, Norton's growing awareness there's something amiss with his body.

Thus we learn he must contend not only with the usual fictive adversaries but an enemy within. This element, I think, more than any other factor, is what's going to drive your book and make it much more than just another hero-against-them saga.

... am late in writing on these matters because have been off feed while finally coming to grips with respiratory problem I have had all year. Mother of all intractable coughs, railroad flat alive with mounds of mucus. Had mulishly decided last year not to take any more medication for anything, but last week ... had to give it up and see a doc. (Hard days nights in Bar Harbor.)

So have (again) quit smoking and drinking, am taking my medicines. [Quit] six days so far and am aiming ... for three months. At the very least. (Commitments should be open-ended and not smack of finality, I have decided.)

Also have stopped thinking lustful thoughts about Janet Jackson's left breast. Yes, I know, that's the mammary that wasn't shown on TV. Which is the reason I had been able to still entertain lustful thoughts about it.

Mac

[March 13]

Hi Mac —

... like you I am battling some body indignity so am not sure how much energy I will have to respond. Was glad to see that [manuscript] was not a Dixie pig....

My ... problems stemmed from a brief few-day trip to N'awlins and Vicksburg, where I think I caught the clap or West Nile virus, or some such. Can you catch the clap from eating a muffaletta?

... it was heartening to see your comments, especially from someone who has a novel stuck to his hand at all times. I sent you half of the novel because I wanted you to tell me how various things are developing without knowing the end game....

RJ

[March 15]

Prostitutes and canines

Greetings,

... I think it is key — and so truthful — to hit on the fact that so many in the city room are not going to be at all helpful to Rob and even try to torpedo him as you have the "cowboy" ... manfully trying to do. (... I remember when I wrote a column in Flint, how some folks did overt things to discourage my little efforts....

Sorry you are feeling puckish.... I guess N'awlins will do that to a well-meaning visitor ... you have to be careful what you eat in that town.... I seem to recall thinking of the place as a humungous fungus creeping moldily along the river ... ah, the smell of stale beer, fresh urine and wine dregs, the sights of wan and skinny female and male prostitutes wafting about amidst the capering and tootling ... was enough to drive a stronger man than yours truly to drink....

Mac

[March 18]

Reynoldses' Southern Lair:

I remember when [a copy editor] started writing doltish alerts to the morningside workers about tidbits he'd fielded while working (or not working) nights on copy desk. So I started aping [his] reports, scribbling or typing such doings as, say, "Greater Auks menacing Genesee Towers" or "Ubly farmer finds 1,500-pound zucchini."

... [He] was the epitome of the stereotype of those old-time copy desk drones ... who lucked into newspaper work more by chance than anything else. Like Tripp, who never studied journalism but hung around a bar where Utica sportswriters convened and next thing you know Bud's a copy desker in sports department. And without having been tainted with absurdities of formal education....

Later, Mac

[March 21]

Great start, strong finish

Roger:

Finished second part today, and it just kept getting better and better as it went along, as if you were picking up steam en route.

The windup — the denouement, as us literary types like to say — was great. It was sharp and quick and moving and affecting, done with a great touch, a sure feel. It hit me where I live.

I've read a bunch of novels, and this one stands with the tall ... would be appalled and aghast if you didn't get it published in short order.

May come up with niggling comments, quibbles, possible polishings, suggestions, but, you have to know this: You did good. You hit a good nail.

More later, Mac

A storyteller's odyssey

[Grand Blanc; April 11]

Confessions of a baseball junkie

Hey Mac —

Yes, I am still alive, albeit recovering from baseball overload. As you may remember, I have been involved in two fantasy baseball leagues for lo, these many years. One of my all-day auction drafts was last Sunday, and the second was yesterday. As Jessica can tell you, the period before the drafts involves literally months of preparation, gathering intelligence.

I could tell you more about the inner workings of each American League player than I could about how the Shrub has mangled syntax. It's baseball, baseball, baseball, all the time. Then on top of that, the Tigers win four games in a row. (Wouldn't Connie be proud!)

Dean Howe had one of the best lines ever about fantasy baseball. He wrote a column [in the Flint Journal] about how stupid it was, how the people involved ought to get a life. He told how it was all based on statistics, and he compared it to going out in the yard in the middle of the night and picking up night crawlers....

So, now the truth can be told. That's what I've been doing since last I wrote anything substantive. And you thought I was busy on my novel. Actually, I did spend one day on it last week, between baseball sleuthing. I took action on four of your comments/suggestions....

RJ

[April 12]

Dear RJs:

Aside to Jessica: Please inform Roger, with all due delicacy, that WIP means Work in Progress, not Work in Procrastination. Also, advise him baseball is no longer the American pastime, and fake baseball is no pastime at all.... Such idle activity is not, in the considered view from central Maine, anywhere near as admirable as drinking screwdrivers in the Hallowell pub....

On to more substantive matters:

48

— No longer give an outhouse rat's bony ass that I have only this machine and books for home entertainment; thought I'd miss radio and TV but don't. Am thinking about deep-sixing telephone too, but that would affect computer. Put that radical move on hold, but threw out answering machine yesterday. I don't know how to make it work right, and do not want to learn, either.

If you folks ever call me, you should know that no cute little message will be forthcoming: "We're in the toilet and can't come to phone right now but if you're not too odious we may get back to you...."

— Yes, Connie woulda been tickled to see Tigers win at outset, but I understand they lost a game the other day, so a pox on them.

— Once again, my team won trivia contest at Liberal Cup. We collected $200. Modesty prevents from going into detail, but one key question I alone nailed among assembled trivialities was: "Has there ever been an opening day no-hitter in major league baseball and, if so, who done it?"

(Yes, Bob Feller shortly before Big War. I think I was only contestant alive during those heady days.)

... Disliked some presidents — Clinton, Nixon, LBJ, Bush 1 — but none stirred animosity I feel for this dumbest president ever.

Don't y'all hate it when you know POTUS isn't anywhere near as smart as you?? FUBAR, in the hallowed words of WWII GIs: Fucked up Beyond All Repair. That's what you get with a guy who brags on being a C-student after being privileged enough to have the best education available to humankind dumped into his lap....

Mac

[April 21]

The Old Loathsome Pines

Dear Reynoldses,

It was very good to hear I've helped and been generously appreciated to boot in re the WOP. (Work of Passion). Am thankful for appreciation but, in truth, I owe y'all a bunch

A storyteller's odyssey

for letting me be involved in a worthy endeavor — one that activates those lately untested talents that I can fairly lay claim to....

It is particularly good for me to have something testing to occupy mind, because just this morning I was shocked to learn that idle senior citizens in Maine are commonly led deep into piney woods — out where Moses misplaced his testicles — and left for dead. Left with not much more than a pat on the head or back and maybe two stale Twinkies before passing over the bar.

Saw a poignant story in The Arostook Avenger about a party of hunters that found three skeletons out near East Moses Mountain and one said to his comrades:

"What remnants you see over there?? Them are those of my granddad, my grandmom and Great Aunt Bess.... They were hardy Mainahs and went quietly...."

Later, Mac

[May 11]

Green Mountain Boy

Hello, RJs,

Just returned to my beloved Maine after four-day visit with lady friend in Vermont. Thus delay in response to the latest missive from Michigan....

In Vermont, [we] ... attended a revue in White River Junction by blacks dubbed "Ain't Misbehaving" and themed on Fats Waller, before an audience of honkies, many of them yuppie flatlanders from Connecticut and Massachusetts; ... played Scrabble games, during which I repeatedly humiliated [her]....

... we gushed over administration's adept handling of abuse in Iraqi prisons. Several Hallowell friends intrusively asked if I "got lucky" during visit to Green Mountain state. I merely note it was exhausting visit, owing to bedroom's ceiling and wall mirrors, the trampoline, the trapeze bars, and baffling profusion of balms, lotions and ingenious sexual devices....

A final observation on the way things are in Vermont: There were five blacks performing Waller revue. It's my suspicion they were the only blacks in Vermont that night.

Later, Mac

[May 14]

Promoting Airman Spooney

RJs:

This morning I fell to musing about "Whores and Hounds" and it struck me that Roger could, if he so chose, promote WOP character Spooney from cameo bit to supporting actor.

It occurred to me that Rob and Spooney are archetypes, two sides of coin, opposite poles among odd specimens that inhabit newsrooms. The odd couple of the newsroom.

Spooney is a drifter-bottle baby of the kind they sometimes got right in old short stories and movies. Spooney is uncredentialed and thinks newspaper business went all to hell once they started hiring high school graduates. He cannot afford ideals but means well, sort of.

Rob is a later version of breed. Not a drunk nor nerd, not a wastrel nor a flash, just a hardworking idealist-realist who simply sets about getting good job smartly done. Thinks it good, along way, to comfort the afflicted, afflict the comfortable....

Interesting aspect of Spooney-Tripp is that, even as his intellectual skills fizzle, he still reads papers and magazines closely, monitors TV, considers it part of his job (and being) to know what's going on.

In a bar, Tripp could, if so motivated, insinuate himself into any group and pick up info about city faces and facts and figures.... Tripp liked to buddy up with local celebs, stars on papers, being somewhat in awe of people who actually show up for work, sober and bright-eyed and even slightly succeed at something....

Later, Mac

[May 16]

RJs:

Just passing along Tripp story, so this note doesn't demand quick response.

My recollection — and allow for human memory's tricks of condensation and confabulation and confusion — is that Tripp and I came out of Green Door [a bar behind the Flint Journal] at closing and spotted [Bill] Gallagher pulling up to loading dock. Gallagher debouched from vehicle and was immediately hailed by Tripp, who worshipfully commenced beseeching Gallagher to let him have a look at his Pulitzer prize and also at the picture of [Adlai Stevenson] with the hole in his shoe.

Tripp expostulated to this effect: "Everybody knows you always carry your Pulitzer around with you, along with that picture ... are they in the trunk? Can we see, can we, can we?"

Surprisingly, Gallagher ignored Tripp as he made his way into the Flint Journal. Suspect Gallagher ... gave Tripp some sort of special dispensation. Have always marveled over Tripp's ability to offend without being hammered into the ground every other week or so.

Later, Mac

[May 30]

Reynolds people:

... Last night [at a bar], a couple of chums, line cooks at another establishment, offered two saucy young blond (blonde) women two Long Island ice tea mixed drinks if they would perform lap dances and salacious gyrations upon an unsuspecting me. So these two comely and buxom females came over and started climbing all over me, exposing their navels, their pubic areas and other body parts. Thrusting their lissome forms in provocative manner, causing me to become very excited, indeed, some observers contended, overwrought.

And I have not yet calmed down.

One wench showed me (flashed, as it were) her breasts, and these were the youngest mammaries I have seen (live, in person) in lo these past four or five decades. To my undying credit, I had the wit to say, "Thanks for the mammaries."

But I don't think any bystanders caught the essence of my great good wit. A bon mot not got. Other than that, not much going here, but I just got three monthly checks and perhaps something as stimulating might occur this evening....

Later, Mac

[June 13]

Dear Reynoldses:

... It was really dumb of Ray Charles to die while everyone but Michael Moore was mourning [President] Reagan. Reminds me of how Mother Teresa screwed up by dying about the same time [as] Princess Diana....

... I have it on good authority that the administration has Bin Laden in custody in Gitmo, and George W., in October surprise, will execute the evil bastard in a Fox News exclusive, using Saddam Hussein's pistol.

Later, Mac

[July 7]

Reynoldses:

Hope you had glorious fourth — mine was spent fretting over fridge, which died, ingloriously, after I had stupidly caused a freon leak while trying to defrost the hoar-and-rime ridden thing. Today I get a new though used icebox, and hope it will take care of perishables better than its predecessor, which, I learned from repairman, was 34 years old and not repairable.

Reason for this brief communication, though, is I was just struck by thought on WIP.

A storyteller's odyssey

At one point you have Rob talking to city councilman about gaming raid, and Rob jokingly asks how much guy lost in game.

This reminded me of ploy I used to use in Miami on police beat when calling a place, like a bar or store, where an unhappiness had occurred.

An example of shifty device was I called a jewelry store that has been robbed; was trying to find out how much robbers got. So I asked guy who answered phone what was the name of the employee that got killed in robbery.

Of course, no employee had been killed, and the guy got so taken up in explaining why this wasn't so that he told me a lot more about the robbery than, I am sure, he had intended to. Including how much was taken.

So it occurred to me that that sort of deceitful move by reporter might be employed somehow in WIP. Just an idle thought. Obviously.

Later, Mac

[July 9]

Hey Mac —

... We got back a couple days early from the Ludington art fair. The good news is we had a good day on Saturday.... The bad news is that rain, and the threat thereof, forced cancellation of the second day. Plus the rain overnight on Sat/Sun caused a bulge in the roof of our booth and it collapsed into a pretzel when I tried to get it off.

So we have spent a few days drying things out and making repairs for our next show in one week. Then we have had to start replacing the inventory that we sold. Businessmen need all the sympathy and support we can get....

Also have had to get my mother scheduled for another round of doctoring.... Unlike your fridge, my mother's plumbing is 87 years old and may be repairable....

RJ

P.S.: I like your idea about giving Rob a deceitful ploy. He's a little goody-goody, and it might take some of that shine off him.

[July 16]

Dear R.J. Reynoldses,

I read a while back that you people had purchased the British company that makes Benson & Hedges, and so quit smoking, knowing you folks have no sympathy for smokers and probably will introduce healthful substances into the product, decrease nicotine, other harmful chemicals, and stuff like that there.

It is a month now since I have had any cigarettes, and am also off the booze and the blunts for that period....

... I cannot sympathize with your misadventures at fair.... The collapsing tent, the loss of profits, the attendant annoyances and inconveniences, show once again that the mindless accumulation of capital can only lead to more and more monopolistic excesses, more big homes for the bourgeois in Grand Blanc and like gated enclaves, further enragement of the proletariat (me) and, inevitably, revolution and a proper redistribution of the wealth.

Speaking of George Bush, a commentator noted he first pronounced Iraq "Eye Rack" and suggested Bush learn how to pronounce names of countries before invading them.

Saw "Farenheit 911" at independent theater in Waterville with chum Maisie. Mr. Moore commits usual distortions, artful omissions, cheap shots, dodgy "facts" and comes up with not much new, but puts it all together well and the local hayshakers were greatly appreciative. Audience treated each known (at least to me) atrocity as a revelation; if boobus Americanus would read newspapers and news mags we wouldn't need such documentaries. (But George's little-boy-lost looks while reading "The Pet Goat" at library in Florida on day of attacks were worth price of admission and Moore performed a public service getting that film out before public....

(It's my recollection I was first "mainstream" journalist to deign to write about Moore.... Think I was first to columnize about him; devoted several whole columns to the rascal, so perhaps this gives me some small claim to fame? What is your recollection?)....

Later, Mac

[Aug. 17]

Hey Mac —

... I hate to be a bearer of bad tidings, but I checked out the history of who reported on Michael Moore first at the Flint Journal. You were the first to write a column about him, as you suspected, but the first to write a news story about him was one David V. Graham. Take a sip of Maalox, and try to get over it....

RJ

[Aug. 18]

Hi RJs:

... I [have] returned to practice of taking an Antabuse a day. I had hoped to start taking a new drug called Campral and put out by Merck; it got approval from FDA late last month after good results in testing on lushes, including brain imaging; supposedly is best thing yet to reduce craving in dry alkies whose brains' pleasure centers get so whacked they keep demanding body get more of vile potions that caused problem in the first instance. But drug, a so-called inhibitory, is not yet available in provinces, so doctor and I agreed Antabuse could be stop-gap until it shows up here.

Stopped taking Antabuse upon arrival in Maine after learning one side-effect was peripheral nerve damage. Which I have, but not that bad, though it is progressive. I'd been taking Antabuse off and on since '62, and no doctor ever mentioned nerve damage result of long-term use until then. Catch-22. Of some small interest here is that Heller's first title was "Catch 18," but they switched to 22 because Leon Uris' "Mila 18" came out about same time. It is just such facts that make me such an interesting conversationalist when I talk to myself in the wee hours.

56

In any case, Antabuse for short period can't do too much further damage to nerves. Neurologist told me couple of years ago, "The good news is you look like you might make it to 85 or 90; the bad news is your left foot won't."

... So every morning I take Antabuse, thereby making it perilous to drink booze for 12 days. Twice, since '62, I have been thirsty enough to drink while some was still in system, and I advise against that....

Regards, Mac

[Sept. 8]

Reynolds bastion:

... hero Kerry was audaciously un-heroed and discredited as a leader; hence the spectacle of a hero stamping his feet and saying he is too a hero. Achilles never had it so bad. But all is not lost, Reynoldses.... So do not go all wobbly. Kerry was written off in New Hampshire, but came back and ... they say Kerry performs best under pressure, like a good rewrite man, say....

Kerry will carry the day. Unless he keeps letting those photogs snap him windsurfing in get-up that looks like a Speedo for older, yet disgustingly healthy, rich bastards. Why doesn't he get into bumper pool?

Later, Mac

[Sept. 17]

Hey Mac —

We are breathing a little easier on the status of our condo. A New Orleans TV station sent out a camera crew in a helicopter yesterday morning; they toured portions of the coast, and as luck would have it, just about the very last scene in the video is of our condo. It shows water from the lagoon in back part way up on the parking level and covering the pool and tennis court and brand new putting green. Our lagoon dock and gazebo appear to be gone.

Our condo faces the ocean on the top floor at the left on the video but we can't see anything but our back window....

57

A storyteller's odyssey

[The eye of Hurricane Ivan] passed directly over us, meaning the winds before and after would have been side to side, hitting the strongest part of the condo on our wing, not directly at the sliding glass door to our balcony....

You probably want to know what happened to your favorite haunts. I would suspect the Barefoot Bar is gone.... Florabama [a ramshackle roadhouse bar on the Florida-Alabama line] went with the first wave, according to most reports. Don't know about the Dawg House....

Roger

Part 3: Naval servitude

When MacLeese began basic training at Great Lakes Naval Training Center near Chicago, it didn't take him long to realize he wasn't going to be an admiral.

At first he thought he had a chance because none of the other guys in Company 224 at Camp Porter had such high aspirations. Then he learned a near-sighted chief petty officer couldn't distinguish him from another recruit.

"[We] were both skinny shrimps, both had black hair and both had contrived to have broken shnozzolas. We were both from Connecticut and both had arms hanging down port and starboard sides."

Enter a savvy recruit from the streets of Detroit. He had noticed that no one counted the recruits when their company assembled in front of the barracks each day.

"He observed that all the company did was march and present arms and pick up things and run from one line to the next. [He] found this activity essentially meaningless and, for two weeks, had spent his days reading and musing behind a woodpile near the fence that enclosed Camp Porter."

That diversion sounded fine to MacLeese. "I vaguely sensed that admirals didn't march eight hours a day and do a lot of presenting arms. They probably read, philosophized and plotted strategy."

The Detroit recruit plotted their daily escape from the sweatiness of boot camp. "He discovered that if we wore incredibly dirty whites and turned our cute little white hats inside out, people would think we were on KP – Kitchen Police – doing the drudgery attendant to serving food to the ravening troops fresh from stressful workouts."

Behind the woodpile, MacLeese conducted a program of self-improvement through reading, with one eye on their company marching briskly by "in a manner that made us proud to belong, after a fashion, to such a fine body of men."

He read and re-read Erskine Caldwell's works for hidden meaning. They played checkers and gin rummy.

Then one day, MacLeese peeked out from behind the woodpile and noticed a line of "purposeful fellows coming across the field." It had dawned on the chief that he had not seen the Connecticut pair in tandem for quite a spell, and he conducted a muster.

MacLeese said the woodpile refugees spent a great deal of their subsequent time at Camp Porter "doing foolish exercises with heavy rifles after twilight. My naval career was doomed. But I found solace. After close perusal of 'God's Little Acre,' I had raised my sights and was thinking of becoming a sharecropper."

Boot camp graduation was a fateful day in MacLeese's life. His third wife, Laurie, said he told her that was when he went to a bar and had his first drink. "He got rip, roaring drunk and threw up." A companion went back to the barracks, but MacLeese went back into the bar for another drink.

Within three years, MacLeese said, he had drunk his way past the amateur alcoholic level. Back then, he said, the A-word was unheard in his circles. "If you couldn't handle booze, you were a drunk and an immoral weakling, too." But he said he was aware of one thing: "I have never been able to drink and guarantee that I wouldn't get drunk."

He also said: "If a man tells you he 'needs' a drink, do not think he merely 'wants' a drink."

Many alcoholics, "or drunks if you prefer," he said, "find the word essential shorthand to remind them of their own peculiar reality.... I'd say 'alcoholics' should consider that antiseptic word not as a primary identification of self but as a description of one of their quite understandable and quite human limitations."

Drinking was not the only vice he did to excess. Gambling was another. In forays to Las Vegas decades later, he had a hard time stopping. He lost every dollar he took with him and borrowed much more.

He wasn't a man who dipped a toe in the water. He jumped in with a splash. When he decided to write poetry, he immersed himself, acquiring books about the art, from beginning techniques to collections of poems and critiques.

Early in his Hallowell years, during one of several attempts to stop smoking, he reported in a phone call that he was using nicotine patches. He had tried one patch, then decided that since one seemed to be taking the edge off his craving, he'd try two at a time. That should make quitting even easier. He was at three patches at a time and counting.

How many more he eventually plastered on his body at once is not known, nor is how he avoided nicotine poisoning.

One can envision his drinking while on shore leave progressing the same way. If one drink made it easier for him to strike up a conversation with women in a bar, well, two would make him more charming, his stories even funnier, and enhance his romantic possibilities.

He "needed" drinks to create a lull in his sensitivities. Drinking made it easier to connect with people, and yet he created an even bigger problem, a new reality, one of dependency and loss of control.

MacLeese would end up spending four years in the Navy and he said "it was by no means a boring hitch since I had five courts-martial and about 30 captains' masts – captains' masts being lesser cudgels used when nobody wants to go to the trouble of convening a court-martial."

In at least one instance, he gained the notice of the local press while he was in port. In 1950, a Newport, Rhode Island, newspaper reported that MacLeese, then 19, refused to follow a police officer's order to move. His penalty: a $5 fine and costs.

While in the Navy, he was occasionally combative, yet never in combat, even though, as he wrote, he "volunteered – a roll of drums, please – to fight in Korea." The captain on his ship rejected his volunteerism "because of all those damn courts-martial. That's the logic that loses kingdoms. Or, at least, police actions. If I'd gotten over there...."

He ended up being forced to go to the primitive port of Cannes, France, and other ports around the Mediterranean in Italy and Spain, and those in the Caribbean, but couldn't get to bask in Korea on a bet. Such was the Navy, where "people could never get it into their heads that not getting to work on time was hardly a criminal offense. No, they had to fancy it up, call it AWOL."

The term was not a stranger to him; he admitted he was "absent-minded" about returning to his ship once he left on shore leave. Or he got sidetracked.

"Once I awakened in a naval hospital ward, surrounded by Marines. They had just come from Korea; most had frostbite. I, an earnest sailor, had just come from a Boston bar where my skull had somehow been fractured....

"I had this big bandage on my head and it appeared that I had been fighting, so I was welcomed with glad cries by the truculent Marines. Actually, I had been knee-walking drunk and probably had just fallen on my head, which was my custom. But I had not the heart to disillusion my new comrades-in-harm."

MacLeese said that although it was boring at Boston's Chelsea Naval Hospital during the Christmas holidays in 1950, it wasn't too bad when the Grey Ladies came around. They would give cookies and candies to the Marines and "sweetly inquire as to the state of their frozen tootsies."

The Gray Ladies mistook him for a Marine, and he "would mutter vaguely about 'bugging out from the Yalu' and speak off-handedly about the 'Frozen Choshin' (reservoir)."

In addition to New England ports, Norfolk, Virginia, was a familiar "liberty" spot for MacLeese and his shipmates as they clattered down the gangway to the boat that would take them from tanker to shore for a night of dodging hustlers and vomit.

"We did not really go to Norfolk. We trod the primrose path to East Main St., a honky-tonk enclave in the city. Norfolk proper was mostly treated as The Forbidden City. Good reason, too. Signs did indeed say, "Sailors and Dogs Keep Off the Grass."

The East Main they knew is gone, he wrote decades later, "stomped out as if it were some repellent beast." The section of "Easy Main" that catered to servicemen was a collection of seedy taverns, tattoo parlors, hockshops, and run-down hotels.

"We'd hit the beach with the more welcome evening tide and 'Easy Main' would soon be aswarm with reeling and roistering swabbies. Trick was to work your way up one side of 'Easy Main' and down the other. We were sucked into each glittering neon nightmare of bustling barkeeps, B-girls, chug-a-lugging gobs and highly suspect civilians....

"We would guzzle beer and occasionally get into brief shoving matches that became battles only on the morrow's recounting. We would yearn for the too-early blooming flowers and proposition them hesitantly, like salesmen without proper motivation. We would tell them sea stories, outrageous lies of loves lost and battles won."

When MacLeese was in dire straits financially, he would seek a spot in Norfolk where sailors and dogs were allowed, and he would "get a buddy to sprawl in the street while hundreds of swabbies straggled by....

"I would tell my comrades-in-arms that my comrade in the street had suffered a fit from Medcrud (a strange malady contracted while consorting with the dregs of the Mediterranean bowl). Needed $5 to rush him to the naval hospital. One night I collected $64 in three hours although my friend did get tired of sprawling in the street."

One day, he and Dick Placek, a sailor buddy, were "stone-broke and trudging down E. Main Street when a loose poodle attached itself" to them.

"Shortly after the poodle joined us, I picked up an ailing pigeon in the street, and no, I didn't get any diseases.

"We were proceeding in stately manner when a hotel bellboy volunteered to 'buy' the dog. I said that would cost him $5, inasmuch as we were quite fond of Pierre, not her real name." At this point, Placek came up with a "divinely inspired notion." He told the bellboy: "You are going to have to take the pigeon, too, fellow. The two are practically inseparable." And it was done.

In 1951, MacLeese was with a group of sailors in the PX on the Norfolk base. A vicious brawl ensued after one of his companions tossed a beer at somebody.

"As I recall, about 60 angered and righteous swabbies chased us out of the canteen. They caught us hiding under some bushes and pounded on us awhile, then called the Shore Patrol." Five hours later – at 2:30 a.m. – a load of six sailors was dumped outside the gates to Camp Allen, a brig run by Marines just back from Korea.

"Buckets were draped over our heads and we goggled darkly. The marines kept us standing at the gate for several hours and every 10 minutes or so some gyrene would slam a billy club against our bucketed heads." MacLeese said this was not the best way to cope with an emerging hangover.

For the next 63 days, they were forced to march to the call of a crazed guard. And march. And march, as the guard sat "smoking happily in a chair," shouting orders. "To the rear, march." Over and over and over again.

The guard "thought it fun to spew out about 50 successive marches to the rear," MacLeese wrote.

"We quickly became a reeling, moiling mob, hydra-headed and collision prone. Blinded by heat, all sense of direction fled, we staggered about, cursing, sobbing for breath. Clearly these gyrenes were violating our military rights, but that was no problem since none of us was aware that we had any rights. Just the lefts and the rights and the rearward marches.

"But here's something weird, too. After 40-odd days of daily marching, we had determined to outlast [the guard], who clearly was in the market for a psycho discharge anyway. We took everything [he] had to throw at us and, in some strange way, were better for it.

"[He] marched us to something approaching manhood. We had goofed up, else we would not be behind bars, but [he] taught us there was something salvageable out of the dreck. Our trip to Marineland had unexpectedly paid off."

Inside Camp Allen's brig, between marches, it was "decreed that no prisoner should sit down between 6 a.m. and 9 p.m. A lot of us prisoners had been used to sitting down now and again between 6 a.m. and 9 p.m.…."

MacLeese was "righteously apprehended for sitting down at high noon and trotted before the Marine officer who conducted 'Office Hours,' which meant 'Beans and Greens Time.'" He was sentenced to nine days in solitary "without condiments."

"Without condiments? At that time I was an avid reader – avid enough to warrant suspicious glances from the more burly West (by God) Virginians – but I could not recollect Zane Grey, Jack London, Mark Twain, Erskine Caldwell or Ernest Hemingway having mentioned condiments. My knee-jerk reaction was, 'Since I don't know what condiments are, maybe I won't miss them.'

"Quickly I learned that condiments meant salt and pepper and everything else a sensible person would put on lima beans and spinach, if he or she were ever forced to make such a decision. I was to get two meals of lima beans and spinach daily for nine days and every couple of days they would throw in some bread crusts. Occasional water.

"They gave me a Bible and I didn't see anyone else for nine days, since the guards shoved the mess kit through a hole in the iron door. There wasn't much to do but read the Bible and count walls."

MacLeese described his brig experience in a column, and here is where, in his later Hallowell correspondence, he admitted to having second thoughts, a weak moment as a columnist. After submitting the column, he went back into it and deleted a reference about using the Bible as a visual aid for masturbation. As he said, there wasn't much to do.

None of his activities, though, "offered much toward coming to grips with this perhaps unique situation: For sitting down they had sentenced me to a cell in which I could sit down all the time.

"At first I refused the food, but shortly realized this was self-defeating. Came the 'Make 'Em Think You Like It' gambit. How about pretending to greatly appreciate greens and beans? What if, in fawning and grateful fashion, I amused myself by praising the guards for bringing me this vile crap, which … the gyrenes always watered to make even more dismal.

"It was done and I am going to have to stop pretending that I unfailingly act dumb. It was smart … because I enjoyed solitary and the delightful exchanges with unseen guards after praising the punishment.… Best thing was that the Marine guards knew I didn't like the menu, but it was a different reaction and they seemed to enjoy it. It made my time in the hole easier.…"

Toward the end of his tour in the Navy, in the spring of 1952, Fireman Apprentice MacLeese was waiting on a dock for a whaleboat to take him back to his oil tanker at dusk after shore leave in Norfolk. The ship was parked in Hampton Roads, the channel through which the James and Elizabeth rivers flow into Chesapeake Bay.

Waiting with him was his buddy Placek and a chief petty officer toting a case of beer in case the whaleboat didn't venture into the rough channel waters. The more the chief drank, and the more he doled out cans of beer to the boat's crew, the less threatening the waters seemed to all. MacLeese and Placek were also drinking, from their own canned supply, crammed hurtfully inside their dress whites.

Eventually, it was "decreed that we would give 'er a try and we set off, bravely and stupidly.… About two beers each out into the Roads, Placek told me that the boat was bouncing and pitching so much" that they would never get to the ship. "Unless we swam," he said.

"I think I said that swimming was not beyond me. Placek then said I was a scaredy-cat who would never swim home. I had no recourse but to shuck my shoes off and dive over the side." Placek followed. "We both struck out boldly, possibly correcting course for Cannes."

During the next 20 minutes, "the crew valorously tracked us down; hunting two demented if wee white whales; the only difference being that when we were finally dragged back aboard it was with boat hooks, not harpoons. Although the latter method was subsequently discussed.

"The crew saved our lives, but during the rest of our journey home a dread silence prevailed" as the swimmers contemplated their punishment and the chief deep-sixed his remaining beer.

The next day, the executive officer held a captain's mast and asked Placek what had happened. He said he had seen MacLeese pitched out of the boat as it bounced atop the waves. Being a former American Red Cross lifeguard, he dove in to save him.

MacLeese gave his version of the events: "I stood up to see if I could see the ship and I toppled over the side!"

The exec "took this bald-faced lie like the officer and man he was." He gave the former lifeguard only a reprimand because he had a clean record. MacLeese, the sailor with dozens of pockmarks, received 10 days restriction.

The punished swimmers were puzzled. Why the light wrist-tap? Why didn't the heroes of the story testify? The conclusion they reached was that no one wanted a court-martial in which it would be revealed that the chief and the boat crew had been illegally snockered, or close to that state.

By following MacLeese's stories about his Navy life, one can hear murmurings of a possible new career after discharge. No one recalled that he faithfully wrote home about his activities but he did write while in the Navy.

He wrote pornographic letters for shipmates at 50 cents a pop. "They said I had a way with dirty words and would probably not go far unsupervised.

"Once I proposed marriage in a pornographic letter for a guy who didn't want to propose, and also told his paramour – a Norfolk barmaid with an IQ of 12 on tiptoes – that he was the illegitimate son of Lord Norfolk, who founded Norfolk, then developed dropsy....

"The girl was willing to accept this proposal and subsequently intimated she would consider it legal and binding. Fortunately we sailed. My shipmate did not have to prove – and could not have – my boastings about his virility and natural advantages."

UNLEASHED

[Sept. 18, 2004]

R and J:

Some storm. Once Ivan got in Gulf I started thinking about you folks and your condo ... a day ago I was watching one of those weather persons who don't have sense to come in out of the rain standing strong on a stormy beach; he was being duly buffeted, but I gave him no mind until caption signaled "Gulf Shores."

First figured your place was high up and in a relatively impervious structure, but after reading email understood the extent of woes. Thought of Florabama earlier, and was disheartened to hear it went, but no surprise there. I remember that crazy wooden old place well — it seemed as if it took ten minutes blundering and goggling in dark depths just to find the bar.

Your report on TV pictures of ... condo and even condo's window, and resultant videotaping and electronic magic acts teasing out sundry images evokes surreal or merely uncomprehending visuals. My hope: examination of video leads to 1972 Alabama State Police documents showing that Lt. Bush stalked, assaulted and slew a Mobile drag queen, got off with three weekends of community service....

TV now sez George leads John in some poll or other by thirteen points....

Later, Mac

[Oct. 5]

Hey Mac —

Just got back from our mission down south, and wanted to give you a quick update. Our unit of the condo was not bad. We had the carpet and pads taken out and probably will need the lower couple feet of drywall removed around the outside walls. Mold and mildew were starting to appear from the rain that blew in. No other damage, though.

Our street looked like a war zone, however. Sand, debris, beach houses strewn everywhere. First floor of our condo [complex] was totally blown out by the storm surge, including office, meeting room, bathrooms. Power boxes,

67

phones, and elevators were also a total loss. Basic structure, though, is fine. Parking lot still had several feet of sand, plus two beach houses blown into it from across the street. Back courtyard was a landfill/garbage dump.

Don't know when we will be able to occupy our unit again. Need power, water and sewer line repairs, and apparently that is going to take at least two months, probably much longer....

Looks like you finally have Kerry back where's he's competitive again....

Roger

[Nov. 6]

Four more years

Hey Mac —

Well, I am making a slow recovery from what Jessica thinks is election-induced depression. I have been napping an awful lot since Tuesday. Today on the radio I heard that the number of hits on the Canadian immigration web site increased by six times on the day after the election....

We have been spending a lot of time lately monitoring our condo, which still doesn't have power restored.... We hope we are going to be able to live in the condo by the first of the year, but are not confident....

RJ

[Nov. 8]

Dutchers:

... Voted for Kerry, and at 4 p.m. Tuesday exit polls and Internet blogs clearly indicated a surprising Kerry lead and probable win. And then came news the numbers were "weird." The liberal TV news shouters were trying to conceal glee over their unspoken knowledge of an apparent Bush loss. That contrasted with the yappers on Fox, some of whom were sour and almost tearful.

First time I voted in a national election and have been extant since Hoover. Next thing you know, Kerry loses....

This is really bad for those who don't love the baby Jesus because it seems clear Bush is going to go hell for leather; he may not be a religious zealot but an ideological fanatic who is, in some twisted way, using religion in pursuit of some cockamamie scheme. He is a drunk and a dry one and I think Twain said the only way to cure dipsomania is with religiomania.

I think Bush is short on book learning but smart in dealing with gullible people and cowing peers and making his fellow thugs happy. He's been "used" but by now he may be doing the using. At least Maine and me stood up for Kerry....

If I was you, I wouldn't go to Canada. Move permanently to Alabama, pass selves off as founders of the Immaculate Baby Jesus Church of the Altered Altar in Norman, Oklahoma. You're both retired master sergeants, served with 101st Airborne ... Bronze Stars, Purple Hearts, NRA, community service up the a-hole. You both like to line dance, drink Jim Beam or PBR, go to barn dances....

Later, Mac

[Nov. 16]

Dutchers,

... Thanks for sending [old] examples of my fevered strivings to rise to wit despite being inside Flint Journal building. Although 25 years hence, it seems MacLeese may have stabbed at skepticism and came up with mere cynicism. And cynicism expressed before age 73 should be looked upon askance. Or so it seems from this craggy perch....

Trying to think of [new title for novel] and have only come up with feeling it should somehow reflect book is about newspapering.... But "Whores" should stay on the shelf and off these streets, methinks.

Later, Mac

A storyteller's odyssey

The only acceptable title

Dutchers,

I spent 212 billable hours on what to name book, and have crafted the only acceptable title. And it is your good luck, Dutchers, that counselors working in Maine can only earn state's minimum wage, which is 67 cents an hour.

I approached task by asking: What is Roger writing about? He is writing about a newspaper reporter who's chasing a city's mayor. Questing after the mayor, tilting with City Hall's rascals. The reporter must fight city hall. Ergo, title of his book must be "Fighting City Hall."

(It is seldom we in publishing can weave such a seamless fit between book and title. A title with universal brand recognition.... It is even rarer, Jessica, for a writer such as Roger, with only non-fiction creds, to be gifted with such a grand title, one immensely superior to anything he's come up with over the years.)

... "Fighting City Hall," we can explain to the less perceptive others, has the immense virtue of being a widely known meme introduced to the world in the latter half of the last century.

We know what memes are, but for less favored we can explain they are creations — or recognition of an existing but heretofore unrecognized entity — of British thinker Richard Dawkins. A meme is a "virus," an idea, mental image, a concept, a bit of lore that flits from human mind to human mind, then lodges in collective memory and consciousness. Like "Remember the Alamo" and "FUBAR" and "immaculate conception."

... And readers — they'd all dearly love to have cojones to fight city hall and win — will buy book in numbers that become annoying or embarrassing in sheer hugeness. Wealthy beyond the dreams of avarice, the Dutchers will, as a mere fillip, give their Gulf Shores condo (in perpetuity) to a consultant capable of crafting the Title of Century....

Mac

Aside to Roger: After Charles Darwin came up with idea of evolution through natural selection and stuff like that,

Thomas Huxley, who, as you remember, was "Darwin's Bulldog," said: "It's so simple, so obvious, why didn't I think of that?"

Am sure something like that is going through your mind, Roger: "So damnably obvious, right before my eyes ... and yet ... so tantalizing, so elusive for me, and yet that cheesy Mac, him with one foot on a banana peel and the other near the grave...."

But Roger, you are in the company of men like Huxley — if not Darwin — and shouldn't go around beating yourself up.

[Nov. 20]

Tweaking the only acceptable title

Hey Maine-ahh —

Yes, I agree you have come up with a perfectly acceptable title and more, one that could grace the cover of my book, one that could make me proud, and for that you should get our thanks and adoration ... and yet, since I said "our," the J of RJ has one quibble. She is not willing to give up said L.A. condo, even in its present sad state, no power yet, no water, no sewer. So I came up with this plan: don't accept the title as is, therefore you don't have a debt of thanks or adoration.

Under this plan, the new working title is "Fighting City Hall and Prostitution." It has a certain style, without the word Whores, to which I seem to have such a great attachment. Now that I think about it, is all prostitution really that bad, doesn't it sometimes serve a purpose? ... Maybe the title should be "Fighting City Hall and Unseemly Prostitution"? ...

RJ

[Nov. 21]

(This message is chiefly to male Dutcher; female Dutcher can read but there is a caveat: she is cautioned there is "adult" or "blue" material toward end.)

Excellent job of tweaking hed, Roger.... I wrote a front-page banner on Gary Post Tribune after MacArthur died: "General

MacArthur Just Fades Away." It appeared in paper after tweaking by [news editor] as, "Say General MacArthur Just Fades Away."

[News editor] was of the Chicago school in which copy editors could slap a "Say" before any headline that might, in any imaginable way, be viewed as needing qualification. It apparently did not enter [his] mind that MacArthur indeed had just passed away, and paper would not be sued over this bold announcement. Or maybe [he] thought story was hoax or false alarm, an exaggeration ... perhaps he believed people did not really fade away? You never know.... [He] was working in Chicago when Dewey Defeated Truman.

Connie was on P-T with me when MacArthur died and she saved hed; I was reunited with it when we got married. But like most ephemera it just faded away.

Glad you see incredible rightness in "Fighting City Hall" and accept praise as my due.... Tell Jessica I infer my modest suggestion of reward for good work has been rejected. So be it. Tell her I forgive her and am stifling resentments over seemingly stingy act, a sort of withholding. But I will not be one of those annoying types who are all-the-time laying guilt trips on friends.

[From "Fighting City Hall and Prostitution," he segues to affixing condoms.] ... All the condoms I have ever worn were affixed by foreign prostitutes. I first tried to affix a condom in a commercial sex act in London because limey prosty did not think it part of her job to affix condoms. I thought this was off-putting, even unsociable. Still, I pressed on. I found the affixing tedious, awkward, difficult and disheartening. Also silly, even droll.

Drollness is no help when plotting sex, even in London, but somehow we got job done.

Mac

[Dec. 24]

Dutchers,

Had this dream last night that a retired couple from Michigan went to Hawaii while all their friends were uncomfortable as usual at home, dickering with propane companies, falling off snowy roofs.... The couple in my dream were fecklessly wandering in the forests and ran into a megagaggle of nenes; the nene, as you-all may now know, is the Hawaiian national bird. Though, of course, it is of Scottish origin, like so many things.

In olden times ferocious nenes were trained to peck at privates of the enemies of the noble Scots — chiefly people from lesser British isles and Holland, the poststamp that unaccountably produces many tall people.

I am now able to interrupt dreams or alter the narrative flow for the better, but this lulu about the Michigan couple — both wearing money belts, you have to have them if you can afford to go to Hawaii and Alabama and god-knows-where-all — became so horrific, the carnage so graphic and deeply disturbing, that I ended the dream, knowing even worse horrors were to come, things too ghastly for one of my sensibilities.

Thank you very much for finally settling up on the cost of the FCH title. I've had that one on offer to Updike, Roth, Mailer, Breslin, Toni Morrison, Maya Angelou, and Joan Collins. Morrison offered me $87, but I turned it down. She was emitting sexual vibes bordering on lust and I don't mix business and pleasure....

It's the day of the Eve before Christmas. Have written three local columns over past three weeks and printed them out on my printer and given them to henchpersons who drop them off a various spots around town — the library, the bars, the grocery store, etc. My henchpersons include the artist wife of the Maine poet laureate; the woman who cleans The Wharf, our most famous bar; a French handyman; a gay bartender-artist ... and two waitpersons named Heather and Maisie.

Now that an Antabuse a day is handily keeping the vodka away, I of course want to write but don't want to deal with any middlemen. So why not just sit in my railroad flat and write local "columns to my friends" in town and let them pass the scribblings around? (Sort of like in colonial times when village idiot would scribble out some fevered rant and post it on the boards by the well near the pond on the green. This appeals to me: screw technology, get retro....)

I have heard some favorable feedback. In any case, I am writing regularly, so feel pretty good about prospect although, as we all know, some folks screw up one-car funerals.

Later, Mac

[Dec. 25]

Hi Mac and a Merry Christmas,

It may give you some warmth and a sense of justice to know that we left Michigan when it was snowing and came back when it was snowing. It hasn't stopped yet. The nenes, or is it ninnies (for coming back), are getting restless. ... We've done nothing but shovel the driveway since we got back and took off our empty thong money belts.

We did see a flock, or is it gaggle, of nenes in Hawaii, but they weren't anywhere as common as the rooster.... they are everywhere, on the hotel grounds, at the beaches, along the road, and even in the wilds of Kauai, which is the only island we went to, except for the obligatory stopover in Oahu.... Did you go to the Pacific at all in your Navy days, or was it just Europe?

... All in all, though, it was a terrible trip. I'm sure it was much nicer in the garden state of Maine.

A couple days ago, we got word that power of a sort had reached our unit of our condo building. So we may be heading down in a few days to do some cleaning and painting.... No phone service yet, no cable, and water service goes out for up to 18 hours at a time. Sounds like Iraq....

Glad to hear you are writing columns again. Any chance your circulation director could add the moneybelt district of Michigan to your route? ... Jessica and I both wish you a happy holiday. Curl up and think about the life of the rooster on Kauai. Perfect.

RJ

[Jan. 3, 2005]

Rim shot

Dutchers;

Always fearful of spelling or pronouncing "tsunami," I never went to the Pacific. Still, naval historians ought take note of an early stab by two of our boys in blue who sought to serve in that theater.

In 1949, [a friend] and I, firemen apprentices off the USS Vulcan and wearing blue suits without navy hats or approval, set out from Newport, Rhode Island, bound for Los Angeles, California. Set off in chill winter with no baggage, no proper clothing, no papers and no money but gamely intent on navigating the continent by foot and the hitched rides shared with the few American citizens who actually supported our mission.

We hoped that there — where bluff land meets the vast and serene indifference of the Pacific — we on the rim of our manhood could begin our journey to the ranks of men who have served east of Suez, where the sun comes up like thunder across the bays, and where a man could raise a thirst and bed both small women and small boys.

Surely, when our eagle eyes first gazed from a Pacific peak in wild surmise, they would have had the same eager rapacity as those of Cortez's men when first they looked upon all that water ripe for voyages of conquest and predation.

There, we felt, we could turn our AWOL selves into the naval authorities, who we sensed would be far kinder and gentler to runaway young apprentices than the rigid fools back east. Probably, we reckoned, we would be assigned duty in Bali Hai or Tahiti.

But it was not to be. The authorities apprehended us in Albuquerque, which is even harder to spell than tsunami, and we were entrained to New York after a week's diet of chili and coffee even worse than that served aboard the Vulcan.

Spent New Year's holiday, four days, with [the lady] of Vermont. Talking and hanging around with [her] for four days while sober allowed me to fully appreciate that the old dear ... paid no attention to my entertaining stories while droning on about her next trips to Florida....

Mac

[Jan. 22]

Ambivalence runs amuck

Dear Dutchers,

Tidings from central Maine are exceedingly — and unaccountably — glad. Why are things going so well? I was wondering just last week. Was writing and off the booze for many moons, doing well. Then, three days ago, I got letter from [lawyer] averring yours truly ... will get about $147,000 [when my] 106-year-old great-aunt in Milford, Connecticut, shuffles off....

Great Aunt Gertrude Noone, apparently the oldest female in Connecticut, was predeceased last year by her sister Esther, who died at age 103. Esther's assets were conjoined with Gertrude's....

Dutchers, we're talking money found in the street here, when Aunt Gert hurries up and dies I soon will double my income and be able to visit y'all and stay in high-rise higher than yours. My roughly $24,000 yearly fixed income seemingly will be supplemented and become $48,000 over, say, the next seven years or so.

[As for the] two old dears ... I remember meeting them only about four or five times. One time I was in a cab with a notorious ... strumpet — and a stone wino to boot I am ashamed to say. There was a hellacious snowstorm and the two of us were on a three-day drunk and frolicking in the back seat; I was working on a pint of something cheap when cabbie picked up two nice old parties who climbed in to sit next to the driver with much sprightliness, and commenced chatting up the hack.

As soon as I heard the voices of the two great-aunts, I knew who they were from hearing them when I was a wee tad. I never found out whether they knew it was me back there ... odds are they did, you've got to be pretty clever to skip past 100 on this ball of dirt....

Dutchers, I want Aunt Gert to be well and live to a ripe old age, all the best. But ... she's already lived to a ripe old age and piling on more years would smack of wretched excess. Because I haven't spoken to [sisters Deborah and Sharon] and their husbands or spawn in three years and five months, I have no idea about the state of Auntie Gert's health, but thanks for asking.

Am thinking [lawyer] wouldn't send this kind of message without, perhaps, having spotted evidence that Gert will not be with us much longer.

I only hope this blizzard currently raging in Milford, Conn., area does not in any way shape or form affect Gert's vital signs adversely. Am so sorry I am up here in Maine and too feeble myownself to make long trip to sit by her bedside now and again. Probably, though, in months after Gert has passed, I'll be able to hit road in Lexus and drive hundreds of miles in any number of directions....

This prospect of money enough to coast has me in a slightly agitated state. I haven't told anyone about this good [news] since I've been pretty much staying home and writing columns to the bar, about which more later.... I want to go over and look at the letter and see if it is really true that I am in line for $147,000.

And please do join me in supportive thoughts about dear Gert. We'll not see her like again.

Mac

[Gulf Shores; Feb. 4]

Scuffing our toes with heads bowed

Sir Alan:

... we aren't quite sure how we should address an incipient heir. Sir seems an appropriate fallback. Being Capricorns, I'm sure we can find some dark cloud in this silver lining down the road.... But that's down the road. For now, we are happy in your good fortune.

We hope a certain someone is not hell-bent on setting a national longevity record.... a word of caution. I would not talk too loudly about your impending good fortune, for fear that Bush might make it a part of his Social Security bailout....

Keep us updated on the situation with elderly relatives, and how about sending a couple of your new columns down south?

RJ

[Feb. 6]

Suitor seeks carnal acts

Dutchers,

This is most recent love letter to Ms. Liberal Cup, the building, and is the sixth such letter, and in this letter I passionately move our relationship a step far beyond platonic and ask Ms. Liberal Cup, the building, to close her doors to all others and have carnal relations with me. And yes, I guess you should address me as sir, but after a couple of months I guess we could return to more congenital forms of address....

Passions flare along the Kennebec

Ardent suitor seeks carnal relationship with Ms. Liberal Cup

Dear Ms. Liberal Cup,

Do you remember when I'd borrow a few scoots from barkeeps ... now and again? Called me irresponsible, you did, said you'd never open all your doors to a retired goober generally broke by the third week of each month.

Well, Cupsie, things were tight for a while back there, me being on a fixed income that wasn't fixed all that well. But, hey, didn't we find out just last week that after the oldest woman in Connecticut dies, I'll morph into a genuine thousandaire? And didn't you brighten up when I told you about that, and suddenly picture me as a somewhat more suitable suitor, huh?

No, well, whatever, and regarding your view I might piddle any oddly gotten gains away, that's flat unfair and so not like the Cupsie I have come to absolutely dote on. Sure, I've been broke a lot during forty months devoted to the wooing of you — those screwdrivers? I know you have to charge for them, but the cost is positively harsh when I'm having six or seven while ogling the alluring inner accessories of you.

And, yes, Cupola, I got lax on taxes, became a bankruptcy survivor, chucked credit cards into the town chipper, got fined for overdrafts ... Oh, sure, no question, I've seen some arrears here and there. As far as my owing the IRS $1,400 in back taxes, mistakes were made; I overlooked filing for two years, so focused on you was I ... and the IRS trusted me to cooperate as we tried to arrange it so it could take installment payments of $75 a month from the bank until my debt was paid and then it could go after Enron.

All last year, Cupsie, the IRS and I couldn't get the job done. We were not reading off the same page. Vital papers that should have been sent from Hallowell weren't sent; certified letters that should have been read in timely manner were read, if at all, days after signed receipt. Senior moments seized their moments.

Then, last Monday, the IRS from Atlanta said in no uncertain terms it wasn't going to take it anymore; it was tired of me kicking it around, and furthermore it said: "This is a formal notice of our intent to terminate your installment agreement 30 days from the date of this notice. You defaulted on your agreement because you didn't pay the additional federal tax you owe. The agreement states that we may terminate your agreement and collect the entire amount of your tax liability unless.... We will search for other assets ... Must pay in full any additional federal taxes you owe ... We will charge a reinstatement fee ... We can file a notice of a federal tax lien, and if we haven't done so already, we may...."

The IRS kept menacing my assets until finally I got a hold of a human who realized he was dealing with a geezer's "memory issues." Soon enough, he fixed it so I could start paying what I should have started paying a year or so ago. I think the nice collection agent [had] the impression I was in a middling stage of senile dementia.

Curiously, these problems have intensified my earnest ardor for you, Cuppums, and it's my fondest wish that henceforth you will open your doors for me alone. And I do understand

79

that such closure might represent a financial sacrifice. So maddened, Cupcake, have I become in periods of arousal, that it's small wonder my financial acumen has been brought into question....

I am drawn to your sensuous web of earthly delights like moth to flame, and to putter around your sinuous bar with her pert little swizzle sticks — this is all I ask as I sit here on Second Street, all by my lonesome on this crazily spinning ball of mud.

Yet still you deny us the throes of rapture certain to ensue in a most noble and novel commingling of kindred spirits, one that doubtless will lead to heights of passion far exceeding the insipid intercourses of lesser beings and buildings.

There you stand, a splendid spirituous structure with a few years on her, true, and me, a survivor of bankruptcy and no spring chicken either. Yet still you deny my cries for consummation most devoutly sought; you balk…. Thing is, we don't have all that much time, and maybe we ought to "get it on," as they say….

Fondly, ardent suitor

[Feb. 13]

Sir Cupsie —

Just a note to warn you that I had my girl send you a couple columns from your erstwhile existence. One seemed particularly apropos because if you are now courting buildings, you should be reminded of your roots, when you talked to bats. I kept one of my faves, a lascivious horoscope….

[HOROSCOPE

By Gregory Guilmartin Cavendish

Scopes, Odd Jobs, Vasectomies

It's been a long, tiring day and I can but hope that my scope for this month is satisfactory. I've just finished cleaning two cesspools, given artificial respiration to two trees suffering from Dutch Elm disease (oaks yet!) and performed three vasectomies at cut-rate prices. I also molested a Munchkin on a Greyhound bus but nothing came of it so perhaps it's not even worth mentioning.

LEO — Aug. 23 to Sept. 24 — Many Leos will wake up this month and find hideous greenish warts sprouting on their hind quarters.... Sometime during the latter part of August you will be served with a warrant and arrested.... Time is auspicious to enter into contractual arrangements with gnomes and trolls....

Time is propitious, also, for sexual shenanigans and the sky is the limit. Don't crimp yourself by solely engaging in sexual hi-jinks with only humans. Trees, toads, watermelon rinds and small daffodils are fun to frolic with, and they won't give you any static. None of this, "I've got a headache, dear" garbage from your average daffodil. A daffodil is game for anything....

Famous Leos — John Wesley Cupernink, a Pennsylvania greengrocer, was the first Rotarian to sit through an entire meeting without doing something foolish. He was also the first Leo to graduate from kindergarten, achieving that feat in 1974.... Horace Fondlemeyer, a Wisconsin Leo, was the most astute businessman within the Leo ranks. It was Fondlemeyer who opened a Nazi memento shop on Miami Beach....]

Our repairs to condo are completed, we hope, and now I am ready to take another look at my novel....

Enjoyed your column. You still have an unmistakable style. You know, maybe you should mention to the IRS about your incipient situation in Connecticut....

RJ

[Feb. 14]

Cup nixes gig bids

Dutchers,

First off, I am courting a building, not "buildings." I am not promiscuous, and neither is Ms. Liberal Cup.

Yes, the IRS might be impressed, but we are still working on getting the money I owe them to them, either by withdrawal from bank or more simply a check from me. IRS says it sent me a form which, if I fill it out, then they will draw money from bank each month. This screwing around has been going on for more than a year, though, and if I introduce another factor into situation it will never get resolved.

I wonder ... I don't want to be calling Connecticut all the time to check up on Great Aunt Gert, so maybe we could get Jessica to call in weekly at the nursing home and say she is an old chum of Gert's and how is the old dear? I know: Jessica could say she would like to visit from Alabama in, say, June. If the woman at this home says, "Oh, I wouldn't wait that long, ma'am, she's almost ready for the high jump."

That way I will not have to sit around the house sticking poison darts into an effigy of Gert, difficult because I don't remember what she looks like. It makes me feel like a really rotten bastard, but there it is…. there's no use scoffing and saying it's not all about me, when in fact it IS all about me and the devil take the hindmost. (I really don't know what that saying means, but I think it applies.)

Thanks for the kind words about column…. [And] thanks for having your girl send me those documents. It was weird reading the Astrology piece because I have absolutely no memory of ever writing that thing….

Mac

[Feb. 21]

Hey Mac —

… As to your thought about Jessica checking in on Gert, I think that's a good idea from Gert's perspective but not so hot from your angle. Jessica has a habit of nursing people along. Probably mean another 10 years for Gert, and a new set of longevity records….

RJ

UNLEASHED

[Feb. 22]

Dutchers,

... I would like for Roger to ask Jessica to forget what I said about getting involved with old Gert, maybe disrupting her morale or circulating false rumors about Gert and the night janitoress up to some form of kinkiness or the other.

In fact, I order Jessica not to get on the horn and start meddling, offering nurturing of old Gert. Nurturing is bad for old people anyhow. Gert's in a high-priced joint and the management has its own devious reasons for trying to keep Gert alive, give her a shot at the world's record of 122 held by some skinny French broad.

I'll sue, and I'll have that condo in 'Bama before you have time to clear out all of Roger's pictures of copulating hummingbirds....

Here is the first of the letters sent to Ms. Liberal Cup:

Sleeping with the stewards

Dear Ms. Liberal Cup,

As you know, I have graced your place wearing my USS Allagash cap with the silver ship amid the gold lettering. Jim Cleaves, the customer who wears the USS Truckee cap, presented me my cap right there in your bar.

While talking to Jim and wife Nancy at the bar the other day, I wondered what they would think if they knew that years ago the Allagash captain ordered me shunned.

Yes, he blackballed me, Ms. Cup. Ostracized, a pariah. All hands were struck dumb in my presence and for two weeks or more nobody looked me in the eye or called my name. It was the "silent treatment" and I guess everyone, at one time or another, has felt at least a smart of its sting, either getting or giving, and getting is worse.

All at once I realized my shipmates weren't talking to me on purpose. Awareness stabbed and cut: I was an outcast. Why me, oh Ms. Cup, why me?

Yep, nobody aboard that tanker in 1950 told me I was about to become a nobody. And splintered memories of that time still snap and spark between my ears. There were about 110 sailors on the Allagash, then homeported in Newport, R.I., and of a sudden all seemed busy ignoring me. I suspect a few had to ask what I looked like so they could find me and shun me.

It was halfway through the first day before I realized I wasn't there. And because I'd committed many sins, I never asked anyone what offense led to the shunning. Come to think on it, Cup, it might have been the stint over the hill in Manchester, New Hampshire. Anyway, if they wouldn't talk to me, I wouldn't talk to them. If nobody's talking to you or acknowledging your existence, how do you ask about what's going on?

You're probably wondering, Ms. Cup, how I got into this pickle. I often didn't come back to the ship once they let me leave it. And sometimes I'd leave it without mentioning I was going away. I was absent-minded and drank a little, too. And I had come to think the only difference between a ship and a prison was on a ship you could drown. Scuttlebutt was the Allagash captain had summed up my standing in this manner: "He's the worst fuck-up aboard."

No, I don't know exactly why the captain resorted to naming and shaming. You don't see a shunning in months of Sundays.

Could be the skipper told his cohorts something like this:

"That shitbird has appeared one time too many before my mast. He's been lectured, hectored, fined, and confined; he's been captain-masted and downcasted, court-martialed and threatened with a most unsavory discharge; this pebble in our shoals has been made to work in the laundry, folding clothes like a titless WAVE; made to clean our latrines.

"We denied him the opportunity to continue as the most inept apprentice in the storied history of our wonderful engine room. And we have warned his shipmates not to go on liberty with him, should he ever again get to go on liberty again, neither on American beaches nor on the strands of lands despoiled by foreigners.

"Yet still he seems not to fully grasp that he is a clear and present nuisance. So let's not look him in the eye or talk to him for a while."

As shunnee, Ms. Cup, I pretended nothing unusual was happening, just as the shunners were doing. We expertly dodged one another in unavoidable close encounters on deck or in passageways. It was as if the other wasn't there. And, of course, I wasn't.

I was quickly relieved of my post as cleaner of the latrine in which the black gang [the oilers and engineers] relieved itself, then rousted from my sleeping rack amid bilge rats, taken to the rancid lair of the deck apes.

But it was not to be my lot to sleep with deck apes, Ms. Cup. I would be sleeping with stewards, the black men who tended to the needs of the ship's officers. This was when the navy hadn't fully integrated, Cup. Six black stewards slept in a remote area in the aft of the swab jockeys sleeping quarters. I got the one empty rack. (The stewards hadn't talked to me before the shunning so we simply resumed not talking to each other.)

The captain and his cronies assigned me two new workstations in the bowels of the Allagash, where even bilge rats were loath to frolic. I guess the captain told his henchpersons:

"You know that hatch near the gasoline tanks? The ladder in that hole goes a long way down, and I'm told it descends to dreck and disused pumps, clutter and suchlike. So let the miscreant work down there.

"Also, there is a half-vast ballast tank back aft, right down there on the scabby skin of our bottom. I'm told that tank looks like the insides of Jonah's whale, only not as cheerful and cozy; let this clown also work there, eliminating rust and making things shine in the glooming of the brown-grey cavern. Give him an electric light with a very long cord, a chipping tool, and a nice bag of rags and wire brushes."

But let me tell you, Cuppess, the ladder down the hatch by the gas tanks plumbed depths, too, only to arrive at a compartment in which you could have swung the bobcat at Dom's Barber Shop if there hadn't been so many ungainly pieces of hard matter crouching all around.

A storyteller's odyssey

A big pump on a scurvy deckplate was surrounded by unknowable hulks of poorly congealed atoms. A tangle of lines, pipes, and wires writhed, and beneath all this ugliness was a bilge full of slime.

The fireman in charge of me never descended to either workplace. He'd peer down now and again, or just clank a wrench on the unsecured hatches. Nobody sat near me or looked at me in the mess hall, partly because of my utter filthiness.

Reeking the malodor of oil fumes and dregs, I arose daily from depths, to break bread with my mates. Ms. Cup, I bet Bruce Mayo wouldn't have let me into your restaurant or bar dressed like that.

Being shunned wasn't all that bad. I got lots of time to myself, and was able to masturbate without fear of discovery. I may have pondered the distinction between port and starboard.

I read pocketbooks: well-thumbed works of Erskine Caldwell, Jack London, James Thurber. Now and again, I'd tap my chipper against a bulkhead, but nobody tapped back.

Then one day people noticed me. Old buddies talked to me. Crew members I barely knew spoke to me. "How you doing, Mac?" Nobody ever referred to the shunning in my presence, and I continued to sleep amid stewards during the period before they shipped me to shore for further detailed instructions.

Now, Ms. Cup, a question: may I still come in wearing my Allagash cap? Can I still come in at all? And what should we tell Cleaves?

—Almac

[Feb. 22, part two]

In re Duke

Dutchers:

Hope an autopsy doesn't turn up any illegal substances or signs of alcohol use in Dr. [Hunter] Thompson's corpse and

86

thus confirm the rumors that he may have abused substances.

In any case, it's a sin and a shame that valuable artists such as Dr. Thompson are violently cut down in their very prime while in Connecticut a selfish old woman wages a determined battle against the Grim Reaper with the sole aim of ensuring that I predecease her.

Mac

[March 7]

Hey Mac —

Just a note to tell you we are both working like a bunch of beavers down here in L.A.

Himself is busy trying yet another beginning to what is becoming his life's work. Herself has booked a flight to Conn. to see if Gert is a better person than Hunter Thompson.

Pumpkin is making new friends and influencing people. Did I ever tell you that nobody knows who we are down here, but when we tell them we are Pumpkin's parents, they know right away who she is. We were actually going into a restaurant the other day, and two strangers yelled at us, "There's Pumpkin's parents!"

We were thinking of shunning Pumpkin because she's getting too uppity, but then nobody would know us.

By the by, absolutely a great column about the Allagash.... OK if I send it to [former Flint Journal colleagues Bob] DeLand and [Lou] Giampetroni?

RJ

[March 10]

Some pumpkins

Pumpkin Person's Parents:

... yes, please share my Allagash exploits with Bob and Lou ... it's about time they realized the extent of valor of those of us who put their cojones on the block when evil North

Koreans were around every corner and none of us knew whether we would survive to sire more cannon fodder for more wars in the fight against evil, the fight that will free every soul alive on this planet from un-democratic existences....

Oh, Pumpkin tale reminds me of Alexander Pope's two-liner: "I am his Highness' dog at Kew/Pray tell me sir, whose little dog are you?"

Mac

[March 20]

Aristotle regarding Bush

Dear Dutchers,

I am a reader of serious shit and this morning at five ayem was reading Aristotle's poetics, his book on poetry and the fine arts, and he refers to dancing, which the Greeks held in high esteem. Aristotle says: "Like the orator, the dancer should aim at always being perspicuous; he must be understood though he is dumb and heard though he says nothing...."

That fits George W. Bush like a glove. He's dumb and insists he be heard though he says nothing, all the while stressing words in the wrong places and smirking benevolently as if he were explaining why the sky is blue to a wee child....

"Nothing will change under my Social Security plan." Yes, just like nothing will change for peons who file for bankruptcy because of the recently passed bill written by volunteers from the credit card industry. No longer will the Al MacLeeses be able to wipe the slate clean, get a "fresh start," the historically tolerant but sensible way of giving people a shot at escaping from lifetime fealty to usurers.

... It could be Bush will still be president before I get my windfall, so now I can continue praying that the stocks in Gert's estate ... keep rising instead of falling.

Here I am worrying about money I don't even have, which seems to be an irony too brutal to bear.

Later, Mac ...

[April 10]

How are things?

Roger and Jessica:

Haven't heard from you in a while. Everything OK?

I have moved and have new Hallowell address. Hope to hear from you soon.

Mac

[Grand Blanc; April 10]

Hey Mac —

Sorry for the lag in communication.

We are back up north, and I have been busy with my dark side — Rotball [Rotisserie or fantasy baseball]. I had one draft that lasted for five hours (until midnight) Friday night, then had to get up early Saturday morning for another draft that lasted about six hours. So as Jessica says, now I can become part of the living again. I've been fiddling with figures and players for the last couple months, but as the drafts near it becomes an obsession.

I think I've told you that these are auction drafts, where you have a limited amount of money and you buy players to fill out your roster. I won one league last year, which gives me a little leeway in the household because that meant an extra $700 or so.

Anyway, enough about me ... did you have a hard time finding a place that would accept the cats and is the location as convenient? How are things otherwise....?

RJ

[April 11]

To the Dutch-Irish People of Michigan,

Picture the Kennebec River full of sullen rage and threatening to inundate Hallowell in the worst flooding since Eighty-Seven; U-Hauls are spotted all along Water Street;

merchants and normal people have been moving wares and belongings to upper floors, loading stuff into trucks of all kinds....

It's a given The Wharf bar will flood, sometimes it floods when there is no flood; owner Dave Bustin says when you have a bar in a basement on the river you expect to get wet. Everyone is told to park on higher grounds. Hallowellians are invited to park in church lots and Christ knows there are more than enough churches hogging the hillside.

Amid all this [I am told] there's a vacancy at [condos] at Water Street and Elm, just three blocks south of downtown.... [Place has] great second-floor window views of Kennebec [and] room enough to swing three cats. The realty office manager ... wondered whether a lone old fart could adequately fill such a roomy place ... for four beings, only one of whom has digits that can work switches and faucets.

Mindful of the Michael Jackson case, which was flaring, I [said] maybe I could get me five little Cubbie Scouts as condoplaymates; [she] didn't get joke or even see it, so I explained I was just kidding around. Why ... do I have to go through life explaining I am just kidding around? Aren't we all just kidding around?

Whatever, the price for this fine rental — built 20 years ago as compared with Joan's place built [about 200] years ago — is too high for me in present temporary circumstances ... but some winter months I paid about as much at Joan's shotgun flat.... [After the washing machine flood, his landlord-tenant relationship with his sister began to fray; it eventually ruptured after nearly four years over disputes about normal tenant responsibilities, such as paying rent each month.]

Meanwhile, I cross Water Street several times a day ... to see how river is doing and it is doing well, a mysterious line of five blue barrels go quickly by and logs that look like partly-submerged rhinos or crocs bob along amid various wood chunks, and ice floes; the river bank, just across Water Street from my apartment with windows overlooking a goodly river stretch, is just about flooded over....

In pursuit of money so I could afford to leave [my previous digs] even before Great Aunt Gert wheels west, I hired a lawyer ... to see if I could tap my $94,500 annuity or whether I could get advance on my share of Old Gert's stash ... pending demise of the oldest woman in Connecticut.

Death, Dutchers and Irishers, is a natural thing.... Indeed, it is said by some grim thinkers that we start to die the moment we exit the womb. So if GAG should perish sooner than later, it is not an occurrence to make a big deal out of....

And I understand thanks to an unexpected note from sister Debby, with whom I have had no contact for almost four years, that Gert's as sound as a pre-Bush dollar and might even last two more years, which would put her at 108, an insufferably long period, really, when you come to think about it, as I often do.

How Gert must yearn for the fuzzily easeful journey through the white lights with Muzak softly in her ears as she rejoins her sister Essie out or up or down there in the Elysian Fields, there to strum on old-fashioned instruments and generally hang out with good friends and warm associates.

Although, and I guess we all in the MacLeese family worry about this, Old Gert might-could go at any time. I have to guess how my three sisters feel because I have now scored a trifecta: three sisters and none talking to me! I am singularly blessed. True, there was a brief bit of conversation with sister Debby, who, all on her own, sent me a package of postcards Connie and I had sent to my mother over thirty-some years.

That was nice and I took it as a reaching out by Debby-Sherry faction to poor old bro eking it out in Maine.... But after a few emails ... I unilaterally canceled our fragile truce; Debby was good enough to write back and wish me good luck in my new American adventures.

But I have friends in Hallowell.... Nine good friends showed up for move; one loaned me the $100 needed to rent a U-Haul truck. When you rent here, they will take a credit card for $100, but will not cash a check because of the bookkeeping involved.

A storyteller's odyssey

As a struggling bankruptcy survivor, I have no credit cards and had less than $100 in the bank, but friend Maisie gave me a hundred bucks, said it wasn't a loan, she was just giving it.... later during moving day, Maisie's mother Janet slipped me a check for 50 bucks while she and her husband, Baron Wormser, the poet, were moving stuff....

Well, we all noticed the rising river ... and a lot of ice floes, more barrels; I was hoping for the stark sight of dead cow legs sticking up into the air, maybe a small house....

And meantime, as the flood reports become grimmer, people on both sides of Water Street are still removing property and wares, and I volunteered to help Boynton's Market employees move stuff, and was busy figuring that my $240 car payment bill, my $400 per month car repair payment bill, my $197 quarterly car insurance bill, and other bills were due and anxiously pending, and the IRS was still wanting $300 come tax day and no I can't pay this year's off in installments: hell, I am already paying off two years of back taxes in installments and you cannot, you vil not, pile installment upon installment ... Or so the dialogue goes in my head....

... Well, shortly before flood was supposed to crest, condo owner tells me we should all be extremely vigilant, a full flood alert, and "watch the river" and park your car on higher ground.

Be assured, Dutch and Irish personages, I expertly braved heavy downpour in darkest night and found higher ground on a firm bluff of grass behind realty office building, all safe and cozy ... and next morning I find car UP TO ITS HUBCAPS in muck and mire; water cascading FROM LAND ABOVE AND NOT FROM RIVER BELOW caused the higher ground to melt away under my car....

This is irony too rich for me to bear without sharing: I sought higher ground to avoid flood and was attacked by water from higher up. Is there, then, no safe haven? ...

Hi:

I had spent quite a bit of time on email just sent, and it was sent inadvertently or maybe intentionally by AOL since I was logged on for a long time while just writing email. I think they automatically send emails if you spend a long time writing them....

Later, Al

Flood matter, add2

Oh, the flood turned out to be a bust. In fact, the Kennebec Journal reported Hallowellians were calling it the "dud flood." There was minor flooding nearest river but nothing like experts had been predicting....

Mac

[April 12]

Hi Mac —

Thanks for the update on the various Hallowell tempests. We gain a little perspective in learning that someone else's frustrations are light years beyond ours. Of course, from your vantage point, that is of no help at all....

RJ

[April 13]

A cuppa

Hi Mac —

Was just prowling through the [kitchen] cupboards ... and came across coffee mug that was gift from you and Connie. It has picture of you with a cat on your shoulder. Cat is black with white nose and feet. Can't recall which member of F-troop that was or is.

Why, you may ask, wasn't the mug out on the counter so we can look upon your likeness every morning? But that's another story. It was with a mug that [son] Ryan created when he was about 5, so you could say it was stored with our family heirlooms.

On a more serious matter, Jessica and I were wondering whether a loan of a several C-notes would keep the IRS away from your door yet again. I know the IRS deadline would come before any check from us would arrive and clear in Maine, but maybe you could borrow from one friend there to get the check out by the 15th, with the promise that a check from another friend is in the mail?

We figure you are good for the money, given that GAG is bound to [die] in the next decade or so. Let us know, and I'll have my girl send off a check to your girl, or whatever.

RJ

[April 13]

Couple of bucks

Hi:

Two hundred and fifty bucks would save me since a nice woman at IRS in Augusta said "any effort to pay full amount" should keep them off my back. So anything you send can help and I can go in there next week with some cash to back me. They seem OK with people if the tardy ones actually make some kind of effort.

I regretted sending that email full of my piteous laments but it was the only way to tell the tale, although subject to misunderstanding ... wrote it because I knew you of all people would not take it merely as a blatant SOS ... wanted to tell story.... I thought of that email as a kind of column under pressure on a ridiculous situation, but good therapy to get it down on paper instead of aimlessly racketing about in my head ... oh hell, there's another lament starting up and I really must stop muttering the blues like an off-brand Hank Williams.

Thanks, Mac ...

Part 4: Right job, wrong number

MacLeese left the Navy a changed man. He didn't "find" himself, as his high school adviser had hoped, but he did find himself to be an alcoholic who often sailed off the edge of the Navy world's conventions. He was altered in appearance, too; he had added a collection of tattoos.

"The 'art' on my epidermis," he said, "includes two women, three birds, a snake, a panther, a teeny-weeny cupid with my sister Debbie's name underneath and a ship wreathed in flags and flowers gallantly sinking. Underneath the ship it says 'Sailor's grave'...."

In an attempt to explain his "snarling, simpering, twittering, hissing and glug-glugging" mélange, MacLeese said most tattooists push designs of women and creatures and symbols. He added that those getting tattooed "are generally smashed and will settle for anything but a chipmunk."

After four years in the Navy, MacLeese returned home in mid-1952 to Connecticut's Naugatuck Valley, where he worked as a milkman's helper, then as a factory worker. On the milk route, he remembered doing more work than the driver, who watched while he lugged milk and milk products into retail outlets, putting fresh milk behind older milk.

He also played a role in a newspaper. It was as the lead in a Page One banner headline and story in the Ansonia Sentinel that reported he had smashed his 1939 Dodge into a car occupied by a teacher and a priest. "I sure pick my targets," he said.

A decade later, he would work briefly on the Sentinel's copy desk.

Joan remembers with delight when Alan came to her house while her husband was away and a cousin was there. "It was the most amusing night." She said he improvised an episode of "Dragnet" and "it was marvelous, very funny, such a treat. He was carefree, in such a good mood, his old self and wasn't drinking. We had a wonderful time."

During that period, he was living with his parents, who had moved to Seymour. That was where he met Barbara, a blonde living next door.

They married in late 1952 in a Methodist church near Riverside School. He was 21 and she 24 (the daughter of Swedish and Irish immigrants), and they lived for several months in a garage-apartment near his parent's former Oxford home, which Joan and her husband had bought.

In 1953, Alan and Barbara decided to "hit the road to see if something would happen and it did," he wrote.

"I got a job in Miami as an usher and a Jerry Lewis movie was playing. It changed my life. After two weeks, I had to quit. I couldn't stand it anymore; he was driving me up a wall. If they ever give an Academy Award in the category of Noisy Lack of Talent, Jerry is home free and he'll cry gratefully for 30 days and 30 nights."

After tending bar, a fox in the henhouse position for him, he decided to apply at the Miami Herald for the job of copy boy, the bottom rung of the newsroom ladder.

"You ran for coffee, you ran for gum when [a] big-shot reporter said to you – you, a Korean veteran – 'Hey, kid, do you think you can find your way across the street? Then go get me some gum. Here's a dime, keep the change.

"I fetched and carried and found some heroes, sort of, newspaper people with talent and wit, competence and concern and a precious sense for the folly of much of it all. People – and I dip into mawkishness – with whom I felt I could belong doing a job I thought I could do.

96

"They paid me zilch and I worked long hours and I would have stayed for nothing and gone back to Jerry Lewis just to finance the job at the Miami Herald city room."

When he first joined the Herald, he had no idea how to behave in an office. Thus it was with a certain amount of trepidation that he entered the city room on his first day of work. "Previously I had labored in factories and happily wallowed in the abundant filth peculiar to those institutions....

"I quickly discovered a happy thing – newspaper editorial offices were full of disheveled muckrakers who might well have been chucked out of some of the factories I'd frequented. Desks were laden with jumbles of clutter and floors were littered with cigarette butts, throwaway coffee cups and paper.

"Joyously I fell into this sty-lish milieu and for a number of years in a number of newspaper offices my innate slovenliness went unchallenged, it being merely standard operating procedure."

He would work in 27 more city rooms during his career. In some, he stopped multiple times for a total of 47 hires in 15 years. He said this occupation "may not be much to some, but it keeps me reasonably content and off the streets."

MacLeese picked up his newspapering skills on the job by observing, reading and doing. His higher education came though books and an inquisitive mind, although he did attend the University of Miami for a brief period.

After a year at the Herald, he advanced from copy boy to police and general assignment reporter.

He described the kind of peace officer he dealt with in Miami: "Ham-fisted, slab-shouldered Neanderthal with bushy eyebrows, sausage-like fingers, a hard-as-a-rock beer belly and a position in the political spectrum somewhere slightly to the right of Attila the Hun."

Those guys, he said, "largely imports from the south Georgia swamps, took courses in 'Police Mentality 101.' They enjoyed beating on black prisoners and alleged that all reporters were college punks with shameless perversions racing about in their pointy heads."

He ended up working for the Herald several times, and also made a stop or two at the Miami News, in the 1950s and 1960s.

"These fine organizations were forced to terminate relations with me on several occasions because I had not yet learned that unrestrained ingestion of alcoholic products doesn't do all that much for the creative process. Also it often precludes one from living up to oral contracts between management and employee.

"Which is to say I didn't make it to work a lot of the time or, if assigned to cover a meeting of Concerned Caucasians in Opa-locka, I would wake up the next day in my car parked on the outskirts of Daytona Beach. Management often concludes from such events that an employee is unstable. (These people have tunnel vision. Supposing a tornado had hit Daytona Beach that morning? They would have had a man right on the spot.)"

As a police reporter, he said: "I helped some TV newcomers at fires and murders (I'm really a great guy) just as old hands in newspapering helped me when I strolled into the old Miami police station on Flagler St. near the railroad tracks."

He also wrote weather stories. One day he wrote a story that got Page One play about a remarkable spell of balmy weather. His lead paragraph:

"The sun is shining again, for the skatey-eighth day, the birds are singing and everybody is smiling. Especially the weatherman, who is obviously on the take from the Chamber of Commerce."

It was in bars, unfortunately, where his skills too often were preeminent, and where his bar-stool companion frequently was one LeRoy E. "Bud" Tripp.

Tripp first became a colleague of MacLeese's at the Miami Herald, and later in San Francisco, and they were partners in offenses against society at both stops.

At the end of their careers, Tripp joined MacLeese at the Flint Journal, where they were coworkers for more than a decade and where Tripp was MacLeese's only serious rival for the honor of having worked at the most newspapers, "including firings, disappearances and righteous resignations."

In World War II, Tripp was the ball-turret gunner on a B-24 named the Thunder Bay "Babe" in honor of Alpena, Michigan, which raised the money to build the plane through war bonds. On March 24, 1944, the "Babe" took a direct hit from flak over Yugoslavia while on a mission to Austria. Six of the crew members were killed in the resulting fire, and four in the back of the plane were able to bail out.

Staff Sergeant Tripp was captured and taken to Stalag 17-B, considered one of the most notorious German POW camps. It became the basis for the William Holden movie "Stalag 17" and for the TV sitcom "Hogan's Heroes."

While some colleagues considered it an open question whether Tripp was rendered certifiable by his Stalag experiences, there was no doubt about his off-the-wall sense of humor. This was the man who would become MacLeese's wingman for many "Hogan"-type episodes.

One such Miami instance occurred at a Biscayne Boulevard piano bar, where Tripp and MacLeese were pretending to be mutes who were also hearing challenged

While discussing issues of the moment with MacLeese in impromptu sign language, Tripp sent the pianist a drink and a tip along with a note requesting that he play the "Colonel Bogey March" (the movie theme for "The Bridge on the River Kwai"). A succession of drinks, tips and notes followed with the request that the pianist play the same tune ever louder because they could barely hear him.

Eventually, the bartender apologetically delivered the message that the deaf-mutes' "Marching" was bothering other customers.

At this point, Tripp unlimbered his voice and cursed, adding: "We were leaving anyway."

Miami also was where MacLeese began to use the telephone as a weapon of perverse pleasure. By this time, MacLeese was marking time late at night on the city desk, amusing himself at the expense of those calling in for one reason or another.

It may have all started with Alan Courtney, who had begun a conservative radio talk show in Miami in 1948. His late night show was immensely popular in the 1950s. He was the type, MacLeese said, who would tell certain call-in listeners "to go gargle with razor blades."

MacLeese was working late rewrite when Courtney got a new telephone number, one digit different from the one for the Herald, prompting misdials.

"People began calling the Herald city desk 10 or 12 times a night, asking for Courtney. At first I would tell them they had a wrong number, but that is basically unsatisfying.... I began identifying myself as Gregory V. Ravendish.

"I would explain rather wearily, as if tutoring a dense child, that Mr. Courtney was getting a hellacious amount of telephone calls and that it had been decided that I would screen them to see who qualified to actually get on the air and talk to Mr. Courtney in person, as it were. I had a particularly outrageous manner of testing the desirability of these callers and I am saddened to say that 7 out of 10 callers would fall for my spiel.

"RAVENDISH: Gregory V. Ravendish here, executive assistant and personal secretary to Mr. Courtney.

"CALLER: I wanna talk to Mr. Courtney about the school bond issue. He's full of hops, why that sucker....

"RAVENDISH: Sir, as I've repeatedly told other callers, we now have a short quiz for a person to qualify to get to talk to Mr. Courtney, who is a very busy man. Would you be willing to take the quiz?

"CALLER: Well, I guess so, although....

"RAVENDISH: All right now, let's move this along, the phones are ringing off the hooks. First, sir, can you tell me who is buried in Grant's Tomb?

"CALLER: Why of course, that's Ulysses S. Grant.

"RAVENDISH: Okay, sir, fine. Now who was the American general who defeated Lord Cornwallis at Yorktown?

"CALLER: For God's sake, it was Washington ... now can I talk to Alan? (Poor fool, he was already talking to Alan.)

"RAVENDISH: Fine, just one more question: Who was the assistant first vice president at Leander State Teacher College in South Carolina during that period, 1840 to 1845 when the president was on loan to the National Planters Association?

"For some reason, nobody ever got the third question and indignant citizens were told that their intellect was such that it was not a good idea for them to verbally joust with Mr. Courtney.

"Many complaints ensued, many persons' noses were out of joint. Inevitably, my cover was blown – by this time I had several co-conspirators – and Miami Herald management let it be known that Mr. Courtney was planning severe retaliatory measures against, as he said on the radio, 'a very big Miami organization.' That would be the Miami Herald."

But Gregory V. Ravendish did not die. He would write articles for little papers in Connecticut, including in Ansonia, be quoted about a number of Orange Bowl parades and games, be mentioned in columns MacLeese wrote in Miami, San Francisco, and Gary, Indiana. Ravendish was even booked by police on the Costa del Sol in Spain for getting into a scuffle with the Guardia Civil.

Ravendish was not his only alter ego newsman. Like "Bob & Ray," a popular radio show at the time, MacLeese concocted other picturesque names. Gregory Guilmartin Cavendish was an amalgam of the names of the U.S. attorney in Miami and a fellow reporter. He also may have appropriated the name of Eisenhower's press secretary, James Hagerty.

In the style of the day, MacLeese would answer the newsroom phone: "City desk, Hagerty" or "Ravendish here." Certainly not "Miami Herald. This is Alan MacLeese. How may I help you?"

At the Herald, the city desk would transfer calls to MacLeese if the caller sounded eccentric. One caller was an inebriated woman with a sexy voice who lived in an exclusive home in the South Beach area.

At her invitation, MacLeese and Tripp decided to pay a visit. Accounts vary on what happened next, with a similar ending.

After ringing for the woman at the gate, MacLeese and Tripp couldn't gain entrance. They were scaling the wall when police arrived.

The cops put them in their squad car and were en route to Miami Beach police headquarters when MacLeese explained the situation. He politely told them who they were, that they worked for the Miami Herald, and were invited to see a woman there but the gate wouldn't open and so were trying to climb over the wall when someone called police. They weren't burglars.

Seeming to be satisfied, one of the officers turned to Tripp and asked if that was his story.

Tripp, going gangland style, said he wasn't saying anything until he talked to his "mouthpiece."

They spent the rest of the night in the Miami Beach jail.

On another night, Tripp again showed his "Hogan's Heroes" sense of timing.

For MacLeese, with no money left to buy drinks in an unsavory bar, the night had degraded to finishing "unattended" drinks from other tables when a fight broke out and he was arrested. Five of his newspaper friends followed him to the police station, where, MacLeese said, a captain was "fixing to let me go."

Enter Tripp. He views the situation and inquires as to whether MacLeese will be freed. The answer is yes. That's when Tripp shouts out:

"Hold on here, officers. This man is my friend. You have hauled him off ... charging that he is drunk. I will not tolerate this. I demand that he be given a balloon test (to determine drunkenness) to vindicate himself. We are not leaving here otherwise."

Several cops agree and the captain throws up his hands.

Two cops haul MacLeese off for testing but he cannot even begin to blow up the balloon. MacLeese said he had as much chance of passing that test as a case of Seagram's.

"Result: Six hours in durance vile, also known as the drunk tank," thanks to Tripp, MacLeese wrote. "Had he not spoken up, I would have been returned to the streets in a drunken condition and could have injured myself."

In Miami, MacLeese said, "us young reporters were very clever fellows, funnier than most upraised truncheons by half, and we dearly loved to safely exercise our keen wit."

He embroidered an example of what would happen to a telephone caller "luckless enough to get hooked up with one of our merry little band" of reporters:

"Caller: Hello, my husband and I are having our 57th wedding anniversary and....

"Smart-ass: Holy Smokes, ma'am, you called one day too late. We did print 57th wedding anniversaries – up until yesterday. Now, though, you must be married 58 years to get an anniversary in the paper. Not to be unkind, but you are up the creek with only the most rudimentary of paddles."

Later in life, as a Flint Journal columnist, he would apologize for such unresponsive behavior. The evolution came slowly, however. Earlier at the Journal, as a copy editor, he would have occasion to answer a reporter's phone and the Telephone Lout would return but his behavioral fever was breaking.

"Caller: Hello, my husband and I are having our 57th wedding anniversary and...."

"Smart-ass: Ma'am, I'm terribly glad to hear that and I would like to help you. However, I'm not on the editorial staff. I'm a security guard, just passing through on my rounds. Actually, we're tracking down a couple of juveniles from Clio who I believe have gotten into the printer's ink. Could you call back later?"

As for wrong number callers, those not involving Alan Courtney, he concocted different dialogue.

"CALLER: Mandy Sue Delilah there?

"ME: No, I'm sorry, but Mandy Sue Delilah is upstairs with a customer right now. She'll probably be through in 15 minutes. May I take your number?

"CALLER: Whaddya mean, upstairs with a customer. Say, who is this?

"ME: Well, I'll take your questions in order. I meant just what I said. Mandy Sue is indisputably upstairs with a customer. Nice chap from New York, I understand. I'm Mandy Sue Delilah's cousin from Caracas, just got in the other night, even though we were stacked up over O'Hare for three hours.

"CALLER: (feebly) Well, okay, I guess.... I'll call back."

In another variation, Mandy Sue or whoever, is up on the roof and can't come to the phone.

"CALLER: Up on the roof?

"ME: Yep. Oh, we've tried to talk her down but she says she's going to stay up there until they, whoever they are, straighten out the situation in Somali and the problem between the Kurds and Wheys in Iraq."

"CALLER: (pretending complete understanding) Okay, well I'll call back later."

But then imagine you are Deborah, MacLeese's youngest sister, and he is home in Connecticut for a visit. She is at the girlish age where the phone is a frequent companion.

A good friend calls her, brother answers, and friend is horrified to learn "that I had suffered a rather untimely demise," Deborah said. The friend "was equally unsettled when told that I had been buried, with little ado, on the hill in back of the house.... I figured, though, that I had a pretty funny brother."

On the wrong number gambit, MacLeese gave a tip of his fedora to Tripp for perfecting the tactic.

One afternoon, Tripp was at MacLeese's apartment, and they were sitting around "swilling copious draughts of Dr Pepper" when the phone rang, the type with a cord, for those following along at home. Tripp answered.

A wrong number. According to MacLeese, "Tripp was outraged at this insolent disruption of our high-minded ... seminar. Still, he was polite, concerned, caring.

"TRIPP: I'm terribly sorry but you have the wrong number.

"CALLER: Sorry....

"TRIPP: Wait, don't hang up.. They are blowing out our telephone lines here and now that you've hooked in they'll have to blow out yours, too,

"CALLER: I don't understand. (I could understand the puzzlement; I didn't understand either.)

"TRIPP: Well, they've got a new policy, [to] blow the soot out of the phones every three months now. What you're gonna have to do, lady, is to leave your phone off the hook and put it in a pillow case.

"CALLER: Pillow case?

"TRIPP: Yes, pillow case. That way you won't get soot all over the place.

"CALLER: Well, I never. Thank you so much."

MacLeese said he wondered if the woman ever did take her phone out of the pillow case. "But I guess, really, that it isn't good to dwell on such matters."

Years later, MacLeese was working for the Flint Journal when he began a column with a story about another wrong number:

"First, I've got to apologize to Karl, even if he isn't in the audience. Reason is I called friend Roger Van Noord of Grand Blanc Township early New Year's Day to vilify him for presumed debauchery the night before. I misdialed, although it took awhile to find that out. Here's the conversation:

"ME – Hello there, you Nordic swine. Feeling rotten today, I hope?

"VOICE – Whaableeah.

"ME – You filthy animal, are you still inarticulate from last night's vile activities? Boy, I'm glad I don't drink on Amateur Night.

"VOICE – Whableahreep?

"ME – Lord, I pity your wife and kid, Van Noord. Have you no decency. Are you still reeling around the house besotted?

"VOICE – Who the hell is this?

"ME – Dave Graham, who is this?

"VOICE – Karl. (Slams down phone.)

"ME – The animal hung up, why would he do that, Connie?

"CONNIE – What do you expect from a Nordic swine?

"I'm sorry. Karl, wherever you are," MacLeese wrote in the column. "Nobody should have to start off a new decade in such a manner, even Nordics."

[April 19, 2005]

Check WAS in the mail

Hi R & J:

THANKS! Contrary to [Journal photographer] Barry Edmonds' oft-repeated jape about "the check is in the mail" being one of the three big lies — it indeed was in the mail on Patriot's Day.

I scooted to IRS in Augusta this morning at opening bell and squared it away that I would pay $300-even as soon as the check clears, then went to bank where they alleged it would take five working days to clear.

That's OK though, since lady at IRS speculated it would take a bit of time. She told me I actually owed $389 for 2004 but said there were exemptions we will discuss later for gaffers in their seventies. I asked her if it helped, exemption-wise, that I was an idiot, and she smiled and said no. Although it clearly does help if you show your idiocy in the right places with the right people. That and wearing my USS Allagash cap gives me a leg up here in Maine, I think.

This saves my bacon, and only truly good friends would give a character such as I more than he sought and I now realize four hundred was actually what I needed to get right with IRS as well as a start on the car insurance, on which I got a 10-day extension....

I thank you-all again and so do Faraday, Fogarty and Finley. I think GREAT AUNT GERT would thank you too, since, reportedly, she is a nice old party.... As Gomer Pyle used to annoyingly say, "Thankee, thankee, thankee." Connie used to get a kick out of Gomer.

Mac

[April 28]

News bulletin

Hi Mac —

Got some news for you. Ryan got engaged last night. We like Jamie, so everyone's happy here....

RJ One

[May 1]

Hi:

Congrats to RJ2! When is wedding? Will two RJs cause confusion? ... Anyhow, tell co-conspirators a geezer in Maine sends best. (As I understand it, marriage is a conspiracy in which two persons contrive to deny the viewing of their private parts to others.)

... We are again on flood watch since it has been raining like a cow pissing on a flat rock for days; yesterday the Wharf, Hallowell's famed watering spot, was indeed a watered spot — three feet of water throughout interior....

... five days after I settled into new digs a [man] banged on door and bustled in like he owned place. [He] sat down at table, pulled out toke pouch from front right pants pocket, and lighted beloved bowl and handed it to me, saying I should "smoke it up" because he had important, even startling, news.

[The man] confided he has "the stigmata" and patted self in appropriate places to indicate ... his version of scarrings J.C. got on the cross. Further, [he] deponed, his stigmata occurred naturally (supernaturally?) and was not scarified up manually like some charlatans have been known to do. [He] asked if I understood what revelation meant. I did not truly understand so he said he's an angel; in fact, a guardian angel. He then asked if I knew who he'd been assigned to guard, perhaps by Gabriel.

Yes, you-all have correctly interpreted my less-than deft foreshadowing. [The man] is MY guardian angel. And here I'd thought he was just a garden-variety [guy].... After a good deal of chitchat, I told [him] it'd be best if he did his guarding by remote control; have not seen crestfallen angel since.

Perhaps my rejection of [angel] may cause Kennebec creek to rise and come right across Water Street as many feared it would during last flood watch. Just looked out window and it's still raining — April brought more showers than folks in rude huts along creek desired — but water hasn't crossed street and I need not, at this point, take car to higher ground....

Later, Mac

[May 23]

Hi RJ1,

... As far as I can see there has been nothing merry about May and all Hallowell hopes June will start busting out all over.

I wrote a caption overline once with a pic of June Havoc; I think it was her or some other famous June. Anyhow she had a prominent superstructure and my caption was "June is busting out all over." In my view that was one of the great headlines that [the copy desk chief] somehow or other let get by him. Although he may have killed it for the red dog edition.

106

Whatever, it has been dreary and rainy for days on end and so low has been my mood that when I saw George Bush holding hands with a sheik of Araby I actually snarled and uttered a strangled cry at the television. You could ask Fogarty, Finley and Faraday if you don't believe me.

My friends the Wormsers have had me over to dinner three times this month, else I would have overdosed on Cheerios, Spaghettios and peanut butter and bread sandwiches.

I use grape jelly and the kind of peanut butter that has crunchy little nuts in it, and it sure beats bread and water or the "greens and beans" the Marines used to serve those of us doing solitary in stockade at Camp Allen, Va....

But at least they never released pictures of me in my underwear, which was regulation white boxers.

Later, Mac

[June 2]

Hi Mac —

We have had a busy time of it, hence my sloth in responding. Went to my mother's for several days for more repairs.... Our next project is to get my mom to commit to going into an assisted living place.... I checked one assisted living hostelry today, and there is at least a year and a half waiting list. I'm not sure my mom [88] has a year and a half to wait, unfortunately. When did your mother start to go downhill?

... We are thinking about going "North to Alaska" if the gas prices don't get too outlandish. Maybe leave about the end of July. Need to get some new pictures for the art fairs....

The other day, I saw a Siamese cat amble across our deck. I mention to Jess: "I think I just saw Charles on our deck." She looks at me like I don't know who Charles or a Siamese cat is, and says "No, that couldn't have been Charles. They [our neighbors] don't let him out....

Two days later, our neighbor comes over and asks, "Have you seen Charles? He got out a couple days ago." Now they have four cats, so I guess when one goes missing, it's not a big deal. The light comes on for Jess, and she starts thinking that maybe I do know my cats, plus Pumpkin for two days had been on point for something under our deck. We thought it might be a skunk.

So we check under the deck, and there are two frightened eyes way in the back in the darkness. Charles. A glad reunion with the daughter next door. Charles has not expressed interest in going outside since. But I am a semi-hero next door....

RJ

[June 5]

Concerning mothers

Dutchers,

My mother made it to 95, and she was still with it mentally but medications were no longer up to fending off heart death; she had been living alone until final hospitalization, died while I was heading east on I-84 and staying [overnight en route] at a Holiday Inn in Dubois, Pa.

Big thing my mother had going for her was living in a separate little house in a community for oldsters in a town that takes very good care of its old folks. Her place was easy to take care of and sisters Sharon and Deborah were always close to hand....

Would Mrs. Van Noord go for some kind of assisted living near Grand Blanc? From what you say about repairs and such, I get the idea she's living in too big and too old a house....

How long would you be up [in Alaska], and are you going to try to nail a shot of male grizzly bear attempting to mount a comely male caribou?

... Do selves a favor and pick up some verses of Robert W. Service, [the poet of the Yukon and] one of my favorite wordpersons, although blue-blooded poets like some I've met think RWS is a real cornball and a mere versifier at that, not serious enough by half.

108

But when you recite, "Now Sam Magee was from Tennessee, where the cotton blooms and blows.....that's putting words together in the right order which is more than many highfaluting poets do. Like "that night on the marge of the Lake Lebarge" when they cremated Sam McGee.

I've been in this new place for two months now and for the first three weeks did not let cats go out on impressive deck on second-floor of building.... So now Faraday goes out several times every day and Finley only occasionally. As for Old Fogey, he's been there, done that. Neither Faraday nor Finley stray very far and, as a matter of fact, they seem a lot smarter than a Midwestern cat named Charles....

I have a Charles story also and I too am hero. Charles ... worked around the house for us. Before Connie died we'd agreed to "do something" for Charlie, who was in his last year of high school and uncertain as to whether he could afford college....

[After Connie died] and just before Charlie's graduation from high school, I gave him a check for $700, saying that's what Connie wanted. I have witnesses to my heroism; does Roger have witnesses? Must we accept his word?

Nobody gets to be a hero if nobody's watching. Ask Deep Throat. Roger could have set the whole thing up, grabbed the poor confused animal and stashed it where he could later retrieve it and then stick it somewhere else and "find" it and then bask in undeserved favorable attention.

Later, Mac

[June 14]

Dutchers,

... Michael Jackson has been decreed not guilty. Already the people in the various blogs are coming up with headlines with all the plays on situation. Jackson "Beats It" and Wacko Jacko "gets off " and plays on the moonwalk. I have my own submission: WACKO JACKO WALKO. A poor thing but I like it....

Mac

[June 16]

Mac:

... Thought you'd like to know. I got my first rejection [of an email query sent for novel] a few minutes ago. Took all of 16 minutes....

"Dear Mr. Van Noord —

"Many thanks for writing. I'm afraid I'm not taking on any new fiction just now. But thanks for writing. All best...."

[June 17]

Reject the rejection

Roger: I once submitted a poem to a poetry mag and when I got rejection I sent back a rejection of the rejection. You might try this....

Mac

[June 26]

Dutchers,

... I keep seeing references to Alaska since you folks indicated you're going there. NYT Sunday style page (today) had lede article under hed saying those who plan to visit Alaska should do so before it melts....

Apparently there's some truth about Alaska "melting." Glaciers melting at faster rate than expected, effects on land and in the water and warmer temperatures are becoming more and more noticeable....

Mac

[June 28]

Hey Mac —

... Yes, I did see that story. One of the glaciers that has shrunken out of sight is one that was recommended to me by a veteran of travel up north. So that's out. And George Bush continues to ask, "What global warming?" ...

Meanwhile, campers are being pillaged by bears probably seeking bottled water to get some respite from the heat up there. I am hunting for my muskrat trapping club, in case I have to beat bruins off with a stick. Those were the days, getting up hours before dawn to trudge down my trap line to pull out a chewed-off leg or stray tuft of hair, and occasionally a real live animal seeking to do battle with my stick or foot.

I'm trying to recall why I did this. Blood lust, getting rid of the frustrations of youthhood by beating animals senseless, the thrill of being outdoors at 5-below. Or did I simply want some spending money? I think it was the latter. I know I didn't think too much about clubbing muskrats at the time. What was your excuse? ...

RJ

[June 30]

Muskrat ramblings

RJ1 Inc.:

I've got to level with you, Roger, about the pathetic way in which I went about trapping and how I may have led you to believe that I was a canny Connecticut trapper of the old school.

To be strictly honest, I never trapped a muskrat.

You know very well that we had to place trap before a muskrat's hole UNDER THE WATER, WHICH WAS OFTEN CHILLY.... Far more better, I concluded, to trap on the land, full of dry air as it is. It's not as cruel to trap a living being on land as it is to trap one under water where, if one is a fellow mammal, one could drown.

I once found a muskrat in a trap, but it was not my trap. And I wounded a muskrat with my tiny rifle but the vile beast escaped in some sneaky way or other.

Another boy used to trap MY TERRITORY and he easily trapped muskrats [and he] accused me of raiding his traps. PILFERING PUTATIVE PELTS. Being non-confrontational even then, I opted to trap the terra firma for minks and foxes and raccoons. But there again I did not show much "bottle" (as the elegant English say) and trapped no animal before its time.

Well, wait, I did trap one and it was a skunk; me and dog Spunky circled around the irate beast; I was wary, Spunky was spunky, darting in and out ... so to avert a dog-skunk fight I shot the skunk dead with my little rifle, which was nowhere near as long as Johhny Wad's member.

You muse on how it was we could cheerfully kill the little animals we were encouraged to prey upon. Well, since neither of us is still doing that kind of thing, I guess the proof's in the pudding. We wuz just normal-enough boys who didn't know any better because it takes a while to overcome our animality in the abnormal situations we keep finding ourselves in.

I got into killing smaller beings while an eight-year-old ... father ordered me to kill a batch of kittens. So I made my killing bones on kittens, put them in a burlap bag, carried them down the hemlock hill to the brook, put a big flat rock over the bag to hold them down in a nice pool with a mossy waterfall.

Another time, the last time I killed kittens, I tied a burlap bag to the limb of a tree and blasted them to smithereens with a big old 12-gauge shotgun, did it like a good and obedient little son. Don't believe I ever told anyone about that, the shotgun thing. Now I just don't recall how it could be that I could do that, but I remember quite a bit of what happened.

Later, I chopped heads off chickens, and turkeys as well. Shot several copperhead snakes, and was glad to have done it. Assisted in the killing of a quite big pig. And earlier than most had been turned loose on squirrels and rabbits, killing my share, and made a fair sniper-killer of treed raccoons in dark of night with serious dogs lunging and frothing about. And there was a lot of fish-killing going around Connecticut then, so I was complicit there too.

By the time I joined United States armed forces, I was a relatively advanced serial killer, so lethal, apparently, that they desisted from throwing me into contact with any of the evil persons the U.S. had then detected and slated for corrective action.

Killed my last fellow being (save for fish creatures) in 1959 while a temporary posthole digger on a mountain in Sonoma County, where the drunken Jack London burnt himself up in a house fire. A little local color there, which I hope you all will excuse. Why must we drag up Jack London's drunken conduct? ...

Mac

[July 6]

Hi RJ,

Have canceled AOL so will be offline until I can get new server.

Mac

[July 16; snail mail]

Dutchers,

Well, if I can't expostulate with emails, I will via snail mail.... [I live] four or five short blocks south of central downtown, and I generally walk it every morning, get a cup of coffee from Slates Bakery and a NYT from Boynton's Market, and sit outside at Slates' tables and read....

This is what we mannerly gentlefolk of the elderly category do every summer morning in Hallowell, with many an eyuh tossed out amongst us. Drink and read and do not fight or fuss, not in the smallest city in Maine, which calls itself "a drinking town with an antiques problem."

We gentlefolk read and drink in continental amity, although we do now and again see rough looking youths and youthesses, some bearded, some pierced, in the general downtown area. We understand they are "street people" and I for one hadn't realized street people had made it this far north.

But the reason I write is to let you know I'll be offline for longer than I first thought ... my iMac was too old to cut the mustard anymore.... So I will find a used but new computer, and there are lots of ads in "Uncle Henry's" ... a famous-in-

Maine publication that has hundreds of ads for hundreds of items.... I really like to recite the lores and myths of Maine and fear I am becoming like some Masshole wannabe who can never be a true Mainah, sad as that is....

The former almac621

[July 25]

Hey Mac —

We are waiting with heart aflutter to hear if you really are back on line.... We are packing up as we speak, getting ready to head out for parts unknown to man, maybe on Saturday. More anon, if we have verification this note is actually going somewhere.

RJ

[July 27]

Dutchers,

You mean the Alaska trek is nigh underway?

Sheesh, I was going to ask if Fogarty, Faraday, Finley and I or me could housesit in Grand Blanc for duration of odyssey. Leave the au pair, and we'll look after her and your small animal friend.... You-all aren't taking the teeny pet to Alaska, are you? A tiny pet north in Alaska? Do you really know what kinds of creatures they have up there? Alaska is where caribous, though merely large deers, are considered merciless predators, conditions being as they are.

When I was on copy desk of newspaper in San Francisco we ran story about a yearling caribou that sprang upon and proceeded to KILL AND EAT a group of wolverines. There was so little left of the wolverines authorities never could establish whether there had been three or four wolverines.

You'd have to keep your huge vehicle and its impressive windows locked and darkened day and night — don't let your smallish pet outside until back in lower forty eight. Truth is, an Alaskan chickadee could carry the little being off for who knows what sort of fate.

But don't let valid fearful worries spoil adventure.

114

And anyhow, from your terse message, am not even sure trip you mentioned is to Alaska ... for all I know, you may be planning to attend a bean supper weekend in rural Ubly.

What happened with computer ... I called AOL to cancel and in the process got terribly irritated by AOLer's insistence that I really didn't want to cancel ... and so on and on until I told her I can never again ply computer because I have brain cancer and am packing for the hospice. I alleged hospice did not allow computers, said there were strict rules about behavior and corporal punishment of inmates, said prayer in ghastly silence was pretty much how most people did their time.

AOLer offered condolences yet remained poised and in control, her modulations arousing me, now that I think about it. She said one of her aunts had cancer of some organ yet was sitting up and taking nourishment after chemo ... and here, Dutchers, I think my tone and air conveyed a manly diffident ruefulness, a devil-may-care air as I said my cancer would not admit of such easy solutions as those enjoyed by the aunt, MY CASE was terminal.

The AOL-er let me cancel, but ten days or so later, after learning it's hard to get a server for such a decrepit machine — they had better laptops during the battle of Iwo Jima — I called AOL and reconsidered my rash act and was told as I re-enlisted, that I will get two months free and my $28 monthly fee will be halved.

Reason I quit was AOL takes monthly payment from the bank. And three times in past four months I have run into overdraft territory. (That's a banking term Roger, and I am sure Jessica will explain it.) And twice overdrafts ... were caused by my forgetting AOL was silently grabbing my money, making my record-keeping pointless....

... So, when do you leave for the melting spot?

Almac

[July 28]

Packing up resentment

Hey Mac —

A storyteller's odyssey

Good to hear you are in fine email humor again. We both eagerly devoured your last. And we admired your fine bit of negotiating skill with the AOL goliath....

Yes, we are leaving soon, date and time to be determined, as I will discuss, and no, we aren't taking Pumpkin. You see, I had this dream where we let Pumpkin out of the van to do her "business" in Alaska, and she didn't return from the bush.

I mentioned said dream to Marilyn (who I think you have met; she was a good friend of Sharon's and was my main backup while I was caring for her). Marilyn now is a good friend of Jessica's and has become Pumpkin's godmother. Me, notsomuch. My standing goes down as Jessica's goes up. Which, I think, is only fair.

Anyway, Marilyn hears about my dream and she volunteers to take Pumpkin for a month or two. Now, the only problem will be getting Pumpkin back, because Marilyn lost her terrier a couple years ago and is still going through withdrawal. If I hadn't had that dream, I think the caribou story would have done the trick.

So, and here's where marital trouble begins, Jessica asks me a moon or three ago, when are we leaving for Alaska. She wants a date certain so she can plan. I do the overall trip planning but she gets everything packed and ready to go based on that plan. End of July is not a good enough answer for her. So to get her off my back I say 3 o'clock on July 30. This satisfies her, even though she notices I didn't say a.m. or p.m.

It's become a bit of a joke when she tells other people. She thinks it might be a.m. but isn't sure. Then as the date approaches, I realize that the date I have "picked" falls a day before the interleague trading deadline for major league baseball. This realization comes a few days ago, and I begin saying that it might be better if we left a few days later, because of northern lights, wind currents, gas prices, and when that doesn't seem to be a valid reason for delay, I say, beisbol been velly velly good to me.

And that tears it, because that phrase is my code for don't bother me, I have to make some decisions on Rotball. Luckily, I have made some money at this in the past, and even have a trophy made from a can of Yahoo on our mantel to prove it. Even if it is only a traveling trophy. So normally that might cut me some slack. But not on trip scheduling.

Now I'm sure you are already on her side on this, but this trading deadline means a bunch of players could be coming into the AL from the NL, FAAB [auction] bids, free agent signings and host of technical fantasy baseball activities that can't be conducted without a computer connection somewhere in the tundra. So things are in a bit of flux here on this trip....

So, we are leaving at 3 someday, and we will try to send you a report of our progress....

RJ

[July 28]

Hi,

Just a note on two subjects. Subject one is when I wrote about terrible things that might happen to Pumpkin UP NORTH, I purposely did not mention her name. Reasons were, naturally profound: I detached my feelings, not personalizing because of forebodings should the worse come to worst.

So I dehumanized Pumpkin to protect my tender if pious sensibilities. And am glad to hear Marilyn, who I met and liked, will be treating Pumpkin in the ways which she richly deserves.

Second subject is my throwaway line at the end of last email in which I coined, yes, coined THE MELTING SPOT in a blinding flash of what can only be called an AHA or EUREKA moment. Think of Einstein....

As you know, I am modest to a fault, but believe THE MELTING SPOT bids fair, if properly MANAGED AND PROMOTED AND CIRCULATED, to become as popular a meme as "melting pot" or "Fighting City Hall" or the rock and the hard place thing, which is really getting worn out anyhow.

Not only would THE MELTING POT [sic] make a wonderful hed for almost any story out of Alaska, it has numberless

117

commercial ventures and applications ... vanity plates, ice cream parlors, taverns ... tanning salons, chili places, ... bumper stickers ... T-shirts ... hot spots around this great land ... well, the list goes on.

So let's make it clear right now where we heard it first, although if you would like to cooperate in a T-shirt or bumper sticker enterprise, I might welcome partners.

Have a good trip, enjoyed last email....

Mac

Dear Sir and/or Madam:

In our previous email we wrongly reported that Al MacLeese's marvelous coinage, "The Melting Spot," was inadvertently presented as "The Melting Pot." That was wrong....

Our grievous error was due to an editing error preceded by a reporting error, and that was itself compounded by an administrative mistake triggered after a correspondent misread some notes or documents or stuff. We regret any inconvenience this sloppiness may have caused.

Additionally, and by way of complete clarification, we failed the test of fulsomeness by not stressing how wonderful we thought Mr. MacLeese's insight on the TMS meme was. We talked with Mr. MacLeese about the TMS, and he said he was now working on a twist, that might fly, if only regionally. It is Mr. MacLeese's idea that Pittsburgh could be dubbed "The Smelting Spot." Or we could make it Gary.

Sincerely,

Letters dept. sub-editor

[Whitehorse, Yukon Territory; Aug. 8]

Sgt. Preston's Lonely Hearts Band

Hey Mac —

We are sitting here in Whitehorse (of "Sergeant Preston of the Yukon" fame), and I have some access to coin-operated Internet. So before my coins evaporate, I am writing you this note. Mentioned Sergeant Preston to Ryan when I called him yesterday, and all I got was dead air. Generation gaps.

We have motored 3,500 miles in six days to get here [leaving home the morning after the Rotball trading deadline], now we are slowing down a bit and savoring the territory. Whitehorse seems to be a bustling town once again after several booms and busts. We did a drive-by of Sam McGee's cabin here, didn't go in, but it looked small at 50 kph. If you tell me I should see it, we'll stop on the way back from Alaska....

Talk to you later, my coin clock is flashing,

RJ

[Aug. 9]

Melting spot memo

Dutchers,

Got message from Whitehorse and am impressed with your progress and also with your prospects, which sound great. File and forget the McGee cabin, you-all need to visit "the marge of the Lake LeBarge" ... Besides, that cabin sounds like some hovel a Volunteer State man would not stoop to enter, not the McGee from Tennessee, "where the cotton blooms and blows."

Have you been overwhelmed by the ALL of Alaska? I think I told you that I read somewhere most folks are kind of awed by it all, and I wonder if the reaction of two hardy Michiganians jibes with that impression.

I think the first short story I ever read was one by Jack London about a Yukon miner who was captured by members of an Indian tribe with a bad rep of torturing white folks for several hours before dispatching them. Miner was given some time before the torture started, and he used time to mash up some leaves and twigs and shit and made some kind of concoction that he began to smear around his neck.

Stupid Indians want to know what whitey's up to and he tells 'em his magical mess has made him invulnerable to

119

knives or axes and sez he can prove it. Puts his head on chopping block, invites surly aboriginal to chop his head off. Which Indian does and then all the idiot Indians got pissed when they realized they'd been cheated out of lot of good torture credits. (I got this directly from "CliffsNotes.")

I read that story in a collection of several London stories and they appeared in little brown pamphlets and I bet if had a few of them in my ditty bag, I could sell them for big money and retire. Oh, wait, I am retired....

Things going OK here ... will sign off hoping to hear more of Roger and Jessica's Excellent Adventure.

Luck, Almac

[Aug. 21]

Civilization

Hey Mac —

We have been in the Anchorage area and parts south for nigh on to a week....

We are in Seward today, and Jessica is at church. I am in an electronics store where they have Internet access. Yesterday we went on a boat tour of the fjords near here and stopped near a calving glacier. It was awesome, and you know my Dutch reserve. Chunks falling off and making waves, rocking our boat. Icebergs floating around, bumping into our boat, crashing into our boat, scraping paint off the hull.

We saw two different kinds of puffins, eagles, seals and sea lions, whales and assorted other minions of the wildlife tourist trade. Connie would have loved it....

Well, I'm being charged at a rate of a postage stamp for a minute here, so better sign off. This is Lowell Thomas, so long....

RJ ...

[Aug. 21]

Hi Dutchers,

Received your email and this is the first time, Roger, that I ever heard you say the word AWESOME. I guess Alaska truly is WONDERFUL.... Read somewhere John Muir advised tourists not to take Inland Passage 'cause they'd never return to wherever they came from.

I'm moving again ... by week's end.... This move is really good news — the guy who owns this condo noted just in passing recently that I seemed to be having trouble keeping up with the costs of condo living (although am current) and suggested it might be good for me to bail before winter, inasmuch as the heating bill can hit $250 per month.

Also, he advised me to stop smoking in the place, but added I could smoke out on the deck, (this is humorous, because when I was serving our country on a naval tanker, they told us we could not smoke on deck, we had to go inside. And now this landlord ... is changing the rules I used to live by on duty while North Koreans and Chinese were acting up although fortunately not on the French and Italian Rivieras, the Caribbean, the North Atlantic....)

Very next day I was in Boynton's Market on Water Street and Jean and Steve Baker, who own store and building, said they had an apartment vacant. Next thing you know I started moving in.... The key part of this deal is the rent is $475, which I understand is a good deal better than the $750 I paid here for the past four months....

So great news here ... Bakers aren't worried about smoking — everybody that works at the store smokes. I pay the heat — electric — there too, but understand, paradoxically, that nowadays electric heat is cheaper than oil or propane....

... won't be long before am actually going out and eating food in restaurants or diners. Have eaten out only three times since April 1, and then only because Janet, the poet's wife, takes me to breakfast. Haven't been starving, really, because Boynton's sells me all sorts of stuff on the arm, and, happily I pay the tab — which averages about $250 a month for the past four months.

But that's for staples as well as victuals — everything from Fixodent to Corn Flakes to trail mix and Spam to some of those pies in little boxes....

... my [new] place is the penthouse suite on the third floor, smack dab in the throbbing heart of downtown Hallowell. There are two flights of narrow stairs leading to my suite, 28 steps and a landing and the stairway is steeper.... Today and yesterday, my guardian angel ... brought his truck ... and we took most of the furniture and I had some help humping the stuff up to the penthouse.

Give you an idea of what it's like to live in Hallowell, twice [we] were accosted by folks who helped [us] lug stuff up the stairs, thinking it unseemly that an older person such as myself should be doing any heavy lifting....

Mac

[Sept. 26]

We be back

Hey Mac —

Just a note to tell you we are back after 11,164 miles of expensive gasoline.... Not sure if you are back at your old email address, so am sending out this feeler. Let me know how things are going and if you are still AOL-ing it.

RJ

[Sept. 26]

Big story brewing?

Dutchers,

Good to hear you are back safe and sound....

I am working on a huge story that I uncovered and have been working for 30 days full bore researching and sending messages on my progress.... [The story involves] big names nationwide in all sorts of business hijinks and subsequent cover-ups aided greatly by manipulating search engines....

Mac

[Oct. 5]

Dutchers,

Well, I have news to report on my sober investigations into felonies past, and must note that two (2) newspapers have rejected my thoughts that I might be sitting on a decent story....

Excuse me if I often seem to be taking the view that it is all about me and not even having decency to ask if you killed any caribou while predating in Alaska? ...

Later, Mac

[Oct. 7]

Hey Mac —

... Things are busy around here because I am acting as general contractor for [handicapped-accessible] expansion of downstairs loo in preparation for my mother coming to stay, maybe as early as next week....

Good luck on getting someone's ear on the [investigation]. Wish I could do some googling, but even if I could there's no guarantee I could be of any help. I can't even balance a checkbook, so big business finagles are out of my league....

RJ

[Oct. 22]

As I was saying...

To the two Dutchers....

... when last I sent a dispatch from Hallowell ... my news morsel had been rejected by two Main Stream Media outlets, so I contacted a couple of papers out West, and proceeded to tell my tale, in all its infinite details, to an ex-mayor of Hallowell, one current councilperson of Hallowell, the county constabulary, the State Police, two bar owners, two Realtors, two lawyers, and several acquaintances who merely met up with me on Water Street and asked how I was doing.... All of this activity essentially ended my self-assigned mission of notifying the townsfolk... and so ... I called the FBI and became an informant....

Aside to Roger: I wrote [an email] to my friend Bob Hardin ... trying to explain how I got into such a foolhardy clusterfuck. I am sending you a copy of it....

Later, Almac

[Attaches that Oct. 21 email]

... I am aware that people who go on little crusades often fall into the very evils they think they perceive, and proceed to become baddies in their own ways. And I am also aware that as a human being I am definitely still a work in progress, the various little guards I have constructed about my ego are, for the most part, keeping me from the real me, but I am working on a project that might let me know more about me.

Because, besides the protestations of each of us, it really is all about me, and I think my me is a good little guy valiantly struggling to get out and play without fear or favor.... and if I win some praise or attention or admiration, why I think I could stand a little of that....

Friend Mac

[Oct. 24]

Hey Mac —

Well, it's 2 a.m., and I am up because my mother has been wandering around the upstairs.... She professed to be all right, then asked, were you sleeping in my bed, meaning her new digs next to RJ's room. I said no, you were alone, in a studied calm voice.

Well, I thought someone was in my bed and I couldn't wake him up, she says. So this is the pass we have reached at Manse RJ.... Through it all Jessica has been a saint, keeping my mother as close to normal as one can....

... Good luck with the Feebs, et al. Sorry I haven't responded sooner. Been preoccupied here....

R Ste. J

[Oct. 24]

Just a note

Roger and Jessica:

I hadn't realized things were so grim, else I'd never written a jolly letter so full of myself. I am sorry about what all three of you are going through but I know you two are strong enough to handle what comes along.

Later, Mac

[Nov. 21]

Lost in space

Hey Mac —

Sorry about the lagtime. We are doing moderately better here. My mom seems a bit more comfortable in these strange surroundings (for her). She still has her spacey moments, mostly at night. But not always at night, proving, I guess, that the tricks the mind plays cannot be predicted....

We have her set for a flight to Texas to live with my sister for a while this winter. That's on Dec. 4, so we'll get a break until we get back from down south....

RJ

[Nov. 22]

RJ-ers:

... Glad to hear the Grand Blanc team is performing well under difficult circumstances.... I remember when Connie's mother Hilda had Alzheimer's or some other form of dementia, and how we moved her into a nearby place [and] finally got her into nursing home in Petoskey.

Last time we saw Hilda she was slumped in wheelchair and drooling and knowing nothing. As Connie [an only child] and I exited building, she broke down, a rare thing for her either in public or private. Came to believe about then that the ones who love and care for the failing oldster suffer far more than the afflicted one.

Blessedly, I suspect, that such dying humans are too far out of the tragic reality to be hurting very bad. Somehow, our marvelous atoms and their wires make it so the sufferer does not suffer more than an organism can bear. Mysterious and heartening if true, and I think it is....

[In new apartment] am surrounded by bakery, barber shop, antique shop, ice cream shop. I can see the Kennebec River, just across Water St., although now, on a Tuesday afternoon, Hallowell is rainy, bleak, and its foothills are soggy as hell because it has been raining more than necessary for several days now, and outside is bleak and wet, but when you're living in a penthouse, you can easily skate through such periods....

Almac ...

[Nov. 30]

Dutchers,

... You may notice that I have changed the preferred spelling and style of my name. The Noone-McLeese is now to be hyphenated and the "a" in the surname McLeese is dropped, eliminated!

... I must explain that when I was a stripling sophomore at Derby High School in Connecticut [sister Joan] talked me into changing my rightful last name, McLeese, to MacLeese.... I went along with this, Dutchers, having been, as ... all have seen, a passive person for many years, but now, during what appears to be another midlife crisis, I have decided to take action and change my name back....

I hope you folks will have the goodness to honor my request in this matter so that we can continue our correspondence with neither hard feelings nor muted hostilities.

Later, Alan Noone-McLeese

[Dec. 14]

High Noone

Hey --------,

Well, we aren't quite sure how to address you anymore. Mac doesn't seem to work with your name change, and calling you Mc seems to put a bit too much of the Irish on you. Seems to be a flaw in thinking, as far as we Scot lovers are concerned, as in we liked you a lot better when you were a Mac. But then I wasn't aware of the family history here. So are you more Auld Sod or single malt?

... Down south ... Red Necks have decided that northern Blue Hairs now will be called Blue Necks. Don't know if this is some Blue state, Red state thing....

RJ

[Dec. 15]

Dutchers,

... Good to hear you have respite from hurtful and stressful caring and nurturing and imagine the two of you are busier than Bush apologists, getting ready to take Bluenecks southward ... Bluenecks, Rednecks, that combo works — am surprised it hasn't come into more general usage. Course, we all remember when southerners called Yankees Bluebellies while clad in grim grey garb.

Have been invited for Yule dinner with a local family for Christmas. Real Mainahs, French extraction. Speaking of families, I got Christmas card from Doug [and wife and sons].... No contact with these folks for many a moon. Some grandfather.

(Outstanding memory of the grandpa I knew came when Grandpa Albion McLeese paid me fifty bucks to drive him from Oxford, Conn., to Bound Brook, N.J. and back. Gramps wanted to get his beloved pisspot, which was in care of my cousin Dickie ... way south in Jersey.

(... we got the pisspot, chatted briefly with Dickie, and headed back to Connecticut. Granddad was starving and kept asking me to stop for food or beverages or to use the bathroom but I would not do it because he had just paid me cash money and I knew if we stopped he would stick me with the bill and I wanted to use the money to get drunk on.

(Dutchers, I just wasn't prepared to waste money on Grandpa, who I never called Grandpa or anything else, and who ate like a horse and had the personality of a hundred-pound bag of wet cement....)

Things going OK here, I keep occupied visiting about thirty different blogs twice a day. The Irish being bogtrotters, why not be a blogtrotter as well?

Happy Holidays if I don't have occasion to be trite and mawkish again before the ominously looming arrival of a time of good cheer, peace on earth, and goodwill towards, etc, etc, etc.

Mac, which is still acceptable usage.

[Gulf Shores; Jan. 7, 2006]

[Email in which Jessica relays the question: Do you frequent Spellbound, an Augusta lingerie store with live models in the window, or are you a model there?]

[Jan. 9]

The pipes are calling

DUTCHERS,

(Clarification: Almac's machine unaccountably switches modes — from modest lower case drivel to upper case CHAOS....)

AM WAITING FOR THEm to HIRE MALE MODELS TO SIT IN spellbound WINDOWs. I AM STILL as COMELY as ever. BELIEVE I COULD appeal, clad in night togs and jammies favored by older potential clients. I could smoke while modeling; [I now have a glass pipe] sinuously shaped like the one Sherlock Holmes was always holding or puffing on....

Should I take modeling gig, Jessica, I will pose in fetching short underwear and smoke in bed like Sherlock, though he did cocaine and "my bad" is sissy stuff next to coke. Grass

128

isn't much worse than catnip, if you ask me, and Faraday and Finley like both.

Whatever, perhaps I've cured my alcoholism with Campral and cannabis; you could say I have made my bad and now must lay or lie in it. My "bad" not my "bed," Roger. Get it? Or are you both not even following me? Did you read right over the subtle and playful business with the catchphrase, "my bad," which is suddenly all the rage? This is a despicable and silly and infantile phrase and that must be why it keeps running through my head. But I AT least am trying to SPiN silk from an abominable corncobbish expression.

OH, yes, along with pipe came … some nice buds grown high IN THE shambling and glowering brown HILLS ABOVE SANTA CRUZ, WHERE HIPPIES or their spawn have been dangling in CLUSTERS FROM THE WALNUT TREES, and redwood bushes, smoking Jamaican blunts and fornicating without let or hindrance since the days of the Haight-Ashbury.

YES, That shocking Augusta window display riled the RABID Christians in the highlands hereabouts, aroused them erect to commit all kinds of Christian foreplay: threatening, proselytizing, tithing and frothing, blaspheming and beseeching and intimidating — and all that while beating off the heteros when not in a passionate lather about the gays and the lesbians and even guys and gals who don't give a rat's ass about sex, much less having it with others.

Happily, down here in the valley THERE ARE mostly just latent CHRISTIANS and even some, full-blown, so to speak, who mean well. There are almost as many non-believers as believers along the river, and a general sense of civility pervades and motorists NEVER FAIL to stop for pedestrians. In Hallowell, Dutchers, cars and trucks and vans often turn around and go back to where they came from when they espy a pedestrian who seems to be struggling.

And, by the bye, the Kennebec Journal ran big feature Sunday on fact Hallowell has lots of gay and lesbian inhabitants, big part of population, and I guess KJ only just noticed this. The KJ'S sudden awareness was apparently triggered during November elections when statewide proposal to eliminate rights on books for gays and lesbians was soundly defeated. Stories headlined the "Gay Hallowell" part in defeating the bigotry of the appalled and aghast Christians.

May have alluded to the burgeoning gay population in earlier emails, but don't think I mentioned Hallowell is fast becoming known as a gay mecca, and indeed folks here put the percentage of gays and lesbians at around 30 per cent of 2,000 souls on board, including Christians, some of whom may play for the Gay Hallowell team.

GENERALLY DON'T MAKE A POINT OF THAT IN EMAILS BECAUSE THAT WOULD BE UNSOPHISTICATED and so NOT COOL. My thought is the subject is not something to make a big deal out of, but then Hallowell is not your typical small city in many ways.

THE LOCALs TAKE THE GAYS JUST LIKE THEY TAKE every other sub-group, with a live and let live attitude and makes this a very good place to inhabit. An anecdote: the Christers muttered in pre-election posters and letters to eds and on TV spots and probably in bingo and massage parlors that Hallowell was a "GAY MECCA."

Day after Christers were slapped down, I looked out the window of the room in which I am typing this and saw homemade sign.... The sign read: "Thank You, Hallowell. The Mecca."

... Well, I am going on and on here or so it seems. Final bit of news is that THEY held a birthparty for me.... There was a big pot of chili and one of my presents was a case of 24 cans of Coca-Cola, and another was five frozen dinners (gourmet) and a cigarette lighter and two sacks of deli-delights for Faraday and Finley [at some point in the previous six months, his old Fogie cat apparently had died]....

Later, Mac

Part 5: Drifting as an ax murderer

For MacLeese, the years from 1957 to 1967 were primarily a blur – with separations, divorces, remarriages and a string of hirings and firings at a host of newspapers. Plus a number of jobs unrelated to newsprint. There was truck driver, lumber yard worker, salesman and posthole digger, to name a few.

Amid the randomness, or Mac-ness, of his landings before he married Connie in 1967, there are as many question marks as solid navigation points in trying to fit 40-some newsroom touch-and-gos into a decade.

He worked at certain newspapers several times during this period. Three seemed to be the usual limit, the number at which editors ran out of tolerance for his drinking. Three strikes and you're out for good. At others, the "umpires" may have granted him an extra swing or three.

One day, when they were copy editors at the Flint Journal, Don Dahlstrom asked MacLeese to compile a list of the papers where he had worked. Dahlstrom saved the list for years before it disappeared. He is almost positive that several papers appeared on that list more than three times, and he thinks MacLeese's record for number of stops at any one paper may have been six.

"I remember being astonished that [a paper] would take him back that many times."

In 1957, MacLeese separated from his first wife (a 1958 Miami directory listed him as a Yellow Cab driver and Barbara as a clerk for an accounting firm but they had different addresses). They officially divorced in November 1958.

By that time, he was beginning to shuttle about the edges of the country, from coast to coast and south to north, working mainly as a copy editor at more than two-dozen newspapers.

"People in the newspaper business," MacLeese wrote, "have a name for persons of this ilk. Drifters. You can always spot them. When the boss takes one around to introduce him to the staff, perceptive observers note the newcomer is making no great effort to memorize names.

"The drifter later buttonholes some debauched – and thereby trustworthy – old copy editor and asks three vital questions: Where is the nearest bar that gives credit, where is the office men's room and what is the cheapest hotel nearest to the paper?

"About a year later, the drifter is but a memory and the only person concerned about his whereabouts is the guy who owns the nearest bar that gives credit."

These newspaper tramps, he said, "roamed afar, collecting and discarding jobs with a fine disregard for position, prestige, security. And wasting much of his creative potential in battles of wits with would-be employers who occasionally asked embarrassing questions."

MacLeese said newspaper drifters seldom listed all of their jobs. "They usually mention about three or four jobs – there is rarely space for more on applications – and they make jolly well sure that they haven't committed any outstanding outrages at the newspapers they list." Why did you leave your last job? "Relocation, of course. It covers a multitude of sins."

He said he belonged to "a breed that didn't fit in; the men who worked for so many papers they 'had to' lie in job applications; the men who never became a part of what was (temporarily) around them." Generally, he said, "we were fairly good workers and so returned repeatedly to newspapers that in unhappier days had fired us."

One wife said he went from sins of omission to commission at certain papers by giving his father's Social Security number instead of his own, in an attempt to make it harder to track his history. Alfred is similar to Alan. By the time the paper caught on, he was likely gone; he was averaging less than three months at a paper during this forced migration period.

Besides the Miami Herald and the Miami News, he worked at five other sizable papers in Florida: the Florida Times-Union, Fort Lauderdale News, Jacksonville Journal, Tallahassee Democrat and the Tampa Tribune. His stops also included dailies in big cities, the New York Daily News, Boston Herald-Traveler, Baltimore News-Post, Washington Daily News and both the San Francisco Chronicle and Examiner.

Falling by the wayside in his memory bank, he said at one point, were "some others that I cannot recollect and who doubtless cannot recollect me, given the brevity of my loyal service."

Most times he left a paper because he was fired. A few times he wanted a change of scenery. "Of course, sometimes I just woke up in a different state and never went back to be fired."

In certain situations, he was not above tacitly inflating his resume.

During one group discussion among comrades, he quietly accepted an "elevation to foreign correspondent status" for reporting in Cuba "when Castro came down out of the hills." MacLeese wrote in a column that it did not bother him back then "that the audience was free to reflect upon the possible heroics I might have performed in Cuba.... I did not interrupt and say, 'No, it wasn't quite like it sounds.'"

He was working for the Fort Lauderdale News in early 1959 when an editor he knew at the Los Angeles Herald-Examiner phoned and "asked if I would go to Havana to interview a Los Angeles woman just arrested there and mixed up in some improbable spy ring with alleged Chinese involvement. Now that's a sexy story.... This was the day after Castro and his army took Havana....

"I asked my boss (at the News) if I could take time off and he said it was okay for me to go for the L.A. paper, but that the News wanted nothing to do with this apparent folly. (The Fort Lauderdale editor's decision seemed based on his conviction that if I got my hands on some money and coupled that with an out-of-town assignment I would get as drunk as three rabid white squirrels and probably be arrested by the fiery Cubans....

("Since a sober Fort Lauderdale News reporter had just been released from a jail stint in Havana for merely doing her job, the Lauderdale editor sanely concluded it would be tempting fates for the News to send yet another reporter, one who would, if personnel files could be trusted, probably already be drunk and with soiled clothing upon arrival in Havana.)

"The upshot was that I got a flight to Havana and arrived drunk and with soiled clothing. It is an article of faith with alcoholics, incidentally, that it is somehow acceptable to fall off the wagon out of town. The thought is that if you get drunk out of town nobody will know about it, possibly including yourself....

"First thing a foreign correspondent should do is contact the folks involved in the story he is covering. My concern was not this war they were winding up, then; it was solely to get an interview of this latter-day Mata Hari so the L.A. Herald-Examiner could play it up big.

"But, alack, the alleged L.A. spywoman had somehow gotten on a plane for Miami just as I arrived.

"So I called the L.A. paper and told them the pigeon had flown with the poop. They jauntily urged me to pack it in and return to Fort Lauderdale. Said they'd send me a check.... Problem was that only one Cubana airlines flight was leaving Havana daily, and there were lots of folks who thought they had priority in the matter of fleeing Cuba....

"And as the days trickled by, seven of them, I found that I now didn't have any money to pay my hotel bill and barely enough to drink on. And I was getting out to the airport late because I was enfeebled by vodka drunk the night before....

"Those were difficult times. Castro was closing the casinos and some (but not all) houses of ill repute.... Horribly, Fidel had put soldiers with machine guns at the doors of all the downtown bars. Think about it: Sometimes it takes a practicing lush his best effort just to totter into a friendly bar."

Eventually, MacLeese said, he swung a loan to pay off his hotel and bar bills. He even prevailed on an American bar owner to help him get a plane out. "Else now I might be editing a prison sheet in Oriente Province, having mastered the Spanish language nicely."

This story is one of many experiences he had while under the influence that he was accumulating in his memory bank. He would tell and retell these stories, most enduringly in his career as a columnist.

One aspect that often got lost in the stories of his escapades and his drinking was how enjoyable newspapering was to him. "There is little of the stuffiness that pervades some offices," he wrote, "and there is a sense of freedom – provided, of course, that you get the job done."

MacLeese did get the job done often enough to be rehired after months and years passed at papers that fired him. He was known for having skill as a reporter, copy editor and headline writer.

One colleague at the San Francisco Examiner recalled a legendary MacLeese Editor & Publisher ad: "Experienced copy editor seeking permanent job. For references, contact managing editors at the following newspapers and ask about Alan MacLeese." Then he listed 25 newspapers.

As he tramped from copy desks in Miami to New York City to San Francisco to Baltimore and points in between, he learned a valuable lesson.

"One of the delights afforded an itinerant copy editor is that if you are patient and peripatetic enough you can write the same head 10 or 13 times and please and titillate your latest boss.

"You bide your time and lurk. Along will come a story about a hellishly hot day.... You will then write, 'Summertime and the living is queasy.' Bravo. Lurk some more and eventually a story will come along about a Spanish leader whose post is in peril. You will write, 'The reign in Spain is mainly on the wane.' More time passes and you are on a copy desk in Kokomo and a civic leader named Clancy will get upset and you can write, 'Clancy lowers the boom.'"

MacLeese said he won $15 for a headline in the New York Daily News that he blatantly cribbed from Flint-area author Edmund G. Love. "The subways got jammed up and I wrote, 'Subways are for Creeping,' taking off on Love's book, 'Subways are for Sleeping.'

"You also wait for the winter when you are not awaiting the summer. I believe I have written the headline, 'There's no business like snow business' at least nine times. On each occasion the slot [copy desk chief] has said 'Attaboy' or some such and I have deprecatingly shrugged my shoulders in the Gallic manner. I have also been fortunate in the number of cases in which sergeants, military or civil, get acquitted of various and sundry alleged crimes. 'No time for sergeants' is my stock response.

"Plays on the old – and no longer valid – expression, 'Britannia rules the waves,' come along but don't hold your breath. A British ship foundered and I came up with "Britannia rues the waves.' The other variation, even scarcer, is for a story in which a British ship does something against the code of the sea. Then you have, 'Britannia waives the rules.''

Although there were benefits for a wandering head writer, there were penalties for one who was forced to wander.

Working in Baltimore, "I wrote a headline about a story in which rain stopped just before a World Series game. My head read, 'Rain called on account of game' and it won a $150 prize. Alas, I had done a midnight flip and as an ex-employee who left under a darkling cloud, I didn't qualify for the prize. A friend claimed authorship, though, and did buy me a drink five years later."

One MacLeese story of drinking and leaving town ended up on a comparative high note.

Late one night, he finished a shift at the New York Daily News and decided to have a "wee dram." The next thing he knew he was in Alabama and wasn't sure how he got there. He suspected a bus ticket was involved.

After realizing he was a day or so late for work, he telephoned New York to assess the situation.

When he explained that he was in Jasper, Alabama, that apparently didn't seem too far out of the ordinary, or maybe someone at the paper had bought the bus ticket. Did he have a toe tag? It was suggested in New York that he make an appearance before too many more days had passed.

In another story involving a bus ride after a toot, he told of waking up on a bus carrying migrant workers to their next job. When the bus stopped, he got off and headed into the field with the others. He figured, what the heck, he might as well help his new compatriots for the day.

After working in the field for a short while, he became thirsty and went to ask for water. It was then noticed that he didn't quite fit the migrant profile and that he was not supposed to be working there.

A third bus-related scenario was much more complicated and perilous: He ended up under investigation for a New Hampshire triple ax-murder.

He wrote several versions of this story. A couple were in columns. The one relied on most here is the last version, the one that is less flattering, the one in a letter to a close friend, the one in which he did not have to show concern for public appearances.

A combination of drugs and alcohol was involved in his, shall we say, irregular behavior. With MacLeese, the drugs were usually medications that were prescribed, obtained over the counter or through other means. His recreational drug of choice was marijuana.

It was in mid-1959, and the story begins with him boarding a bus in San Francisco just weeks after he was jailed for falling asleep drunk while conversing with a Golden Gate Bridge toll taker. He was in his managing editor's car.

136

MacLeese said he had spent $400 working undercover trying to find vice after dark in a less urban area north of San Francisco. He spent the time getting drunk and cavorting with pimps and prostitutes. He claimed he was pretending to be drunk as part of his assignment and really didn't find any vice.

The tollgate incident may have been why he was on his way to look for a job in Baltimore, home of a Hearst paper. As he rode east he was ingesting prescription sleeping pills along with two fifths of "slurping whiskey." The blend didn't travel well, for one who had not had a fight in two years.

First, he "jerked a soft-cheeked sailor from his seat after ascertaining he was fondling a sweet young girl who ought to have had no truck with the likes of him. I told her all he wanted was to get laid, and she could sit with me and be safe."

Then he "knocked the heads" of two Oriental tourists sitting in front of him "looking about curiously as inscrutable celestials will."

At this point, the bus driver ordered MacLeese to stand near him "gripping a silver rail with both hands." West of Omaha, the driver stopped the bus, which MacLeese told him "was occupied by a cabal determined to ridicule me."

After "neglecting thirty-some fares to give me time to take some air," the driver continued to Omaha, where MacLeese proceeded to sucker-punch an outsized Air Force Academy graduate inside the bus station and a fracas ensued during which two Shore Patrol men wrestled MacLeese to the floor.

Parenthetically, MacLeese said he was arrested by two Shore Patrol men in Albuquerque, N.M., in 1949, when he was in the Navy, and he asked: "What are Shore Patrol persons doing in Albuquerque and Omaha?"

By the time of his trial, "a scant three hours later, the erstwhile cadet was manfully bearing 12 stitches and being forgiving as hell. The ex-cadet told the jurist that he bore me no ill will inasmuch as my mind and body were both unsound; he pointed out that on the bus I had accused him of using a clicking instrument to destroy my precious mentality."

MacLeese said he was jailed for 27 days "as a mentally deficient derelict, having only a Santa Rosa, Calif., library card and bus ticket for ID."

About 12 hours after his incarceration, he wrote a "well-reasoned" letter of complaint to the local paper. The letter went unanswered.

"Perhaps this was because of my blurted and defiant contention to two burly homicide dicks that, as long as they had captured me, they could clear up the triple ax-murder I'd done – not in Fall River, Mass. [of Lizzie Borden fame], but in Keene, N.H. – in the fall of '54. Which I had also belligerently confessed to on the bus to most of the uneasy riders."

The detectives took me to be fingerprinted and stayed to watch the process, which went smoothly.

"You're pretty good at this, Mac," one said. "Done it before, I'll bet."

Well, yes, he had done it before. He had been to jail before, too. And as he entered the cellblock, it occurred to him, "in a flash of Connecticut Yankee ingenuity, that a display of toughness was the way to go. A bold act would persuade my sleazy cellmates to not try to rape or hit me or make fun of my dated tattoos."

He kicked a card table away from four startled players, one a weight lifter. "I later learned they were playing hearts."

MacLeese said his gambit worked. "I wasn't raped or made fun of, just battered to the floor three times (the weight lifter) in the urinal area, awakening two hours later with a different nose, dislocated jaw and ringing ears.

"After my richly deserved thrashing, an inmate approached me as I sat ruefully on a bench. He lighted a match, held it in front of my eyes, then declared that this person had been taking drugs. This gave me a certain cachet, as we say, when doing county time."

The Omaha officers checked back East. Fortunately, no one in New Hampshire knew of any unsolved triple ax-murders. "Good news and I was glad I had been so specific."

As for his dated tattoos, which were of poor quality and had become blurry with age, he took to wearing long-sleeved shirts to hide them. His sister Deborah said he became embarrassed about the tattoos and did not like anyone seeing them. About his "Debbie" tattoo, she said: "Frankly, I was proud beyond reason that he had my name beneath a cupid on his arm."

Within a few months, he had made his way from Baltimore to Miami, where he met and married his second wife, Joan, in a classy ceremony, with a hotel reception.

He soon ventured again into the supposedly glamorous world of foreign correspondents with the promise of a long-term job.

A newspaper friend, Bob Hardin, had gotten a job with United Press International in London, and he "conned the people there into hiring me," MacLeese said. "All I had to do was to show up in two weeks and the job was mine."

Hardin would vouch for hiring MacLeese several times during their careers, and each time it cost Hardin, mainly in credibility, as MacLeese squandered the opportunities. None of the other instances would rival what happened in London, however.

MacLeese quit the Fort Lauderdale News and he said that "nine days later I was on a plane to London, having invested my life savings in this closely considered career move. I would become a foreign correspondent ... and buy a trenchcoat." His wife was to follow him to London later.

On his arrival in London, he missed connections with Hardin at the airport, and he took a cab to the Piccadilly Square area. "Although everyone that knew me had advised me not to drink in London (or in Fort Lauderdale, Pottstown or Pawtucket), I gravitated unerringly to a pub after renting a cheap flat. I would watch the folks playing darts, call Hardin and UPI on the morrow. I would...

"Several morrows later, as dawn's smudgy fingers clutched the venerable London cityscape, I woke up in the bowels of a Fleet St. newspaper building. Presses nearby were rumbling, as was my stomach. I was sleeping on newsprint. A pressman strolled by, greeted me familiarly. 'Have an orange (juice), Yank,' he said.

"It developed that I had spent considerable time with the pressmen over the past days, to say nothing of several doxies who frequented their circles. I was broke and feeling poorly and supposed to start my career as a foreign correspondent in the British Isles that night.

"I rang Hardin up. We convened and it was concluded that I needed several days to get myself in working order. Hardin ... called UPI and said that I had to nip over to Brussels on business and would be several days late starting."

Hardin and MacLeese then obtained "more suitable" quarters in Chiswick, a west London suburb. "I put Fleet St. and its riotous pleasures behind."

After several days recovering in Chiswick, MacLeese ventured back into London on a Sunday, the day before he was to start work. Hardin mentioned that MacLeese would be welcome at a UPI staff party at a home that night. MacLeese wrote: "It would be good to have a little civilized talk after the barbarisms of Brussels," even though Brussels existed only in his imagination.

MacLeese had a few drinks before the party, and he arrived "in high good humor and set about ingratiating myself with my future workmates and superiors. To do this sort of thing properly, one must assert oneself. Surely UPI doesn't want any yes-men in its ranks?

"That's how the argument with my boss-to-be started. I thought The Associated Press, UPI's keenest rival, was superior in several ways, all of which I was familiar with. I think I threatened to quit UPI."

MacLeese's next moves were to become "ensconced prettily on a magnificent white rug." He then proceeded to burn it with a cigarette, then spill whiskey on it. "It was about this time that I became quite ill, and shortly after that, the boss fired me seven hours before I was to start work."

When Joan arrived, Hardin told her, to save the marriage, that he had been misled about the job.

After traveling through France, Spain and North Africa, MacLeese eventually returned to the Hollywood (Florida) area. He and Joan had separated and he was without a job.

He found himself hitchhiking north on U.S. 1 with no fixed destination and 75 cents in his pocket. His financial handicap prevented him from taking a bus. He recalled sitting alongside the road angrily telling himself something like this:

"MacLeese, you jerk. You lost your job, left the homestead and sold your $600 car for $135 cash money. Your suitcase sits in a ditch in Hallandale, you shredded your driver's license and fed it to an ingrate of a hamster on a treadmill in a bar in Dania. Defiantly (desperately?) you ate your last $20 bills in that very bar to the audible dismay of the assembled sozzleheads.... You dummy...."

He had hitchhiked on three continents, including Africa (en route to Casablanca) and Europe. The journeys of hitchhikers, he said, often hold more attraction than their destinations, if any.

"A cop swerves his vehicle to a halt as I trudge through the northern limits of Fort Lauderdale.

"Cop: Let's see your ID.

"Me: I lost it in Dania.

"Cop: What kind was it?

"Me: A driver's license, but I gave it to a hamster.

"Cop: Oh?

"Me: Yes, but I have a 1959 Baltimore library card.

"Cop: Get in. I'll carry you to the Broward County line.

"Me: Thank you, officer."

His connections to Baltimore went far beyond a library card, and his memories were skewed by booze.

140

"I have a warped view of Ballmrr, I suppose, having worked three times for the Baltimore News-Post [the third time it was called the News-American], a newspaper owned by the Hearst family."

Ballmrr, MacLeese explained, is its name to Crabtown natives, and when a newspaperman got a job at a Hearst paper, "it was said that he had 'taken a turn for the Hearst.' Or, more imaginatively, it was said that he had 'gone from bad to Hearst.'"

"There was good and sufficient reason for this gallows humor," he said. Copy desks on Hearst papers "were penultimate pit stops for the drunken and improvident copy editors of the land. If you couldn't get a job at a Hearst paper, it might be time to think of becoming a security guard."

In Ballmrr, MacLeese was introduced to the miniature. Each morning, "most of the copy editors would visit a bar on corner of Commerce and Pratt streets, to load up with 'minnies,' small bottles of whiskey which were then placed in pants pockets for the arduous eight hours that loomed."

He said that of the 12 editors on the copy desk during his three tours in Baltimore, there were as many as eight certifiable drunks, those who had a "drinking problem" that was more often management's problem than theirs.

"We clanked en route to our seats; as the day wore on we clanked less, tacked more."

Many clanking trips to the rest room were made during the day, and "nobody in in the city room had to look up to know that a copy editor was bound for relief of one sort or another.... To be sure, the clanks subsided as the day wore on. Who can hear one hand clapping?"

One day, MacLeese entered the men's room to find the copy desk chief there, "mournfully peering into a wastepaper basket. 'Look,' [the desk chief said], indicating the basket. It was not necessary for me to look, I knew that therein lay about 25 minnies, since I had been responsible for five of them.

"'It doesn't seem fair,' [the chief] said, 'Most copy desks have one or two drunks, tops. On my desk, though, the majority is drunks. The inmates have taken over the asylum.'"

MacLeese said he "clucked but didn't get too close, fearing he'd smell the vodka on my breath. I was hoping he'd leave quickly because I wanted to have a benevolent upchuck."

On reflection, MacLeese said that perhaps "the pronunciation of Ballmrr stems not from the natives' aversion to enunciation, but a long-forgotten group of seven or eight drunken copy editors. We never had trouble saying Ballmrr, even at 9 a.m...."

That he was a problem drinker during his years BC (Before Connie) is a given. To some he showed remarkable on-the-job talent, to others he was nothing special.

Llewellyn King was working as a copy editor for the Hearst paper in Baltimore when MacLeese was hired there for his last time. By then, King said, MacLeese was a legend. King was warned: "MacLeese is coming, don't lend him any money."

King called MacLeese an "extraordinary talent and an exceptional drinker."

Now a publisher, syndicated columnist and host of "White House Chronicles" on TV and Sirius XM radio, King drew on superlatives in describing MacLeese. "The most remarkable man ... the most charming human being." Even when he was "blind drunk, he was not unpleasant ... he was such good company."

MacLeese, King said, had an "extraordinary capacity with words" and was a gifted headline writer.

Jim Houck, who worked with MacLeese in San Francisco, said a lot of people were impressed with MacLeese's work on the copy desk there.

Houck wasn't aware of MacLeese's exceptional drinking problem, though, until the night of a poker party. "At some point Al passed out. After everybody left and [the host] went to bed, Al woke up and drank every bit of liquor in the house. He didn't show up for work for several days."

MacLeese also was a no-show when his father died, and drinking was a factor.

He knew exactly where he was when his mother died in 2001 at age 95; he was on his way to be with her, but that was a different era for him, in time and condition. When his father died in 1958 at age 52 from heart problems, MacLeese was out of the loop. His sister Joan thinks he was in rehab.

According to Joan, his drinking problem was one reason their mother didn't let him know of their father's death right away. Joan and her husband, James, were living near her parents.

Joan said that when Alan confronted his mother about it many years later, he asked her: "Why didn't you call me?" His mother replied: "Why should I call you? I had Jimmy." The reference was to Joan's husband and the implication was that Alan would have been of little help or solace. He was considered someone who couldn't be depended on in a crisis.

Deborah, his youngest sister, said "he was not the brother to whom you went with problems or for any kind of assistance. You took him on his terms."

Her feelings about her brother evolved as she got older and as his drinking problems became more of a family burden.

"I remember when I was little and he would come home and I would be so thrilled that this was my brother, this nice-looking, smart, tall guy who clearly had an adventurous life far away from the valley. Nobody else had a guy like that in the family and it made me feel special."

Although he was appealing – "funny, intelligent, quick with a joke" – she remembered him turning "whiny and pathetic" when drunk. She said he was "a particularly sensitive and defensive person [who] took offense when none was intended."

Later, his entertaining stories about drunken revelry could dredge up less happy childhood memories, "snippets of bad times relating to Alan ... trying to locate him in local bars, expecting him to call and need to be bailed out of some difficult situation in some faraway state, my mother needing to wire him funds that were supposed to bring him home but which instead got used for another (or extension of the current) binge."

Deborah said she "grew up knowing that an alcoholic cast a shadow over an entire family and that his needs, because they were usually urgent, trumped those of the rest of the family."

[Jan. 15, 2006]

Masturbation cover-up finally exposed

Dutchers,

I just now had a morning smoke ... and started websurfing and suddenly ... I thought about how, while in a Marine-run stockade I pulled — please excuse the expression — [time] in solitary with only a Bible to comfort me.

Fast-forward, now, to 1970s while a vivacious Flint Journal columnist, [when I wrote I] had occasionally masturbated with Bible as visual aid. Some passage about snowy breasts or thighs(?) triggered the acts, but am just guessing. My acts may have been impelled more by boredom....

But wait ... the nicely worded masturbation reference never saw light of print! Re-reading masterful prose in proof, I cravenly and, to my everlasting shame, edited myself —

causing the precious masturbation reference to be deleted before it could reach customers who doubtless were queued around Flint paper dispensers knowing this was one of the days my popular column appeared ... and I betrayed them, wimpishly took it out....

I could have brazenly admitted masturbating while imprisoned and in a sacrilegious manner.... So, a crucial failure of nerve, Dutchers, and that's the backstory of my early retirement, subsequent problems, the whole nine yards.

It was this instance of losing my cojones that led to behaving boorishly at the Green Door, like the time while mentoring [a reporter], I petulantly hurled a glass of vodka against a dining room wall....

... it was a betrayal that made a mockery of my special relationship, my mission, if you will, with my beloved newspaper, and Roger, you being a former top official at the paper, I hope you will accept this missive, delivered HONESTLY in my halting and fumbling way, as my sincere attempt to apologize to the management and staff of the Journal....

"The Old Masturbator from the Faraway Hills"

[Feb. 4]

Hey Mac —

... Have you read Basket Case? I assume you have. I gave it to Jessica to read down South, and her reaction was that you had written it. I think that's a compliment for both you and Carl H, the Miami Herald columnist....

RJ

[Feb. 6]

Dutchers,

Carl Hiaasen — admit it Van Noord, you had to refer to his last name by initial because you had forgotten how to spell it — is one of my favorite popular writers, right up there with Elmore Leonard and John Sandford and Robert Parker.

UNLEASHED

I've read most of his books, save for the ones he wrote starting out with Montalbano, another Herald staffer.

Indeed, if my recollection is accurate, the Montalbano person was on the Herald when [it] illegally deported me from Miami to New York City in the year of our alleged lord, 1965, or thereabouts. I had been working as a copy editor in the new Herald building on Biscayne Boulevard, and one day I had off from work so got drunk in bars along the boulevard, and ran out of money so decided to go to the Herald city room and borrow some money from some fool who might loan it to me.

(... bear with me here because this following story is true and may be used in court testimony if I finally decide, after all these years, whether I wish to pursue recourse through a legal venue to bring me the closure from pain and agony over this traumatic incident I so richly merit.)

So I get to the city room and people are working away and I espy [an editor] sitting all by his lonesome off at a big desk. [The editor], who I did not know at all well, was laying out the front page for the next day and I sat down opposite him, grabbed some pencils and layout sheets, and proceeded to explain ... the finer point of a craft that I had practiced in many places for quite a spell.

I do not well recall the exact timing of events, Reynoldses, but ... a reporter, and then nondrinking drunk, was instructed to take up a collection of money from those assembled in the vast editorial edifice so a ticket could be purchased from the Greyhound people to transport me, shanghai me if truth be told, to New York City.

This was done, and with [the reporter] guarding me, I was removed from the building and we went to my room and got my suitcase and then [the reporter] purchased a fifth of something and I was taken to the place of the greyhounds and put on the bus.

... so that is how I was ... sent packing like a crate of oranges. And, because the Herald had ... purchased whiskey for me, I was thrown off the bus in Jacksonville, Florida, arrested and woke up in the Duval County Jail with one shoe, a brown shoe if I remember....

Mac

145

[Feb. 15]

Dutchers,

... yesterday I started out to take my pipe to the sink but saw my glasses were on TV so decided to take them and put them in my pocket, but then noticed stick of butter still on table and melting and was going to fix that when saw the fly, yes there are flies in winter in Maine, was on butter and reached for swatter but realized TV was on without sound and broke stride to fix that when it struck me that clock on stove didn't match time of clock on tv, and hastened to fix that when phone rang and ere I could answer realized had left Finley locked in closet and then pizza, ah, never mind....

Mac

[Feb. 15]

Hey Mac —

... You were on the mark about me not trying to spell [Carl H's] last name. I can never remember whether it has two A's or two S's. Those Nordic types (or should it be Noordic?) should simplify their spelling, or fix that sticky typewriter key....

RJ

[Feb. 19]

Advice and counsel earnestly sought

Dutchers,

As you-all know, I've been impeccably handling personal finance despite my advancing age, but even fairly robust elders must occasionally ask our slightly younger friends for advice.... So if reformed banker X will please pay particularly close attention concerning validity of financial scheme and its rationale ... and then get back to me ... I would like that very much. Perhaps you-all will even learn a dodgy trick or two from an older codger, case of an older dog teaching younger dogs new tricks?

UNLEASHED

In any case, I was close-reading the NYT around the first of the year and read the first of serial stories in weeks that followed that reported, in one form or another, credit card companies were keenly aware that beaucoup millions of Americans declared bankruptcy in 2005 — most of them smartly seeking to beat the new bankruptcy law that now makes [it impossible] to flee SCOT-FREE like I did a couple of years ago, cheating my betters of thirty-four large, and proud as a peacock about it too.

Well, and here's the nutgraf, the credit card people came right out and admitted they are ardently seeking new customers among ranks of the recently bankrupted because, and get this, NONE OF THESE millions and millions of FUCKING DEADBEATS owe anybody any money!! (Double exclamation point mindfully tacked on.)

See, Dutchers, I had been getting credit card solicitations for months and months but pitched them w/o opening because I naively thought I would be rejected for a "pre-approved" card as soon as they found out they were dealing with bankruptcy survivor.

So and but then: about four or five months ago old iMac went hoarse, then totally lost his voice, no longer groaning and wheezing when laboriously dialing up, and no longer bleakly saying you don't even have any spam. And on top of that, iMac, he developed "typetwoerroritis" and whimsically shuts down shop if I so much as start to call up "porn" or "sex with male quails."

And so then I hear from poet there is guy in Moosehead that could sell me a computer and install it and could be trusted with my life to make sure that I would know how to operate it before he left the building. And he would bring along a scanner and a printer and some kind of animal that kills viruses.

It is here, Dutcher, where the wisdom of the geezers pops up ... there is such a thing as "pattern recognition" in the brain's workings, as dictated by the frontal lobes, and every time we do something of a certain nature why we ring it up as a pattern and the older we get, the more patterns we easily recognize.

So I saw, in my wisdom, that I could apply for these cards and likely get accepted because I am a deadbeat and don't owe nobody (on the record I hasten to add) any money!

So I applied for Mastercard Platinum card and was approved over the phone, that yes by god they checked me out and my card would arrive in ten-to-fourteen days and Bank One, which indicated I was quite likely to get its card in seven-to-ten days. And I will be pleased to do business with them because they offer a $5,000 credit limit while the Household Mastercard has a limit of [$2,000], which I deem as almost an insult. But a deal is a deal.

It will be seven years, a long hard slog, before I can again declare bankruptcy, and my well-thought out plan counts on the Democrats getting back in power long before then, and they will promptly return bankruptcy law to where it was when I declared bankruptcy for the very first time. And if need be, I can then have another go at it, at least according to plan.

Mac

Oh, I will now be able to have new computer and scanner and printer installed in March so plan is to use card (or cards) only for computer and then now and again to keep the usurers from disqualifying for not throwing enough interest their way....

aMac on iMac

[Feb. 19]

Free advice (worth what it costs)

Hey Mac —

Am dispatching this note ASAP before my girl thinks up some reason you shouldn't do the credit card bit. She agrees, yes, you should have a new computer and printer but is not too sure about the scanner and the floating island so you can use computer in the new hot tub.

We are going through the same problems now with laptop on which I am writing, hoping to complete this note before it freezes up. So we are shopping, too.

My girl adds, however, that after you buy said computer on credit card, you should take said credit card or cards and cut them up and toss them in trash. This will avoid temptation to use on routine necessities. But you would still have the numbers (if you write down those sort of secret numbers on back), so you could still use over phone in emergency to order new sex toys or whatever from the Home Shopping Network....

The only other option she will accept is to put credit cards in Ziploc bagful of water and freeze them in your fridge, so it would take time to thaw them out and prevent using them on whims.

If you neglect to take these safeguards, she says, she will fly to Maine and beat you about the appendage sticking above your shoulders. Or she will take steps to have GAG strike you from her will, which must be accruing lots of interest....

RJ

[Feb. 20]

If this be terrorism....

Dutchers,

Ms. Dutcher apparently is unaware of severe penalties Bushco metes out to terrorists — especially those who would threaten to beat up a 75-year-old disabled Korean War hero, an enfeebled relic who is also a recovering booze addict and an ... outlaw consumer (and a bankruptcy survivor to boot) who is merely trying to better his lot while waiting for his ship to come in.

And Ms. Dutcher's suggestion (edict? fiat?) that I put the cards I will soon have to play with in a Ziploc bag in the ice box is the coldest statement that I have ever heard a banker make. In any case, I am being very proper about this matter.

With my card in hand today, I went to Gardiner Savings and transferred $1,000 to my checking account toward the cost of the computer-scanner-printer ... the guy who's selling me the service has now gone off to Kenya, where he is, in his nice Christian way, helping the natives. Prolly tearing down houses that Jimmy Carter put up with shabby southern lumber.

Why is it that every time I enter a transaction, it is much harder for me than anyone else? For instance, the card was approved and they told me I would get it in xx days and it didn't come and I called several times and finally found out they had lost an entire shipment of cards and one of them of course was mine. And that they had to kill my card and birth a new card!

There were letters from Household bank telling me my card was coming, and then telling me ... it wasn't coming but finally got someone to feel so sorry for me they Fedexed a new card within two days of my final impassioned entreaty in which I was thinking the clincher might be if I threatened suicide over the phone, but we didn't reach that point.

Perhaps Ms. Dutcher could explain to me why banking people treat me with such cavalier, well, uncaringness?? And what's worse, I had to explain to the Christian computer seller-installer that the delay on my part was because my credit card got lost in the mail.

Yeah, right, most non-Christians would say, but the Christian was forgiving and even told me he would trust me with just a down payment but he had to leave for Kenya right away. So I won't get the computer until early March and that's only if the Kenya cannibals don't kill him and cook him.

Alan McLeese

[March 13]

The incident at Moose Ramble

Dutchers,

Bear with me now inasmuch as I am sending an email on my new ViewSonic (IBM compatible), lots-of-kickass-bytes, and I am now on a high-speed computer that responds with the speed of dark to my every command and has persuaded me, against my earlier modest denials, that I am indeed a master of the universe; I have a machine that yesterday showed me a moose that bellowed and today astounded me even more by showing an animated and suggestive video of a woman shaving a stuffed beaver.

Nothing is beyond me now, except most of the wonders I have seen have been by accident and it still takes considerable brainpower for me to merely access my ... email. But I can browse my blogs, and read all manner of shit, including the fact that I turned up today: There are fifty billionaires living in New York City, and 29 of them are Jewish. Probably some Dutchers in there, but they were not enumerated.

... when I was at the Hannaford market today I whipped out the Bank One card, you'll be impressed by this, Jessica, and gave 'er a swipe for a $45 food bill that included food and catnip for Finley and Faraday. I felt empowered by the card, Jess, and I look upon today's purchase as practically food for free because who knows, in the final analysis, how much of this money I will be able to pay back?

Well, enough about such crass subjects, the other big development here is that I have re-contacted sister Deborah, and now it may be that I shall be reconciled with the sisters, their various spawn, and also I may see Doug [and family] ... sometime this spring when they visit ... Maine, where Doug's wife's sister has a "Cottage near the Beach."

I hope you folks are doing OK and I am well and, in fact, I hear that Great Aunt Gert is doing well as well. Debbie sent me pics of GAG and I must say that she looks like she's good for another twenty years or so, give or take a month or so.

Also, Debbie sent me newspaper article from Bridgeport Post about Great Aunt Gert's 107th birthday ... and GAG's thoughts over the centuries, three count 'em, three. I will now do the things I need to do to make sure this message is sent. This machine is frightening, it knows so much, it can even tell when I get excited, aroused....

Later, Almac

[March 23]

Back from dove hunt in Texas

Hey Mac —

Yes, we are just back from an 1,800-mile side trip to the tip of Texas, primarily to keep an eye on my mother while my sister and her family took a break from said duties for a week or so. Took us two days to get there, and two days back, so we've been gone awhile.

They live in Harlingen, which takes us past the King ranch and town of Armstrong, near where CHENEY SHOT A MAN IN THE FACE....

Mom seems to be doing about the same....

I am writing this on our new laptop computer, so no more excuses about frozen or lost emails, I hope. By the way, Jessica says that because of your gene pool (where GAG is giving signs of living to 127) you might want to reconsider whether she will die before the credit card bills come due....

RJ

[March 25]

Dutchers,

... I have been busy making breakthroughs in expert personal banking practices despite some cut-and-run carping from even the tent of my friends, the Dutchers.

My friends here in the city of Hallowell, however, all agree I am not only canny but gifted, even prescient in the way I have been handling my affairs to the point where today is the 25th of the month and I have sixty dollars in my wallet and $1.65 in the bank with an annuity check due tomorrow with more than four hundred scoots in it, the payout is reaching record numbers in the three digits because the market has hit its highest point in five years, and I knew that this was going to happen five years ago sitting in Drake's Tavern in Bridgeport, and that is just one of the reasons I am prospering like a Dutchman in Aruba.

Despite my credit card acumen up the wazoo, some people like Jessica will say I have shown no aptitude at all for handling my affairs and point to decades of throwing money around like a drunken sailor or newspaperperson. Some people, like Jessica, seem to think that merely because they have worked for banks that somehow they know more about banks and credit cards and canny timing than I do....

Consider this, if you will or may: I recently borrowed a skosh under two large to buy the marvelous computer I now sit before for a grand total of $1,569.71; I did this three weeks ago, and have been billed for a total of $48. Shoot, I paid off [that bill] and now will not have to deal with [it] until next month's minimum payments.

I know full well, Roger and Jessica, that they may come after me with a vengeance, they are already figuring out that while I have no interest on purchases I have made, which have been minimal, but they are going to slap me silly with the interest on the 15 C-notes (banker jargon) but that day is far in the future and today I am ... reading with avid interest how the Washington Post hired a plagiarizing grifter as a blogger. I applied for a job at the Post while working at Washington Daily News and the only flaw in my application was that it was written while drunk in a bar in long hand, and mailed, if I recall correctly, with an incorrect return address.

Almac

[Grand Blanc; April 6]

Boggled up in Grand Blanc

Hey Mac —

We are back home and have been greeted with myriad missives forwarded from a new more powerful computer. I have spent a bit of time trying to make sense of it all, but the going is tough because when it comes to high finance and rich connections, my brain to work does not seem, as they say in German. It boggles, I guess is the English translation.

... I hope you have found a blogger that can help you make some hay out of these alien entrepreneurs' crop circles....

RJ

[April 7]

Hi,

Sorry I haven't written more lately but that's because I am writing more lately. Once I realized I was dealing with a rather large story — unless I am madder than a Danbury hatter — I sort of decided, as I went along finding out stuff and zapping emails to [a Los Angeles blogger], that I should share more of this story.

I decided I would [share] all the emails of all the stories I was batting out to [the blogger] with my wonderful friends from Grand Blanc [and four others, including sister Deborah].... It should be noted at this point that I did not tell any of the recipients other than [the blogger] that I was going to do this because I was so busy googling and smoking some very very choice stuff of the Burmese strain.... Happily, only a small percentage of the recipients ... cut me off as barrage of emails intensified....

Mac

Jessica ... you might remind Roger that he is a former newspaperman and as such it is always his bounden duty to comfort the afflicted and afflict the comfortable.... he, Roger, should start exerting pressure on his friends in high places ... [and] help his good friend get a hold of some notoriety....

Later, Almac

[Forwards April 7 email from sister Deborah]

Hey,

How are you doing? (Other than madly working on the computer day and night).

At this point I've gotten 4-5 copies of some of the [emails]. I'm thinking that when you don't get specific responses to emails then you are not sure if they have reached their destination. Don't worry about that — anytime an email is undeliverable it will be returned to you with a reason it was not delivered....

This is certainly a complex story with which you are dealing. Can't imagine what the end result will be but you folks are clearly following some interesting lines of inquiry.

Good luck!

Love,

D

[April 11]

Dutchers,

Hey Rog, Jess, could you folks do me a small favor, now that we're all in this neat little loop together? See, I have been sending info to two newspapers and perhaps, oh, say fifteen vendors of the news, complete details on what I know about the [investigation] ... and yet, after more than two weeks of emitting words to the outer world have received no assurance from any of these fine wonderful dedicated news sources that they are doing anything....

As the former managing editor of the Flint Journal, Rog, are you feeling empathy and warm regard and kinship for me out here by the fire station in Hallowell while the Kennebec River slides by, ominously. So would you, Roger, maybe ask somebody in the loop whether progress is being made in our joint efforts?

... Yes, yes, Jessica, I know, WTF don't I ask somebody in an official position myself, instead of trying to con someone else into doing something. But I cannot do that, Jessica, owing to my longstanding fear of rejection.

Someone must act, because if this unknowingness must end, ere I have to return to those meetings they hold in the dank basements of churches and you have to make your own coffee; Rog, Jess, don't send me back to the church basements, those uncomfortable chairs generally reserved for Christians....

Mac

A storyteller's odyssey

As you well know, Roger, stress and a lack of information can cause an arid drunk to topple off his wagon, maybe stagger out the hallowed interior of the Wharf and plunge into the river....

[April 11]

One last turkey hunt

Hey Mac —

I'm packing for the left coast of Michigan tonight and will leave early in a.m. Going to meet assorted relatives at my mother's house to start cleaning it up before putting it on the market at some point this summer, we think. Be gone for several days, then when I return, am leaving for one last turkey hunt with Dick Cheney....

I think you had suggested me calling someone and lending my considerable girth to your cause. Didn't sound like a good idea from your point of view since I still can't make sense of all the machinations.... All they'd have to ask is why this is a story worthy of investigation, and the impact of my call would tumble like a house of cards.

You are the man, and the one who is able to respond to such inquiries.... But I enjoy reading about your efforts to give voice to your suspicions, so keep forwarding copies my way. When I will be able to get at them is another matter, since I will be out of pocket for at least 10 days....

RJ

[April 11]

Hey, can you do me this one little favor?

... Roger old buddy, if this thing we're working on results in a little notoriety for those involved, well, if anybody asks, could you kind of forget all about that crazy story about me supposedly going around bragging about having been [hired] 47 times by 27 different papers.

It's key that we remember that that was total bullshit because when I got hired at the Kennebec Journal ... well, not to put too fine a point on it, I told them I'd only worked

156

for maybe five or six papers; I feel bad ... because it was good of them to hire me at the age of 72....

So when they realized that the extent of my computer abilities was to keep sending stuff to warehouses in Ulan Bator, why they gently ushered me out, which was the right thing to do, and of course I do feel bad still about the time I showed Stephanie my broken [arm] and [told her] that I did kind of suspect it was broken ... but dammit I didn't want to miss any work.

So Rog, are we cool? Oh, one other thing, no big deal, but about all the trouble I got in in the Navy ... let's not go there at all, and as for those times while hitchhiking in the fifties and sixties, it is true that I often would up and be perceived as a tramp at worst, an itinerant at best. And you should never show a library card from Baltimore as the sole means of ID....

Just so [these subjects don't come up] among the members of our group, I'm going to make sure that this email goes only to you....

Mac

[Group email sent April 25]

Remarkably lucid and irate post

Folks,

I have decided to pitch in on this project ... [with] a virulent and exasperated post....

Impassioned, yet caring and sharing, I suppose I will not write anything like that again until I can find another place on the web and figure out how to make them let me utter my piteous pleas, which grow hollower and hollower here in Hallowell, and my shell-like ears are already turning pinkish and an angry red as I sit here alone wondering what my comrades in other journalistic trenches are doing....

I got drunk tonight for first time in two years, I am celebrating, we have brought them out into the light ... and that is something, because nobody else seemed to give a rat's ass....

MacLeese

[May 16]

Hey Mac —

... We have now cleaned out my mother's house, except for the furniture and memorabilia and other items we want to save.... The end of the month, Jessica is flying south to pick up Mom and fly her back here....

I talked to Mom on Sunday and there still was ice on the pool in southernmost Texas. She had gotten up in the middle of the night a week ago, and was using all the towels in the house to stop a flood in her room. Maybe she was watching too much weather channel. So we are a little apprehensive about this next six-month visit.

Haven't seen any update on [your investigation]. What's been going on with that lately?

RJ

[May 17]

Dutchers,

... as I look out my eastern window the water is creeping placidly by ... and we laugh ... at the plight of others to the south, the Massholes and their ilk, because all of the woes are downstream of us....

What can one say about the next six months with an out-of-control mom? One has to laugh so as not to cry, I guess, and the only solace is the probability that mother nature mysteriously manages to guide our way to an easeful death even though that may not appear to be the case to those innocent bystanders....

You asked about [the investigation] and will not be surprised, I am guessing, to learn that the probe is ongoing.... In the meantime ... the Kennebec Journal declines to respond to my entreaties about the fate of my 250-odd emails to it.... But I have called scores of other outfits and soon the whole world will know that I am a crazy old fart....

Later, Almac

[May 31, snail mail, with check for $461.72 enclosed]

Hi, Dutchers,

No, GAG did not die; indeed, sister Deb sez she's probably good for four more years.

But I have other resources: A [guy] who says he represents a Hong Kong bank wrote me and practically forced me to accept an unsecured loan of $5,000, and by the fourth of June that check in this mail is good. The added $61.72 must be used for a dinner for two at the Olive Garden nearest you, and it should cover tab & tip provided Roger lays off the linguini.

Al

Oh yeah, and thanks!

[June 6]

Hey Mac —

Thanks for the largesse in the mail. Someday you will have to explain how you arrived at the $61.72 for the trip to Olive Garden. $30 for each of us and $1.72 for my mother? Decaf coffee for her.

There was some grumbling from the banker side of our operation here — OK, a lot of wailing and gnashing of incisors — over the Hong Kong vehicle for the check, but we don't need to go into that in detail. Something about credit card interest rates and loan sharks, stuff that us mere consumers don't understand, much less worry about, unless our wallet turns up empty on a Monday....

RJ

[June 8]

The new banking which oldtimers don't get

Rog:

In addressing this communication to you I do not mean to exclude Jessica, but since we will be talking about banking, and I make references to Jessica's outmoded views, it's best that we just talk man-to-man and pretend she isn't listening.

I got a letter from some nice young fellows who work for a Hong Kong bank on Western Avenue in Augusta, and those altruistic guys, not Asiatics, incidentally, have branches all over Maine and in their personal letter they were nice enough to send me, ... they asked me, and I quote: "Alan MacLeese, could you use $3,100?"

For Pete's sake, Rog, since I lack gees to buy new fake teeth, new fake glasses, and a new windshield for my Babemobile, and the Depends — that's a joke, and why you took it seriously bothers me — and what with the prices these days for herbs, the horror, the horror.... So I gave a quick call to the ppll that offered me $3,100, but noted, casually, that I would not reject any genuine offer to loan me five large....

Now Jess would say they are really going to nail me down the line, but Rog, who knows what ... I might do when push comes to shove. If GAG dies, then I can say to the Hong Kong [bank] and the credit-card distributors, I spit on your piddling loans, and here I will pay you off and don't bother me anymore until I am about 108 or so and by then can make a bundle off my incredible longevity, and so, Jess, where's the downside here?? ...

Almac

So, when ... the Hong Kong bank branch called, Rog, I said I could use three large, but, no, I won't go to your stinking office, show my badges; you call me up and let me know, and they did and, contrary to Jessica's received wisdom, Roger, and mark this well, have fifteen thousand scoots of credit and my boyish and accommodating personality, so how can I lose??

have been hurt like that beofe, Rog, so to go to their offrice, even though pre-approved, no.... I would onlyh come over there whenthe loan was a don e deall.

Dutchers,

In the previous transmission there were errors toward the end, and they were caused by transmission personnel on this end.

When you get to the point on the previous transmission where the words cease to make any sense at all, that is probably the point where you should realize that from thereon there will be nothing but incoherent babbling, and there is no point in continuing reading and you should all throw up your hands and say, well, beyond this point is the pale, nothing good gonna happen here, so just stop reading until the codger signs off.

Almac

Yours in sports

[July 17]

As I was saying...

Hey Mac —

... we have been busy, lo these many weeks of silence. Ryan and Jamie got married on Mackinac Island, so now there's officially another RJ in the family....

My mother didn't go ... we decided that would be too risky and she would be too confused.

Just a few minutes ago, she asked me: "Now who is Jessica married to?"

... Jessica waves hello....

RJ

[July 22]

Working on the webroad all the livelong day

Dutchers,

Am still working around clock on [investigation] thing which is reaching proportions that boggle my mind. It's grown bigger than my original target....

Still posting every day on five or six top blogs, and the whole thing should pop on the lame stream media within the week, and then it's Katie bar the door.

Later, Almac, who has now been workin' this job since March 25, and that's a whole lot of searches and clicks and posts....

[Aug. 6]

Intelligence from the provinces

Dear Dutchers,

Let me say at the outset that I know you, and the rest of my remaining friends, if any, think I am crazier than a shithouse rat. I deduce that from the fact that no one who knows me or has been emailing me has contacted me in months, and, as far as I can figure, I have two friends left, perhaps, and they are engrossed in mourning the passing of Eldon Auker, the landlord from Grand Blanc who wouldn't give me and Connie our deposit back. Well, Dutchers, you see what happened to Auker? He is dead, d-e-d, and I am still around....

Yes, Van Noords, I am still working on the webroad ... still working on the job I started last September, and it has grown, exponentially, and they will be talking about this in the caves where the remnants of the MSM [Main Stream Media] raggle-taggle crew goes to expire....

Later, Almac

[Aug. 7]

Hey Mac —

First of all, let me say in response (a la Lloyd Bentsen) that I know crazy ... and you are not crazy....

So unless you think Jessica and I are living in your house and sleep with you in your bed, the jury is still out....

Where can I find some evidence of progress you ... have wrought? I couldn't even follow the links the last time I tried....

RJ ...

[Aug. 7]

Rog,

... That brief post in early April was first thing I posted on Web. I now have scores of posts all over web ... any interested person should be able to follow the trail.

... a chess player such as yourself should have no problems although, admittedly, the conditions you are living under are extreme, and put my situation in the shade, but these are interesting times I would guess for the both of us.

Almac, who wishes at least one friend would show at least a mild interest in what he's doing because it ain't chopped liver we are making here.

[Sept. 15]

Hey Mac —

I have a few moments today between chasing my unsteady mother with her walker (being Dutch she insists she doesn't need it), and I am using this peaceful time to let you know that I am sending forthwith an article published in the latest issue of Michigan History magazine, no less, about one Bill Gallagher, photographer of national note.

So how has it been going with you? I try to keep up with your [investigation] by checking your postings. As I told you before, I have a hard time dealing with or even gaining a basic understanding of these matters of high finance and big business. I read the "CliffsNotes" version ... and I guess you can blame this on George Bush and all his shenanigans, but I can't find something to get upset about.... What am I missing here? Or is it just my attitude lately?

It's pathetic, but all my stories lately seem to be about dementia.... this week, Jessica and I were fighting about who was going to get the chance to go out grocery shopping.... We laugh about it, so that's a good thing, I guess.

RJ

A storyteller's odyssey

[Sept. 17]

Hello, Van Dutches,

Well, here I am still in Hallowell, and what can I tell you? I feel bad about your situation, and I do not know what to say; indeed nothing I could say would mean a shit, so fahgedaboutit.

Connie and I lived with Hilda, out-of-her-gourd for several years, and finally shipped her to a home. It was horrible, no matter how you sliced it.... Life is an underwater bicycle race, and nobody wins, but nobody loses either. Because, of course, there are no winners. I can only see you folks doing what Connie and I did, which was to put Hilda in a home.

Is there not a point where one realizes that one has a life all one's own, and that life is short, and that, perhaps, now, at this point in time, that you can let go ... take her to some other place where she will be OK, relatively, of course, and you folks can relax and enjoy the rest of your fuggin' lives?

Perhaps, Roger, your mother is somewhere where she doesn't really hurt or know, and perhaps the time has come for you and Jess to cut the cord, and live the rest of your lives in the ease and happiness that you both so richly deserve? Just askin'.

Almac, or as I now prefer to be known, AlHallowell.

[Sept. 18]

... I think we are gradually coming around to your way of thinking and the reality that you and Connie had to face. We are steeling ourselves to keep her here until after Thanksgiving, when she is supposed to go down south to live with my sister for six months.

... at that point, after my sister gets a feel for how things have ... disintegrated, we can [discuss] the next step....

RJ

164

[Sept. 18]

RJ:

... [Hilda] wanted to go [to nursing home in Petoskey], and, pure luck, it was a great place, but the very first time Connie and I visited her there she was non compos mentis and drooling. Connie and I walked out of the place and Connie broke down on the sidewalk and I could only clumsily comfort her, because, well, by then I was, rotten bastard that I am, somewhat relieved that Hilda was not really suffering, she didn't know what was happening, and, voila, me and Connie were off the hook. [Hilda died in 1986, seven years after being moved to the nursing home.]

We are not constructed to suffer too much, and eagerly look for an out, an egress, and, what the hell, that's only human.

Alhallowell ...

[Sept. 21]

Got the Gallagher. Was incensed to see that the dead [Flint Journal sports editor Doug] Mintline got quotes but I did not, and I was the guy who didn't twitch a muscle when Gallagher set off a cherry bomb about four feet from my chair in the slot.

Gallagher later said he admired my calmness, but then added it was probably because I was sedated from some chemical or another....

Alhallowell

[Sept. 21]

Dutchers:

... [L.A. blogger's] essay, fueled by my assiduous research, appeared on Silicon Valley's top online mag, ValleyWag, and has subsequently spread all over the Web, much like the dew that covers Dixie, and that, oh joy, the New York Times "What's Online" gave [him] about ten grafs, was dismissive and only you and I and [him] know why — because the NYT blew the story, and I have written three separate letters to ... the public editor, and if it weren't for that trivial war in

165

Iraq, the spying and the lying and the denying by the U.S. gubament why [we] mighta gotten more ink.

It's shit like that, J and R, that is throwing a monkey wrench into my golden years.

Alhallowell

[Oct. 2]

Are we all on the same page here?

Dutchers:

I was taken aback to see that Rep. Foley from Florida dictated a non-email the other day informing society that he "strongly believes he is an alcoholic and has emotional problems" that need to be attended to in rehab. [Foley resigned from Congress after sending explicit emails to teen-age pages.]

Ah, Dutchers, how many times have I sat down at my typer at various newspapers and announced that I strongly believed that I needed to go into rehab ... and on four occasions there I was in Florida entering the Avon Park Rehab spot for another 30-day spin.

And now, there is Rep. Foley, bending over backwards to get himself right in a Florida rehab place. Right away I wondered, Dutchers, did Rep. Foley slip off to Avon Park, is he strolling the same hallowed corners and orange groves that I bestrode, curing my alcoholism on four separate occasions?

Then I realized, after reading four thousand articles aggregating on a website ... that Rep. Foley was going to a private place near West Palm Beach, not the lovely spot by a lake full of bream and surrounded by orange groves and you had to make ... wallets in the morning, pick oranges in the afternoon but then you could dance away the night or play bingo, whatever....

Onward, upward, from Hallowell.

[Oct. 28]

Dutchers:

... the whole world is going to hell, with an able assist from the Repugs, and the tiny little victory that right-thinking, read left-thinking, folks will achieve when Dems take over House and possibly even the Senate, won't make a bit of difference in the big picture, because ... [George Bush has, in] his egocentric messianical nuttiness, begun the process of setting two billion Muslims against, roughly, two billion Christers, and now everybody knows who the enemy is and, perforce, we must kill each other, thanks to George and like-thinking morons.

Other than that, Dutchers, things are going well here, relatively speaking.... I meet more and more people in low places, and, although it has been raining fiercely for several days, and we expect 70-mph winds momentarily, I am unafraid ... like that character in Li'l Abner, I don't mind dark clouds overhead, even if they are targeted at me....

Alhallowell

[Nov. 30]

Dutchers,

You will be interested to learn about the Machiavellian tactics your correspondent used ... over the Turkey Day gladnesses.

Seems that I had no invitation to dinner for Thanksgiving and, ergo and thus, I was doomed to spend a septuagenarian's nightmare of loneliness on the one day of the year that I have revered, the mass killings of hordes, gaggles, of the most stupid bird on the face of this planet.

Still and all, I let it be known to various friends, some of whom actually brought up the subject, that I would be alone for the holidays, yes, but I had my Bible for solace and would put some macaroni and cheese into the microwave, and then me and the cats would chow down on macaroni and kibbles.

At no point, Dutchers, did I ever indicate that I felt distraught over this situation and when discussing it I tried

167

hard not to bite my lips and cast my eyes downward and awkwardly tousle my curly locks.

Well, Thanksgiving Day came and it was about eight at night when there came a knock on the door and it was my friend Charlee ... a comely twenty-year-old, bearing a complete turkey dinner in some kind of cardboard container, a whole apple pie, a container of eggnog, a jar of pickles, and a goodly slice of pumpkin pie!

So Charlee and I hung out for a bit ... and she went on home and then the next morning, a Friday, there came a knock on the door and there was my friend Bill ... and he is holding a huge bottle of vodka, and thrusting it into my reluctant arms, averse as I was to start drinking from it right away.

So Bill and I chatted about this and that for a while, and he went off to his home ... and then there came a knock on the door and it was another friend ... bearing about 30 cans of a local brew that is more potent than any other beer made in New England....

Then, a day or so later, I was walking by the Liberal Cup and ... a friend named Laurie, dragged me in off the street, I was merely innocently passing by on Water, and she and her lovely daughter bought me two holiday drinks.

So, Dutchers, despite the fact that I modestly, if repeatedly, declared that I was not discommoded at all by the prospect of a Thanksgiving without the family, and was visibly stoic about the whole heart-wrenching thought of an elderly, enfeebled Korean War Veteran who may soon be on the wrong side of the grass, so let's do a miracle on thirty-fourth street, or whatever street that was on the geezer.

Pretty good town, Hallowell, eh? Hope you guys had a lighter tune for the holidays....

Almac

[Dec. 6]

Hey Mac —

We are finally coming up for air after Jess flew my mom down to Texas [and] we fled the country for some needed

R&R in Toronto.... [We] returned home to find our sump pump had failed, leaving us with days of carpet cleanup in the basement. I just got done spraying the basement with antimicrobial Febreze, on orders from my superior. Ever tried to get high on Febreze? Whew!

Toronto has changed and yet it really hasn't since two couples went there decades ago to [not] watch Fiona on Fire. Couldn't find any trace of Fiona but the hotel TV still has some X-rated goodies for those so inclined....

RJ

[Dec. 7]

Dutchers,

For lo these many months I have wondered, idly of course, as to the state of my Great Aunt Gert's health. And for all these months, 23 of them and counting, I have been isolated from [my] three siblings.... And the other day I realized that I ... am the only one that has no clue as to Gert's day-to-day progress in her apparent search for immortality. And it struck me how unfair that was, and I know I could just call up a sibling and find out something, perhaps, but something deep inside will not allow me to contact any of [them].

The unfairness of my situation hit me the other day and I had sudden thought that was actually quite sensible. Why not, I thought, write the lawyer for Gert's trust, who surely would not resent an inquiry, crass as it might seem, as to the state of Gert's vital functions....

So I wrote his law office ... and just kind of mentioned that, well, how was Gert doing? [I said] I was planning certain moves and exploring business opportunities and wondered if, perhaps, I could be expecting some sort of check in the mail in the foreseeable future.

And here, Dutchers, is the response I got, and you can well imagine how tickled I was to learn that Gert bids fair to becoming a "super centenarian" and my understanding is that term applies to folk who clear 110 and are still not breathing heavily.

So, it's always good to hear that kinfolk are not feeling poorly, are sitting up and taking nourishment, are, in short, in fine fettle.

And, Dutchers, I am kind of proud of myself that I took some positive action in finding out something about Gert. And now I can forget about any concerns of profiting from Gert's demise, any prospect of a more easeful eighties, and can concentrate on my work with orphans and widows.

Good to hear quality of life is on the uptick, and I have little sympathy for persons who have basement problems. My take, people who can afford basements instead of crawl spaces are just asking for it.

Almac

Part 6: Suicide is not painless

MacLeese had many low points in his life, but early in 1962, in Bridgeport, Connecticut – freshly divorced from his second wife – he scraped bottom.

Not much is known about his first two wives. He didn't talk about them. Piecing together the contemporaneous evidence of his activities, it is likely he continued the drinking and disappearing act he cultivated in the Navy. The relationships could have been sabotaged by that combination alone.

As for his Connecticut environment, he wrote "there are redeeming things about Bridgeport, although none is apparent to a lonely stranger. I worked for the Bridgeport Post and you had to bring your own pencils to work, if that limns the situation."

After several weeks on the job, and convinced of his "innate undesirability," he went to a bar to lose himself among uncaring strangers.

"I would tell the world, which hadn't noticed, that I couldn't care less and would shuffle bently off this mortal coil…. Leaving the bar, I trudged desolately in martyr-like fashion to my hotel. Don't ever go to a hotel like this one. It was a place where winos went only to vomit or urinate. There were ungodly wails from next door, but I did not investigate, cultivating my own woe.

"So I took my bottle of cheap whiskey, a tipple to check out with. There in my room I drank it all and then smashed the bottle, using it to slash my wrists – four strokes, two to a wrist, and crimson bubbled. This was going to beat the hell out of Sominex.

"What went through my mind? That it was all rather unimportant if you had been paying attention. That the divorce, a subsequent firing for cause and the loneliness were good and sufficient reasons to give it up. And the scars are still there and I would show them to you but you don't want to see them and I really don't want to show them.

"It illustrated the chanciness of life. The cheap hooch was finished and I almost was but I fell onto a table holding a telephone – an affectation for this kind of place. The sometimes-desk clerk heard the buzzing, saved my life and today I don't know his name. He found me in a pool of blood on feces-encrusted linoleum – gifts of forgettable strangers. Soon an ambulance wailed through the night to Bridgeport Hospital.

"Skilled strangers there sewed me up. And then the police came to take me to a cell in Bridgeport City Jail, a rather special place for people who damage themselves.

"So I chewed the stitches out with my teeth and it is fortunate that turnkeys occasionally check cells. Back to the hospital, where they may have grown weary of these particular repairs. Then on to the "County," that being Fairfield County Jail.

"Several days later, stone-sober and as reasonable as I get, they took me in'cuffs and a strait-jacket to the insane asylum. Sorry, there is no better way to say that. In that year, mental hospitals were insane asylums or worse. Those at the hospital that weren't disturbed were busily working on the proposition."

Fairfield State Hospital in Newtown, Connecticut, had as many as 4,000 patients, from alcoholics to the insane.

MacLeese described what it was like on the huge campus: "Men masturbated openly, children bullied adults, women groveled on floors. Those that weren't groveling on the floor were beating their fists into it, but somebody would generally come along to sedate them. Padded cells were available; that's where they took the enraged man who kept seeing buffaloes.

"In short, people did what they thought was reasonable but nothing was reasonable.

"We would sit in our ward, back slap against the wall, our peripheral vision outstanding. You had to sit against the wall – who knew when Henry's medication would wear out? It is no good to say we were paranoid, you had to be paranoid to maintain your expectations of leaving alive someday."

His sister Deborah has memories "of very tense, uncomfortable visits with Alan" at "Newtown" during his stay. She was 15 at the time.

MacLeese "spent three months there, treated leerily, because I was labeled an alcoholic and drunks were second-class citizens in mental hospitals. I asked a doctor, 'Why do you have me in maximum security with rapists and murderers and child molesters?'"

The answer: "You tried to kill yourself twice in one night. That's a good enough reason."

MacLeese guessed the doctor was right.

"Several months into my confinement and out of my depression, I decided that suicide was too final a gesture at 31," he wrote in a column about his experience, and he found a moral in his story. "Life's real and imagined pains are supportable one way or another. Life beats death, even without reports from the other side.

"Sobering, but even suicide tries can be made too much of; we should not make a life out of the night we tried to end one. Yes and yes again to life. Those thinking of suicide should try to rethink. Life may be a bitch, but why not stick around and see what they're going to do to you next?"

After his time at Fairfield State, he was tried for trying to kill himself. The state put him on two years' probation and said he couldn't leave Connecticut. He would leave, though, before the end of the year.

Chastened by his experience in the "fidget factory," MacLeese began taking Antabuse to force himself to stop drinking. He would have an on-again, off-again relationship with Antabuse, and a successor drug, Campral, for the rest of his life.

Immediately after leaving Fairfield State, he took a job 35 miles north, in Litchfield. He became editor, "a glorified reporter, actually," of the Litchfield Enquirer.

MacLeese's first business card there said: Alan N. MacLeese, Editor, Litchfield Enquirer, Connecticut's Oldest Weekly."

He said that "lacked a certain panache, lacked even an uncertain panache. Presto-chango: Al MacLeese, editor, Litchfield Enquirer, Connecticut's Weakest Oldie." His wry sense of humor was back.

"While the pun 'weakest oldie' had the virtue of almost unvarnished truth, it did not evoke rich chuckles in Litchfield – the town that sheltered Benedict Arnold and, not satisfied with that, then presented us with the nation's first law school. Litchfield has been torn between guilt and guilt ever since."

(MacLeese also had a "humorous" card printed when he began writing a column for the Flint Journal but nobody laughed much then either. Except in the newsroom. It read: "Al MacLeese, Flint Journal, headlines, columns. Fairly cheap. Cesspools cleaned, some yard work. Own transportation. Call 767-----.")

A Litchfield native with a sense of humor noticed his work. Such as a column about a "mangy cur" that was nipping his heels on his way to work. Or the Memorial Day parade headline that said something like: Only in Litchfield – Red Cross rides in Cadillacs.

Laurie, who then was a proofreader for a publisher, knew MacLeese was in trouble in a town that loved dogs and the Red Cross. She wrote him a letter saying he was a wonderful writer but did he want to be tarred and feathered and run out of town?

MacLeese invited her down to the newspaper to continue her discussion. The rest, as they say, is history.

The two were married three months later, on Aug. 23. She was 24, seven years his younger. To her, he looked like Gregory Peck.

During their courtship, he had gone to Fairfield hospital in Newtown for AA meetings as often as three times a week. Although he went to the meetings, he wasn't a true believer in the AA philosophy. Laurie said he didn't do the steps. Probably because many of the steps focused on seeking help from God, and he was an atheist.

Did that make him more vulnerable when depression, fueled by his normal companions of guilt, remorse and recrimination, built up and he became defensive and edgy? No definite answer there, but his usual cure for what he called the "blues" was the bottle, not AA.

Drinking took forethought when he was taking Antabuse; when he found the pressure building, he had to plan a fall off the wagon. He needed to stop the pill for 12 days, the time it took for the medication's effects to wear off and he could drink again, or the result was not pretty or pleasant, which he learned from experience.

After he and Laurie were married, they went directly to Baltimore, where he took a copy editor job at the News-Post and received cash awards from the paper for writing the best headlines.

One day, three weeks into their marriage, he called her and said: "Laurie, I'm in a bar."

174

He was sober with her until then, and had at some point stopped taking Antabuse. His drinking got him fired in Baltimore within three months.

Next was Keene, N.H., where he worked as a reporter, and she was pregnant. In April of 1963 they left for Miami and the Herald.

At a party shortly after they arrived, Laurie said, "a beautiful blonde wraps herself around Alan like a snake and indicates they had a past. We were invited to her wedding, and Alan took me to a boutique and bought me a black tube dress with an overdress of organza and a giant pink 'picture hat' with a big brim and a cabbage rose on it. I never felt prettier."

In July, MacLeese covered New York Gov. Nelson Rockefeller at the National Governors Conference in Miami Beach.

While the governor was talking with reporters, MacLeese asked a woman standing nearby if he could put his reporter's pad on her back to help him take notes. Sure, the woman told him. Laurie said he chatted with the woman while he was taking notes. At minimum, he must have said that he liked her dress, maybe even that his wife would look good in it and that she was about the same size.

A day or so later, the MacLeeses were recipients of a box containing a sleeveless dress with an off-white top and a turquoise blue bottom, Laurie said. The woman turned out to be Happy Rockefeller, who had married Nelson just two months earlier.

Like many stories involving MacLeese, this one was unbelievable. A search of film clips from that conference, however, showed Happy arriving at the hotel wearing what appeared to be the very dress Laurie described.

He continued to drink in Miami, and he would disappear, without a word, Laurie said. Once he was on the loose drinking and he found himself in Georgia. She said the Herald sent someone there to bring him back and dry him out.

At AA meetings, Laurie acquired evidence that he would bet on almost anything. His wagers normally ran the gamut from horses across the board and 519 trifectas to whether a final score would be an even number or which fly would leave the wall first.

On the occasions that Laurie went with him to AA sessions, he would bet her which half of the other couples there was the alcoholic. The clues could be misleading. Those meetings, he said, often were held "in a dingy room over a dingier bar on downtown W. Flagler St., which aspired clumsily to skid-row status."

Thinking she might be lonely while at home during the pregnancy, he gave her a male Siamese kitten, which he named

Mokus. He said it meant crazy, but in the AA, it was a term for a newly sober state of mind. An aspiration for him?

Laurie created a nursery for their coming baby, and after she was done decorating and furnishing it, he wrote a column about it, she said. The punch line: "If the baby has a black, furry face, I'm giving it back."

At the time of his nursery inspection, Mokus was sleeping in the bassinet.

Their son, Alan Douglas, known as Doug, arrived before their first wedding anniversary.

Fatherhood didn't stop his drinking. That October, he ended up in Avon Park, on a lake in central Florida, for a 28-day rehabilitation program, one of four stays there during his career.

During another of those rehabs, a woman patient came up with an idea to "get things organized so we all can have fun." The plan: An Easter egg hunt, "although most of us stated quite forcefully that we would prefer to sit by the lake and sulk about past indignities."

While the woman and a partner industriously hid the eggs among the saw grass and palmettoes the night before Easter, MacLeese and a buddy crawled behind them, noting where each egg was deposited, then later relocated the eggs.

On Easter morning, "30-some alkies morosely trudged out." One muttered: "Let's get this silliness over with quickly so we can eat breakfast." That was not to be. Everybody was growing increasingly irate because no eggs were to be found.

"Say," MacLeese remarked, "perhaps we should hunt over there by the dock. I'll bet that's where the Easter Bunny has hidden these eggs."

Suspicious glances and "a stampede to the dock area followed, and we discovered more eggs than you would expect to find lying around amid the rotting oranges and scurrying palmetto bugs. We harvested, then lunged for the chow hall, where eggs are not painted foolishly."

The next weekend, a bottle of beans was installed in the recreation room. Guess the number of beans and whoever came closest won a carton of cigarettes, cancer being preferable to alcoholism.

MacLeese denied he and that same buddy snuck into the recreation room, but he guessed 1,766 and his buddy 1,768. "There were 1,767 beans and we didn't want to be too obvious. We had to split the smokes, dammit."

Laurie said that when he got out of Avon Park the end of October, he resumed drinking.

After getting a job at another paper, this one in Miami Beach, and barely working long enough to learn where the men's room was, he wore out his welcome in the Miami area. They had to leave.

Next stop: Gary, Indiana, at the Post-Tribune.

Laurie remembers Gary as a beautiful city with gorgeous parks even though it had black ash raining down from the U.S. Steel stacks. When drinking, Alan had contrasts, too. He could be funny and charming but lurking in the background were the problems, the fallout from imbibing to excess, that made him an employment risk.

One night, they were at a party, and the wife of the paper's editor, who hadn't met MacLeese before, asked him: "What is your capacity?"

His answer: "About a quart a day."

"I laughed so hard I was hysterical," Laurie said.

In Gary, he would come home drunk late at night and be found lying on the floor inside the door the next morning, Laurie said, adding that he was never physically abusive to her.

MacLeese said he had never hit a woman, "although several have hit me repeatedly." One, he said, "gave me an interesting scar over an eyebrow" when she "chucked a (full) beer can at me one night."

Gary was where MacLeese met Constance Valerie Reed, who would become his fourth wife three years later.

Connie also worked at the Post-Tribune as a copy editor, for less than three months in 1964, and to cut expenses, she shared an apartment with two men. The MacLeeses went to their apartment once for a visit.

Then, when he didn't show up at home for three nights, Laurie called the paper and asked Connie if she knew where Alan was. Connie said he was at her shared apartment. Laurie went there and dragged him home.

MacLeese worked in Gary for about nine months. "By that time," Laurie said, "I knew that when he came home with a certain look on his face, it was time to pack up a U-Haul for his next stop."

That would be San Francisco.

Baghdad by the Bay, and "the sinful ways of its boozy denizens," as he put it, spawned several of the most renowned stories in MacLeese lore during stints there at both the Chronicle and the Examiner. Stories that would be repeated, and handed down like heirlooms, to succeeding generations in newsrooms.

Like when he was dispatched to cover a Golden Gate Bridge Authority meeting, a lengthy affair, and he ended up at a bar and did not return for days and days. His editor, on his return, asked: "Did you save your notes? We might still be able to get something in."

Like when he spent his day at a grog shop until his shift began. Commendably, he arrived for work on time – but at the wrong paper. He was a familiar face, and the slot put him to work. Eventually, MacLeese realized his error and slunk off. Such mistakes could happen in San Francisco.

Like when he and Bud Tripp were driving north of San Francisco after an all-nighter. Tripp "jerked the wheel upon spotting the San Quentin prison sign, roared up to the front entrance of the joint, jumped out, tried to scramble up the wall. To 'break in' where others try to break out.

"Two guards ran out, one with gun in hand," MacLeese wrote. "I believe I talked them out of an arrest, and was smug when they let me, the responsible one, drive us away."

Tripp, when asked why he wanted to break in, responded that he "thought it would be newsworthy if somebody tried to break in, instead of tiresomely breaking out all the time."

Although Tripp could indeed make MacLeese look like the responsible party, there is no doubt that MacLeese could screw the pooch very well on his own.

Laurie said his drinking and disappearing act eventually reached the breaking point. She filed for divorce in 1965 in San Francisco, and they separated, with the divorce becoming final a year later.

At the filing, she was granted custody and allowed to take their 2-year-old son to Connecticut. He was given visitation rights, which he never exercised, and he allowed his son to be adopted by Laurie's new husband after she remarried in 1968.

MacLeese had already established a tradition in San Francisco, a sentimental exercise involving the Golden Gate Bridge.

"On the several occasions that spouses have seen fit to discard me, I have been in San Fran" when the legal papers arrived. "I began a heartwarming custom of chucking the divorce papers" off the bridge.

Decades later, Laurie said she wasn't bitter.

She laughed when she remembered the times when a bartender would take his wallet and put it in the cash register for safekeeping. "He would call me the next day, and I would push the stroller to the bar to pick up the wallet. That bartender rolled my husband for me."

178

She had other memories: "He gave me the world, Miami to San Francisco. Pregnant, I swam with dolphins.... And we had dinner at sunset at the pier on Cannery Row.

"He was tortured and tragic but beautiful and brilliant, so talented. He made me feel special."

The period after their separation is a swirl of anecdotes and a couple of conflicting memories.

MacLeese moved to the city's North Beach area, which was popular with writers. In the previous decade, it had been the home of such Beat Generation luminaries as Kerouac and Ginsberg.

For three months, he apparently lived in an apartment vacated by Bob Hardin, who had gone to Spain. MacLeese doesn't mention Hardin in his column reference to the apartment but he does say its former occupant was a writer who "had left a manuscript of an exceedingly well-written novel in the joint."

Hardin believes he left behind copies of two works in progress, including one novel with a character based on MacLeese.

The manuscript MacLeese found in the apartment gave him an opportunity for cachet as a "real" writer, as opposed to "scrubby newspaper writers."

"For several months I would tote the manuscript into bars or flaunt it before damsels I was able to entice into my apartment. People began referring to me as 'that writer' and I got a lot of free drinks before somebody swiped the manuscript. Probably some bum who wanted to con people into thinking that he was a writer."

At times in his career, MacLeese admitted being envious of successful writers he knew.

One was Denne Petitclerc, a scriptwriter for "Bonanza" and a fishing buddy of Hemingway. Another was John Keasler, a longtime Miami News humor columnist who had written a novel, "Surrounded on Three Sides."

At the San Francisco Examiner, he bumped into Frank Herbert, a Living editor there. He was working on "Dune," considered by many the best science fiction novel of all time.

Laurie said he was surrounded by talented young writers and he felt depressed because they were writing books or had books published and were asking him why he didn't write a book.

As far as is known, MacLeese made only two ventures into serious writing. They were many decades apart, both highly tentative and both quickly died.

The first took place in the late 1950s, a synopsis for a proposed movie script. The treatment was a joint project with Hardin when they were police reporters for rival papers in Miami.

Hardin said their idea, a Western parody about a Harvard-educated Indian guide forced to conform to stereotype to suit his Army employers, was funny, but when they showed the synopsis to a newspaper editor, he discouraged them.

"And Mac was easily discouraged. He had no reservoir of self-confidence until he met Connie."

Hardin said they were young, "sensing we had some talent but [were] not too persistent – in Mac's case, not the least bit persistent … it took almost nothing to knock him off his horse."

More than 40 years later, he pitched another friend an idea for a joint novel, which he titled "The Harvesters," focused on the "evil" of hunters who kill fellow mammals in wholesale legalized and ritualized slaughter.

The proposed plot: Three retirees attempt to bring deer hunting in Michigan to a screeching halt by becoming ecoterrorists through killing and stuffing (or mounting) random human targets before displaying them about the state in various poses, including strapped like a deer on a 4x4 hood.

In a seven-page letter detailing his proposal, Mac wrote the friend: "You have shown the discipline to initiate a project and get it done. I haven't, but perhaps between the two of us we can do this." Carrying out such an ambitious project by himself, he knew from experience, would be imperiled by a lack of focus and self-assurance.

MacLeese's novel idea probably could evolve into a Coen brothers movie or even a sitcom in today's blood-thirsty, vampire-laced climate, but his friend didn't want to touch a topic as intense as serial killing in the wake of the death of his wife. The proposed joint project was stillborn.

Plagued by unrealized aspirations, MacLeese's dreams were beyond his ability to harness his talent. His insecurities, coupled with ambitions beyond his command, made him more susceptible to demon rum.

In September of 1965, MacLeese was one of a handful of copy editors laid off as a result of the merger of the Examiner and the News-Call Bulletin, and he was drinking, according to fellow copy editor Jim Houck.

Houck was told by the copy desk chief, Bud Liebes, that MacLeese said that "if they wanted to lay him off they had to give him a plane ticket to Connecticut, otherwise he wouldn't go. So the paper bought the plane ticket."

The Examiner's editor gave the ticket to Liebes and told him "to take Al to the airport, put him on the plane, and stay at the gate until the plane pulled away." Liebes said his instructions included a caution: "Make sure the son of a bitch doesn't get off."

"Bud said he did exactly as told," Houck said, adding: "I do have a vague memory of Bud Liebes calling Al's sister in Connecticut and, I assumed, making sure she was going to pick him up at the airport."

His sister Deborah said she did receive a call from someone named Bud, in the middle of the night at the family home in Connecticut, but it wasn't to pick her brother up at the airport. She said the caller "indicated Alan was not doing well" and it would do him "a world of good if I came out to visit him and set him on the path to sobriety."

Deborah said she was 18 at the time "but thrilled that someone thought I could bring my big brother to the straight and narrow. I used every cent I had and flew to San Francisco, saw Alan briefly, drunk and pathetic, and spent the rest of my time there wondering where my brother was and whether I could afford the cheap hotel stay" before flying back to Connecticut.

"It was one of the great heartbreaks of my life. I was at sea in a big city (I had never been to anywhere bigger than Derby, Connecticut, before that) and the great gesture I had made to my big brother was received by a whining drunk."

She doesn't remember how she met up with him or how they ended up in the cheap hotel where they stayed.

"The visit was very scary for me and I felt lost. He disappeared a few days after my arrival and he was drunk the entire time I saw him. What I thought would be an adventure was a nightmare."

[Dec. 10, 2006]

Roger,

Although I do include Jessica albeit with a proviso that ... we are driven to write about penises.

... I was reminded of a naval experience ... and I feel that now, nearing the wrong side of the grass, I should pass this memory along if only for the good of the race, and to momentarily explore the phenomenon of why short men often have long dicks.

A storyteller's odyssey

Back in the late Forties, [I served in the Navy's] black gang, the oilers and the engineers, and we had a little short sonofabitch ... Kraut and he was about just tall enuff to get into the Coast Guard, where you could wade ashore in case of any problems, and he had a dick about a yard long.

This little bastard used to parade around the ... living quarters, shared by Norway rats, with his dick hanging out, barenaked, and none of us ... guys used to do that despite the perception among some of the public that all these Navy guys were either queer or rough trade, one.

Anyhow, many of us tars were irritated by this little shithead's flaunting of his yard-long unit, and one day he made so bold as to wag his dick, as he flounced around the compartment, flaunted it ... and this Indian guy named, predictably, Chief Wahoo, leaped up from his seat at the poker table and grabbed the offensive little big Kraut by his member, and proceeded to drag [him] up the gangway and out onto the aft deck, all the while threatening to throw [the Kraut] over the side if he kept on flaunting his manhood before those of us who were, arguably and obviously, less endowed.

After that significant event, which I witnessed from a front-row seat, [the Kraut], paradoxically, never again flaunted his private member before his largely unappreciative, although hugely impressed, auditors. There's a moral here but I will leave you folks to figure it out.

It is Sunday morning and I am now about to read Frank Rich's explanation of why Bush is toast, although, myself, I think, in that case, I'll have an English muffin.

Mac

[Dec. 21]

Anniversary of sorts

R and J:

... [Seven years ago] Connie had her stroke. I know she was in hospital about a week ... when I was asked about pulling the plug. Pulling the plug, doesn't that sound so ... something. Anyhow, I used to be hypercritical about folks who zealously marked such anniversaries, and I guess it is

182

natural, to wallow a while in how wrong things are, or seem to "are" but what can you do?

The Buddhists have it right, between the imponderables, birth and death, there is a whole lot of stuff that seems quite similar to suffering. Way to look at it, I think, is that we all have been granted a front-rowish seat in this universe, and I suppose we should be happy for large favors, although if it had been up to me to design humans I would have tried to make it so that they didn't have to be continually eating, drinking, digesting, defecating and then doing the same godamned thing over again the next day and so on and so forth ad infinitum or, at the best case scenario, ad nauseam.

Anyhow, [before] pulling the plug on Connie, [I responded] to questions about why she had so many bruises on her body upon death, apparently folks thought I might have battered Connie or something, although the fact of the matter was that Connie, toward the end, kept falling down, and was heavy on the wine, an ironic thing, no, having being married to a drunk and then having to turn to the stuff while she was dying.

I knew she was hiding bottles of wine all over the house, and found them when I was cleaning up, but what could I say, a drunk, could I remonstrate with Connie about DWD — drinking while dying. No, of course not, inasmuch as she was the only one who ever really loved me....

I got your Xmas card or Yule card and you must consider this as a holiday greeting as well, although I remain an adamant atheist and detest Christianism....

Alhallowell

[Gulf Shores; Jan. 2, 2007]

How the old dog observed New Years

Hey Mac –

Happy New Year from us to you and yours. We have just arrived down in Gulf Shores....

I took ours (Pumpkin) out on the beach for the first time this morning, and she was extremely excited for one who is now more than 80 years old. Maybe you remember her passing you in longevity some months ago. She bounded down to the surf, after depositing about a dozen logs in two stops about two seconds apart on reaching the sandy side of the road.

Logs, to the uninitiated, is a manner of describing and quantifying defecation, and to Pumpkin it appears to be a way of marking territory. To me, the usual method of marking territory would be much more preferable because I wouldn't have to stoop to pick up the remains....

And stooping has become a problem for one who now mainly carries a cane on the plain. Actually stooping is less of a problem with the cane. The cane gives me a vehicle to be homo Erectus. Tomorrow I may try out my bicycle to see if that is still an acceptable form of exercise.

RJ

[Jan. 12]

Breaking news story out of Hallowell

Dutchers,

It is my considered opinion that a cane is just a cheap crutch for low rollers, and I have often myself been told to avoid canes like banes, to despise their very existence, enabling tools at the worst sort, no moving parts, no magical ability to take photographs or make telephone calls or provide lesbian porn.

"You're using alcohol as a crutch, Alan," I have often been told, just like a godamned cane you see these gimps using. "Pull up your socks, too, Alan."

Informed by such harsh experiences, I inferred all canes, crutches are bad ... even if you think you need them, so were I you, Rog, I would opt for the bike, and if Pumpkin can't keep up, well, throw 'er to the coyotes or the wolves.

I had two canes, Irish walking sticks, when I emigrated to Maine, but they are gone now, history.... My Irish walking sticks were stolen; one from a bar in Bar Harbor and the other from car outside of a Margarita's in Augusta, where I had stopped for food....

Later, Almac

[Jan. 12]

Oversight in previous post clarified

Dutchers,

The hed on the previous post indicated breaking news story, but then the text did not really have all that much news.... But there was breaking news on the Hallowell-Milford front, Milford being where my sainted Great Aunt Gert [now 108] resides....

Well, Dutchers, on my recent birthday I got an email from my sister and we have resumed the normal discourses we often see between kinfolk who are not at war.... The reason I consider this breaking news is simply because now I am in the loop, for two years I have wondered in solitude as to how Gert was doing.

I admit it, I am aware that if Gert dies my fortunes would vastly improve. Is this wrong, Dutchers? Think not that I sit around pondering these morbid matters all the livelong day, but still, surely, you can understand that a person such as myself ... needs assurances that nature will take its course in my family just as in others? ... Or no?

Almac

[Jan. 17]

Longevity

Hey Mac—

... My mother turned 90 last week, no match for GAG, but still the longest living person I can think of in our family. When I mentioned that to her, she made the perceptive (especially for one with dementia) comment that living long doesn't mean much if you don't have good health.

I have been riding bike down here, so am getting some exercise, which make me happy. And I have good balance, so long as I don't stop.

RJ

[Jan. 18]

To my biker buddy in 'Bama:

... the winter just hit about a week ago here, we had been getting a pass, but now we are getting some snow, sleet. A true-blooded Mainah recently was discussing the mild fake winter we have been experiencing, and said, disgustedly, "Shit, we might as well be living in Delaware." Now there's a remark that epitomizes the true Mainah, an admirable type although far too hardy for me to try to emulate.

I [used] my new insurance cards ... Tuesday when I finally went in, after a month of hacking and spewing mucus all over the recreation rooms in the penthouse here, and the doctor told me that I have "bacterial bronchitis" and I said I thought I'd have walking pneumonia and he smiled and said. "That's what we call bacterial bronchitis, too."

He said that, miraculously, it did not seem that my lungs were anywhere near as fucked-up as they should, given my admitted use of Benson and Hedges and various brands of MaryJane. He asked me how my drinking was doing, and I said that (I had rehearsed this so the quotation is remarkably near the actual remark), "I think it is fair to say that I am drinking more than the average person but quite a bit less than your average drunk."

The doctor, a man of Irish descent but postmodern proclivities, said that that sounded like "progress" and he gave me a five-day regimen of an antibiotic and today is the third day of treatment and this hacker's hack is actually subsiding and it was a great relief to me because I had begun thinking that the envelope, lung-wise, had perhaps been pushed too far....

Mac

186

[Jan. 24]

Longevity bulletin

Mac —

Montreal woman dies, making a Conn. woman the oldest woman in the world. Now I know what you're thinking but not yet. The oldest woman in the world is Emma Faust Tillman of East Hartford, where she gets her milk from the same dairy as GAG. Tillman is 114....

RJ

[Jan. 25]

Dutchers,

Yes, I know about the [woman] in East Hartford — knowledge of [her] can only goad Gert into greater efforts.

Gert's like Woody Allen, who doesn't want to attain immortality through his works, he wants to attain immortality by not dying. There are, in fact, quite a few centenarians in Connecticut, and if Gert ever passes to my greater reward, I'll use my part of her stash to move to that pleasant land of steady habits....

Almac

[Jan. 30]

Suspect in nursing home death

Jess tells me this morning that the oldest woman died after a four-day reign (rain?) in Conn. Hope you have an alibi....

[Jan. 30]

You speak of the wrongest oldest woman

Dutchers,

My heart leapt, like a gazelle gracefully bounding over a lazy hyena's back, when I got Jessica's bulletin about the oldest woman in Connecticut expiring.

But, dear Dutchers, Jessica zeroed in on the wrong old Connecticut broad. The oldest woman, of whom Jessica spoke, is some Negro person from East Hartford Conn., not that there's anything wrong with that, but one more properly identified as an African-American woman who is not, was not, Gertrude Noone, the lovely Anglo-Saxon woman with whom I am most vitally concerned, a relative, a kinswoman, the person who I care about more deeply and intensely than any other human I have ever been associated with over these many long years....

The older party that increasingly consumes my waking hours, here in my solitary fastness, is a mere stripling of 108, and only the baby Jesus knows how long she will persist in denying me my birthright, my way to an easeful eighties.

Dutchers, I will bet that youse have inherited SOMETHING in your time on this post, but things don't seem to break my way. Why am I put in the pernicious place where, sitting around in my garret, with no washing machine, no dryer, desolate and sometimes chilly, where even the smelt in the Kennebec are complaining about the weather, and me in the insufferable position of awaiting the death of a presumed loved one.

Problem is, Dutchers, that this person, this Gertrude Noone, ignored me for decades, coming, as she did, from the rich part of the family ... and then, all of a sudden she wants to leave scoots to me....

Dutchers, I have told friends of my dilemma, and some think it deplorable the way things are breaking for me, a deserving and amiable oldster. And some friends, I suspect, think I do not have a great-aunt on the cusp of leaving the coil and, not so incidentally, leaving me something large; they believe I am shamming to gain sympathy and get free drinks.... This is a canard up with which I will not continue to put.

This is having a truly bad effect on my character, which, heretofore, has ... never been brought into question so strongly as in the run-up to Gert's fearfully anticipated rundown. How did I get chivvied into this situation, Dutchers?? What is there, about me, that seems to encourage this kind of, well, dirty low-down treatment. Eh?

188

[Jan. 30, continued]

... Yeah, we do notice that more and more folks [are] dying. And, alack, more and more folks we know. I started noticing the dyings in the Sixties. Most of my friends were drunks, mostly ten or fifteen years older than me. Don't ask why they were older — I didn't like kids when I was a kid. Anyhow, the dedicated drunks I knew started dying off in their fifties. I was close to several, maybe more than several such drunks and they seldom made sixty. (Tripp being the exception that proved the rule.)

Then, I started noticing even contemporaries that weren't drunks were dying on both flanks.... And, since this is all about me, I wondered if there was any sense to be made, and I think it makes no nevermind, play it as it lays. That's my final analysis, all the rest is chit-chat, and yes, I know, how can there ever be a final analysis.

But wait ... a final analysis ... our lives may well have meaning if our kind honorably survives and finds the key to make the universe work ... and we will have played a part.

Good-old blue-eyed Bette Davis, and you can't stop me if I've palmed this quote off on you before, said, "Growing old is not for sissies."

... I remember Bette Davis from when I was in high school, and I thought she came across as far too intelligent and tart, even, for what I dimly perceived to be a sex object.... But then I cottoned to Jane Russell and Ava Gardner and did not give a rat's patoot for a skinny snip such as Davis who did not seem to have much in the way of boobs....

[Feb. 16]

Dutchers:

So I was dancing with a darling at the Wharf when an old friend I happened to see....

It was the floor actually; I fell and banged self up and, after being laid up a bit, had an epiphany, the fabled aha moment, and decided to return to the Pill, which, if you recall, is the one that makes drunks not care about drinking, and took the first doses the other day, and will no longer be a menace to the (few) non-drinking dancers.... I used my wrist to break my fall, and I am glad I did not use my left elbow, cause that's already been broken and sensitive to being smashed up against the floors and sidewalks.

While I was laid up — six days in penthouse high above food but unable to access the food owing to inability to put clothes on without wincing piteously, word spread through the upper levels of Hallowell society.

[One friend], Laurie ... visited me daily, bringing milk and bread and potato and macaroni salads and tapioca and a chocolate cake and a roasted chicken and English muffins and shepherd's pies (2) and also some litter for the cats, food for them, too, although they shared in the chicken, and paper towels, sugar, an NYT crossword puzzle book and daily issues of the NYT, and a warning that if I need anything else I should call her or she will hurt me.

Laurie was angry because, when I had bacterial bronchitis, I didn't tell her about it until I had recovered. Laurie also got me those little Trax or whatever they call them that you put on your shoes while walking the icy cobblestone sidewalks of Hallowell so U don't fall down and break another elbow.

Dutchers, take some counsel from an older senior, and try to avoid falling down. What happens when you fall down and break something is that the hospital gets you, keeps you for several days patching, and that is plenty of time for you to get a deadly infection fromsomesickbastardinthenextbed and, voila, you are well on the road to dying of complications from some small broken and relatively unimportant bone.

(I'll not even get into the visit from the herb person in my life, nor the well-to-do chum who left Benjamin Franklin on the kitchen table during his visit; subsequently he said he would not take Benjamin back and that I should, as is the wont of some of us, spend Ben unwisely.)

... Later and if you have friends who drink don't let them drink and dance.

Almac

[Feb. 16]

Hey Mac –

Jess (after gasping at your predicament and taking a few breaths) says: Don't you know the floors get harder as you get older? ... Maybe you should go dancing with your Great Aunt Gert, winner takes all.

Thank god you have some good friends that will check in on you.... The Wharf sounds a bit like the Florabama, pre-Ivan. Where you could see an old woman dancing while sucking booze from the nipple of a baby bottle so she wouldn't spill a drop. Now they still only have about half of the complex open and don't even sell beer in long necks....

Well, take care of yourself, hate to see your portion of GAG's fortune go to some Baptist Church.

RJ

[March 5]

Hey Mac —

... Have you read any of Frank McCourt's books, especially "Angela's Ashes," his recollections of growing up in Limerick? I've just tumbled across a bunch of criticism from people who say he made up a lot of the stuff. I guess I realized that the book was not meant to be a scholarly work. Not sure why these Irish critics don't appreciate a good storyteller. I thought Irish meant storyteller....

Hope you are back on your feet....

RJ

[March 8]

Dutchers,

... As to McCourt, I thought first effort fine but and then it all turned to relative ashes, and not Angela's. Some early critics faulted him for allegedly drawing the long bow and excessive Irish affectations, but, hell, he's Irish with the gift of that tongue. He grew up the same period in which I grew up, and the situation in Limerick was, I am sure, a lot worse

191

than the situation in Connecticut, which wasn't all that terribly great.

In Angela, I thought it sounded real, but subsequent stuff seems (to this common reader) pedantic, even slyly pompous, with whiffs of self-congratulation.... And of course we must factor into this critique the traits common to all common readers: jealousy, envy, hatred of the success of others, and so forth....

Later, Al

[March 14]

St. Patrick's Day looms, but who gives a shit?

Dutchers,

It is amazing how ... pills make the question of drinking moot, the subject does not arise to roil the mind, and this at first is disorienting — the great good such magic beans could do for humans. A little tweak in the brain and a person's defining characteristic becomes irrelevant, inoperative.

So who gives a care about Saint Pat? My main memory of a St. Paddy's Day involves a month or so in the Fifties when I was a police reporter for Tampa Tribune. My first day on the job was right after St. Patty's Day, and I checked blotter to see how many Irishers had been booked as drunks on the night of such a solemn occasion.

Several obvious Irish names were listed, and I wrote a saucy account, which netted me richly deserved kudos. Of course I was able to write with a good deal more insensitivity and callow humor than you could get away with these days. About same time the paper ran hugely humorous piece with cartoon about a drunken brawl at an AA meeting.

Back to my St. Pat tale: it was known by Tribune bosses I had had what was nicely referred to as a drinking problem. But they went ahead and hired me and first week was fine but then I got paid and on three straight payday nights was arrested by Tampa police as, wouldn't you know it, a drunk. So it turned out that the new guy that wrote about the drunken Irishers getting arrested was merely doing a little field work.

How could I get arrested three times on successive Friday nights when, up to then, such a thing had never happened? Who could have predicted such a series of events?

But enough about me. Did I tell you I got email signed by two friends who demanded I write about my life; this is not first time this idea has been broached, but it was made out of the blue from unexpected quarters, and it was in writing too, so maybe it isn't a bad idea.

Am always thinking about writing, generally have ongoing narrative in head. You know, quietly talking to yourself, making it up as you go along? Is this what everybody does? What do the Dutchers think? Not about me talking to myself, but about me writing about myself. All sorts of ways to write about a life....

Later, Almac

[March 19]

Hey Mac –

... As for your memoirs, you may recall that Jessica and I have been begging you to write them for lo these many years. So that's still a good idea. In fact, if you don't, I may just ask someone else to write them in the unlikely event that you pass before I do.... I wouldn't worry about how to write it, just write it, not self-consciously, but as a letter to friend. Your letters are publishable as is. So release the dam....

RJ

[March 28]

Dutchers,

... Sister Deborah and I have been emailing like it was going out of style and the only new development in the Gert Watch is that Gert, who prefers to be called Gertrude, well, Gert is now deef as a post. The misspelling of deaf is intentional in case Roger has his red crayons unsheathed.

Thank the baby Jesus that going deaf in one ear and being unable to hear out of the other is not terminal. When Gert dies, I am going to go to Ireland, the land of my people, and visit County Cork, which apparently is where Gert's folks are from, and I am going to go to a glen or a dale and sing "Danny Boy" and lie about on the Auld Sod, eating prates and catching moonbeams. Is this a plan or what??

Almackennebec

[Jamestown MI; April 13]

Gone again

Hey Mac –

We made it home and are gone again. We are in Jamestown now, trying to make arrangements to put my mother's house on the market, and a bad market it is....

So are your crocuses up yet in your garden? Ours have been up and now are frozen in the revival of winter in these parts. We are really worried about our hyacinths, as I am sure you must be about yours.

I'm going to miss the I-Man. He was the most entertaining show on morning TV, but I never could figure out why MSNBC let him get away with what he did on the air. I mean, he even verbally abused the hierarchy there and they let him get away with it, all because of his good ratings, I guess.

Then he steps over the line ... while he's going with the flow in some side conversation with Bernard, and that's it. Why didn't he understand the difference between casting aspersions on public people, like calling Hillary worse than a nappy-headed ho, and doing the same with semi-private people?

... I can hear people saying now, like Playboy magazine readers, I just watched the Imus show for the interviews. And they were great interviews. Where else could you get Tom Friedman talking at length about the Middle East? But I liked the show too for its unpredictability. You never knew what was going to come up or who was going to say what.

The Rob Bartlett essays were priceless.... I suppose it's only a matter of time before Imus shows up on satellite radio. So do you think he deserved what he got? ...

RJ

[April 13]

Diamond-cutters are a man's best friend

Dutchers,

I really want to address the Don Ho situation, but first have stunning news which may be of great interest to other men — and their helpmates — who are, shall we say, of certain ages.

In a high-tech lab in Silver Spring, Maryland, scientists not long ago revealed American men who reached age 76 in January of 2006 are finding their penises have grown an average of two-and-a-half inches.

It's a new element in the waters, the scientists say, and too involved to explain to some laypersons. The growth sometimes occurs overnight, though I don't want to get anecdotal here. But I can confirm the true stunner: aside from the good gain in yardage, which is that the septuagenarians' erections have become hard enough to cut diamonds.

They're been hushing this up — the Viagra-Cialis people, that crowd — while gerontologists try to figure out how best to present evidence to general public.

In some ways, this is disconcerting. In other ways, it seems to open new vistas for men and women who love them. And, I suppose that works for the other team too. So what's the upside? The downside? Can I put aside my personal involvement and make rational decisions here? Will there be unintended consequences? Should I buy some new clothes?

Roger and Jessica, this is not something I want bruited about. Best to keep this under our hats. For now. Am concerned that, should word get out here, it might give me an unfair advantage over other players in the town.

As to Imus, I too once enjoyed shtick and watched on MSNBC for years. And on radio before that. Lots of funny stuff if your ox wasn't being gored. Cool to listen to Imus diss the big shots, speak "truth" to power, draw in the insiders in the press, the movers and shakers.

But for me, Imus began to seem not very funny, more and more of a mean-spirited bully, an ego-ridden power-hungry jerk who was cruel to the little people, and sick as a dog half the time into the bargain. Yes, he was talented, driven, smart and gutsy. A veritable prince in the charity game, as he would tell you at the drop of his hat.

Bartlett and Larry and Bernard and Chuck were and are funny and talented and good at what they do and [their] Dr. Phil-Falwell-Clinton-Gonzales-Hulk-Kennedy-Carl-Cardinal Egan often inspired.

What got me though was the gradual realization that all these humorists were under marching orders to say bad shit because Imus had learned it was no longer safe to deliver the dirt, let the boys do it.

And then last week a bunch of college basketball players activated Imus. I suspect he thought of them as stick figures on a screen. Worse luck, they turn out to be humans doing no apparent harm, folks with families and stuff like that there....

Shockjock and poor man's Charlie Rose to the stars of the press, the bigshot pols, the movers and shakers. The Russerts and Schieffers and Williamses and Brokaws and Mitchells and Barnicles and Goodwins and Matthews and Dowds and Riches and Rooneys and Gregorys and Oliphants and Thomases and Alters and Finemans and Bidens and McCains and Dodds and Liebermans and so forth.

These people helped make Imus more powerful than was good for him or anyone else, and the regulars are now disdained as folks who winked and nodded as Imus abused them and others with an increasing abandon.

Many of Imus' respectable ... buddies made good bucks as he flogged their "books" on Amazon, fueling his ego by revealing what a kingmaker he is, how much they were beholden to him. Good old boys. In my view, every good deed Don Imus has done was done for Don and he got huge dividends in self-satisfaction....

Imus' relationship with the celebs is the real story here. Imus courts big shots because of the power and prestige their presence on his show gave him. And the celebs courted Imus, held their tongues, kissed his ring....

Imus and enablers bring to mind Oscar Wilde's famous quotation about the English gentry that hunts foxes from horses. "The unspeakable in pursuit of the uneatable," said Wilde, who probably wouldn't have made the cut at Don's table....

Later, Almac

[Jamestown; April 14]

So did you have inside info that Don Ho was going to die, at 76 no less...?

And someone I sleep with who prefers to remain anonymous says to stop pumping yourself up, if you get her drift.

[April 15]

Dutchers,

I swear on a stack of atheist tracts I did not know Don Ho had passed over the bar in the Sandwich Islands. Did not understand reference to Don Ho in your response, thought the reference was to the former director of The Wrinkle Farm.

But then I found that yes, Ho is no mo. At, and I could hardly credit this news, the now magical age of 76. This is big, Dutchers!

It's clear we are here discussing one of the possible side-effects of the enlargement development. Imagine an elderly person, perhaps not as "centered" as your correspondent, suddenly gaining yardage with a diamond-cutter as a bonus, so to speak.

Poor Ho: awakens to greet a new day and has to go and well, we can infer the rest, a heart attack, the very sort of side-effect I had envisioned!

197

This confluence of events, and my uncanny subliminal awareness of what had transpired in the land of the nenes staggers even me, and speaking of that I am hurt by Jessica's flip remark that I am somehow "pumping" myself up. I didn't ask to be thrust into greatness, and it is not my fault I lived to be 76! And in such magical times! And I think, by and large, I'm handling this new thing very well but will need more supportive feedback from Michigan to get me through.

It's bad enough, all the storms that have been hitting me.... Skies are glowering on the well endowed as well as lesser members of the community.... I (well, we) may be doomed. And then of what use is my diamond-cutter? ...

Mac

[May 2]

Dutchers,

How are things going out there? It kept raining all the time here in April but now that it is May, the rain has gone away.

Connie always recited this bit of verse on May 1: "Hurray, hurray, the first of May/Outdoor hanky-panky begins today."

Al

[Grand Blanc; May 3]

Hey Mac –

When last we talked, I think I was making plans to put my mother's house on the market. I hired a Realtor on the 19th, and lo and behold, in a terrible home-sale market, we got an offer the next week. We made a counter offer on Sunday night and it was accepted on Monday night....

The big news around here, and maybe you have heard, is that Booth is closing its Lansing Bureau. I've enclosed a link to the only story I've seen so far. I've been in and out so much, I might have missed something in the Journal. Didn't Connie work for Washington Bureau at one time? ...

RJ

[May 4]

Dutchers,

Read about Booth bureau on E & P site on Internet. Checked other sites and found no stories other than the same one you sent.... Connie did work at Booth bureau in D.C.; she was first female reporter hired by that august bureau, and was working there when we got married.... Bureau then was a Potemkin kind of place, full of pomp. If you wrote one story a week, they'd give you some time off to recover....

The impudent bureau chief took Connie aside before we got married and avuncularly advised the plighting of this pending troth was not a good move, careerwise or anyotherwise. The chief had checked my priors and found me wanting.

I never did like people who worked for bureaus of papers in American capitals. They miss stories, pad their expenses, steal office materials, and don't even have the redeeming qualities of being shiftless drunks. I don't want to talk about this anymore....

I envy you people getting a rare chance to once again use those skills perfected during the career years, the dealings with the workmen and the Realtors and the bankers and the movers. These are needful challenges to keep us on our toes with noses pressed to the grindstones, shoulders to the wheels and eyes on the balls.

But then suppose you folks are making a nice little buck wheeling and dealing while I keep getting discouraging reports ... about the activities of Great Aunt Gert. GAG recently attended an annual Connecticut centenarian gathering and was, for the third year in a row, the oldest person amongst all the droolers and dawdlers.

As is her annual reward for being oldest of the old, Miss Gertrude gets to make the ceremonial cut in the big birthday cake for other geezeresses in the throngs. Sometimes you can see a male geezer, or someone who looks a geezer ... but then you probably find the fellow is only 42 and works security.

GAG gets interviewed and quoted and photographed at these events. ... GAG was moving along briskly with a walker at this year's gala when cameras zoomed in. GAG quickly handed the walker off, a mere accessory.

Each year, Gert feeds rapt interviewers a different ... "secret" to her longevity. This year, GAG averred that the secret was to "get up early, go to work, do a good job, and then go home." The last time Gert had to go to work, much less do a good job, probably was right after VJ Day in the Big War. Also and FYI, GAG now weighs eighty-eight pounds and her vanity, always impressive, grows with each passing year....

So my friends make money and hone their useful skills, raising their self-esteem exponentially, while I sit here helpless before the forces that seem determined to deny me my rightful inheritance in a timely fashion.

Almac

[June 8]

The Auld Sod revisited

Hey Mac,

... we go to closing [on mother's house], which with a POA needed only my signature. A POA really is powerful (maybe you could get one from GAG and handle her affairs, taking your allotted amount in trust, as it were)....

So closing was on Friday. First day of [garage] sale is Saturday.... [After garage sale], we drive back to Grand Blanc, unpack, and about an hour later, get a call.... Our mom had fallen and broken her hip [in Texas].

The sequence of events was mind boggling .... Sale of house, selling contents, leaving house. Mom breaks hip hours later.... She's in nursing home now. A big page in our family history has turned, so what are we doing now?

... we're going to Ireland! Tomorrow morning. Something I didn't talk about because I feared it might get canceled for any number of reasons....

RJ

[July 3]

Confessions of a former police reporter

Dutchers,

I was just reading an obit on a science writer named Gormer, and the lead of the story said this Gormer person "dug into his science beat with the guts of a police reporter." Right away, I thought, gee, I am a former police reporter and I do not remember too many heroics.

In fact, Dutchers, I remember some really mealy-mouthy timid exchanges with police officers.... One time, a huge detective, a native of south Georgia, kicked a chair out from under me because this was a police station, not a fucking parlor for police reporters to laze about.

My response to this crudity was not a timid remark, but no remark at all, and I was glad when the snappish detective departed, muttering about the Yankees, and I don't think he was a baseball person.

Another time, I remember chancing by a closed door in the police station and hearing the smacking of fists and bouncing of a person off the walls. Having seen a large rough "buck Negro" (not my term) go into the room with three buck whites a bit earlier, I knew that a Civil Rights offense was taking place.

What to do? Well ... no sense for me to make waves here, besides I'm off in a half-hour and dearly wish to return to the Village Barn tavern across Flagler Street.

One time, a police official in the city morgue approached me to shake hands and I found I was shaking a hand that wasn't his. It was the hand of a ... floater on the slab in the room. They need the hand to do the ... floater's prints. With an insouciance that I did not feel, I pretended not to notice I was holding a dead man's hand, and politely returned it to the police official and sauntered off.

Also, once, as a police reporter, I was assigned to go to a house and knock on the door and verify if indeed famous gangster Meyer Lansky was living there. Turned out he was, but as I tip-toed by the house, I thought what if some mafioso aide opens the door, and that I am not confronted

A storyteller's odyssey

by the reportedly relatively amiable Lansky, and he hits me or snaps at me or something?

So, Dutchers, I did not knock, and told the city editor nobody answered the door and what would a rich crook be doing living in such a modest house anyway? Could give more examples, but have made my point. All police reporters are not gutsy.

I have not responded with my usual alacrity to your last post, which I guess was about three weeks ago. During that period, I somehow lost all the files that I have saved, and now cannot look up old emails to respond separately to each of the astounding activities which you people got up to before fleeing to Ireland.

Incidentally, this is now the fourth or ninth time you folks have informed me that you were hieing off to some exotic locale, places of course that I cannot myself visit owing to the fact that GAG is now homing in on the big 109 figure, and still reputedly smarter than a whip, brighter than a bathroom fixture, and healthier than a horse, though weighing just 84 pounds, and she still gets pissed if you try to help her rise from ... seat or throne....

Meantime, I have spent several weeks dealing with disgusting side-effects of medications. For a while there I didn't write any emails, but now seem to be less lethargic, and am eagerly looking forward to the Glorious Fourth tomorrow. Faraday and Finley and me will be the only mammals left in downtown Hallowell for the Fourth; the town is already deserted and it just dawned on me that, for most folks, yesterday and today are part of a long weekend that ends tomorrow.

Am back on good terms with sister Deborah, and she visited me for lunch last week.... perhaps I can start getting some real inside dope on just how well Miss Gertrude is getting on.

Hey, if Debbie tells me, she hates to say it but Gert is ready for the high jump, I will bear up, take the hit in manly fashion. And get on with my life. Yes, we'll not see her like again, and may the lass from the loins of folks in the Auld Sod have a fair wind at her back and a soft rise in the road.

Later, Almac

202

[July 4]

Back from the Auld Sod

Hey Mac,

Yes, we are indeed back from Ireland, the land of Polish waitresses, and things seem to be prepared for you to assume a position of power there. I learned that the president of said country, commonly called Polski West, is a woman who claims to have the last name of McAleese....

Of course ... I was told that the president has no power. But she must at least have a swanky home in which to receive George Bush or provide digs for a distant Maine relative. The power in the country is held by the prime minister, some Polish emigration official in disguise....

As we toured Connemara, the current "troubles," the Polish situation, cropped up in an odd context. Jessica was ordering tickets for us to tour an abbey, and a Polish woman was dispensing same. Jess asked for one senior and one adult ticket. The woman, incredulous, said, "One senior and one dog? No dogs!"

Because the economy is booming in Ireland, the Irish don't need to dirty themselves with menial labor like being a waiter or sitting on their arse to collect tickets. The Polish are the illegal aliens who do those jobs there, although they aren't illegal.... So the Polish waitresses and waiters take your order, and then you wait to find out what they think you actually ordered....

In Cong, where much of "The Quiet Man" was filmed, we took a walking tour and then decided to walk to the nearby Ashford Castle, where ... John Wayne and the rest of the cast stayed during the filming 50-plus years ago. I paused on my cane in front of what we had learned was the Rev. Playfair's house in the movie when an elderly gentleman came out.

I'm thinking it's Meyer Lansky, and being a good police reporter, I strike up a conversation. I learn that he had lived in the house for 60 years. Then I learn that he was Wayne's double for the film. He used to go fishing with Wayne on

Sundays during the filming, if Wayne wasn't too hungover from the Guinness....

Talk to you later, or sooner if you come into some money.

RJ

[July 6]

Scribes to the tribes

Dutchers,

... McLeese is our original family name.... There are McLeeses listed as writers or chroniclers in the thirteenth and fourteenth centuries under the Gaelic name for McLeese that I can never remember, so they were hacks of the clan's version of history.... Have long been aware jackleg relative was [married to] president of Ireland, but never boasted about it — as Roger was good enough to point out, the Irish prez hasn't got the clout to order piss poured from boots....

Here is an aside to Jess:

Some day when Roger's mood is good and he can handle a little setback, there is something you need to tell him. In that part of Ireland in which "The Quiet Man" was filmed, there are, 24/7, men on duty and well paid to tell tourists they were doubles for John Wayne.... Ask him if the guy tried to borrow money? One of those faux Waynes is notorious, and will make plays for the women tourists, too.

So Jess, you really need to tell Roger he has been gulled before he goes around telling [friends from the Journal] about his latest major tourist coup and gets himself in so deep he'll be too embarrassed to ever return to that lovely land across the Irish Sea.

I do not, Roger, incidentally, believe a word of the blatant bullshit about Polish people taking over Ireland, doing all the scut work. If that's the case, how come we're still getting Irish maids up the wazoo at the docks in Portland and Boston and New York. What is this, some nasty Polish joke?

... Oh, and incidentally, "The Quiet Man" was Connie's all-time favorite movie, and I liked it as well. Never been a Wayne fan, but it seemed in that movie he demonstrated more depth than generally credited with. And have always been a fan of Victor McSomethingorother. McGlagen? McLaglen? Some kind of mick.

Later, Mac

[July 6]

Yeah, well, you had to have been there, to look John Wayne's stand-in straight in his good eye and assess his credentials like any police reporter. Plus, he came out of the Rev. Playfair's house, ergo he had to be the real stand-in. Or maybe he saw Wayne riding his bike one day. It's Ireland, and he wants to tell a story. Ireland, the land that time forgot to teach it Polish so the tourists can get fed....

I think a letter to the Irish Mary might be in order, just to see what she's doing about the Polish situation ... I mean churches were advertising Polish masses....

RJ

[July 8]

I Have Confirmed the Report

Dutchers,

Roger, you were right and I apologize. There are a lot of Poles in Ireland; I myself confirmed this via Google. I googled Polish Immigrants in Ireland and it is true, there seem to be about 200,000 of them, and I should not have doubted your report. I can't imagine why, but it was news to me about this development. I knew that Ireland was doing well these recent years, but the Polish part somehow stayed under my radar.

I should have believed Roger right off the bat, Jess, and the same holds true on the Wayne matter.... It must be because I am relatively poor and live all alone and cannot travel to exotic locales like my rich friends, that I brood and question the honest affirmations of my friends, the Dutchers....

Regarding the skis and the stoshes invading Ireland, various Net writers note many similarities between the Poles and the Irish. I hadn't thought much about this, but they say the Polish joke "started out here as an Irish joke," the bog trotters being one of the most popular targets in 19th-century America. Indians weren't all that funny.

As for Ireland today, I get feel from reportage that it's a happy mix, the Polacks and Micks, both groups alike enough and energetic and smart enough if pointed in right direction.... Bet you could whip out a humorous essay [on subject] without much drudgery. If you people ever stayed home long enough with your poor lonely little dog, that is. But, hey, I don't want to make anyone feel guilty here.

Later, Almac

Part 7: Sharing a bed, long-term

After MacLeese left San Francisco in 1965, one of his landings late that year was at the Flint Journal. It was another touch-and-go.

The Journal hired him as a copy editor, and he was ready to apply his mental file of clever, punchy headlines he had written any number of times at any number of newspapers. He knew the "events described in these headlines would recur with only names changed. History is the same thing happening again."

But MacLeese was not destined to write any headlines for the Journal anytime soon. His history repeated itself.

"The editorial powers had decided that new head writers should sit in the Journal 'morgue' for two weeks reading up on Flint history" before headlining stories about Malaysian ferryboats sinking and Mexican buses plunging.

"I was put in the damned morgue [library] on my first day at work. And I had been anticipating writing a neat snowstorm headline to get me off to a flying start: 'Here comes the zinger, we're going to have a blinger,' maybe."

Instead, he was handed a history book about Genesee County pioneers and was told there were plenty more books where that came from.

"I was affronted at being put on the sidelines, although I could not be assertive about this because it was known by Journal management that I had a track record as a 'bottle baby.'

"Bottle babies were drunks. In those forthright times, advertisements for headline writers sometimes read: 'Copy editor wanted. Nice town, good scenery, fine hunting, fishing. Outstanding civic groups. No floaters, drifters or bottle babies need apply."

MacLeese stayed in the Journal's library a few days, then he visited the old Brass Rail on E. Kearsley Street. "Fell off the wagon, sullenly. There followed several days which cannot be recounted with precision. I disappeared from the YMCA, leaving my suitcase.... The Flint River was dutifully scanned.

"Meantime, I had set in motion plans to migrate to Houston." If he could not get to write headlines in Flint, he would go to Houston was the logic.

Connie Reed, whom he had met in Gary the previous year, was then working in the Detroit area as the Wayne County bureau chief for the Ypsilanti Press. She loaned him the money to go to Houston, where MacLeese had a friend, another copy editor bottle baby, who arranged an interview for MacLeese at a paper there.

In Houston, MacLeese roomed with his friend while awaiting the interview. "But my friend had mostly vodka in his icebox and I was unweaned."

The friend "lived 20 blocks from downtown and had no car and I never saw a bus. All of Houston seemed 20 blocks from downtown. Even downtown seemed 20 blocks from downtown. Every time I would try to walk downtown for the job interview, I would grow faint and wobbly in the harsh sun and totter back to the apartment for a belt. This may be where the term Sun Belt came from.

"In the apartment sat the icebox with unused lemons and vodka bottles in various states of use. They were never half full, always half empty. Irony heaped upon irony – they would not let me work in Flint and I wasn't up to it in Houston.

"It worked out. My friend lured me to a plane after buying me a cowboy hat. The plane carried me off to New York."

MacLeese had come full circle within weeks. He had left New York to go to Flint.

In New York, his new hat blew off in a "windy stone canyon." He soon blew, or was blown, out of town, too, to Boston. While working at a newspaper there, his big concerns were to get back to his hotel in the downtown "Combat Zone" unmugged and to get a pint or at least a six-pack along the way.

He was still finding himself at home in, or getting lost in, a city's seamy underbelly.

Early one morning, "in Boston's pre-dawn, I accompanied a pimp and a whore into a slum. Turned out they were setting me up for a mugging, and who can blame them?

"The pair and four male confederates who came out of nowhere jumped me on the steps to a basement apartment. They expertly ripped all my pants pockets, taking my filthy lucre. They held me down and the boss mugger sat on my chest pricking a knife against my (pale white) throat. This focused my attention since it seemed the boss mugger might bloody his knife, so maddened did he look.

"Scared silly, I told him, attempting calm reason, that his group, while understandably involved in its work, was off-base. 'Why didn't you just ask for the money? I was going to blow it on booze and women, so it's no big deal … no need for overkill.' (Poor choice of words, this last."

The boss mugger grunted and let MacLeese up. The band climbed the stairs and started off down the deserted street of mainly abandoned tenements.

MacLeese said he followed them and called out: "Hey, have the decency to leave a couple of bucks so I can get a cab. If I walk I'll get mugged or killed for nothing."

The boss mugger "turned, seeming caught between snarl and smile, then blankly let three dollar bills flutter to the street" before loping off.

The moral of this story? "When cornered by dangerous humans, do something unpredictable yet non-threatening as a last resort. It may throw them off. (Like Dan'l Boone grinnin' at that ba'r.) And if unpredictability doesn't appeal, avoid pimps, whores and bears, you fool."

Why was he consorting with prostitutes when many women were attracted to him? The answer might involve a lack of self-confidence.

Llewellyn King, who worked with MacLeese in both Baltimore and Washington in the mid-1960s, found him to be "incredibly appealing to women." One woman King knew thought MacLeese was "the most gorgeous man she had ever seen."

King told the story of MacLeese and a babe at the Baltimore paper "that we all lusted after." MacLeese was able to hook up with her, and to get out of work, he called the desk to say he had broken his leg. The couple headed to a motel. The next day MacLeese showed up for work as normal, without a broken leg. He was canned.

With women, MacLeese could be funny and charming but in certain situations he was insecure. "I have long suffered from the ghastly fear of rejection, which strikes most who have been unable to convince themselves of their overwhelming attractiveness to women."

To that point, he told a story about an incident in a piano bar in Boston. "So classic was my tale that a psychiatrist at a drunk farm once accused me of making it up. Alas, it is true.

"I was sitting at the bar, cap tilted back to appear rakish, despite natural handicaps. Exchanged glances with a woman across the bar who had wildly careless eyeballs. After two hours of ingesting liquid drugs, to soothe the central nervous system, I decided to approach this beautiful Bostonian, who I fervently hoped was improper.

"Nearing her seat at the bar, it occurred to me that she was going to turn down my hesitant invitation to dance with ill-concealed disdain. Each scenario I had played in my mind entertained this possibility. By the time I reached her side, the best I could blurt was: 'Frankly, you uppity female, I don't give a damn if you dance with me or not.'"

MacLeese said: "It is this sort of assurance that has followed me through life."

He said he once told a woman: "I love you, you son-of-a-bitch." She replied: "There, there, friend."

Even though he may have lacked self-confidence, that didn't mean he wasn't competitive when it came to women. He told one story where he stayed in the arena too long and was forced to improvise.

Another babe at a bar was involved, and he was having success impressing her until a well-dressed baseball player sidled up and tried to insert himself in the conversation. MacLeese had to urinate but he knew that if he left for the rest room all would be lost.

The ballpayer elbowed his way between MacLeese and their common target. MacLeese had to go but he also had to stay.

With the ballplayer now firmly between them, MacLeese saw an opportunity to go and to stay. He micturated, to use his word, in the ballplayer's sport coat pocket. The ballplayer didn't see that coming and he was stunned – for a moment. During that moment of confusion and consternation, friends of MacLeese took the opportunity to spirit him out of harm's way.

By 1967, MacLeese had followed Connie Reed to Washington, D.C., to work as a copy editor for the Washington Daily News. Connie had joined the Booth Newspapers' Washington Bureau as its first woman correspondent in 1966. Booth was a chain of dailies in eight of the larger Michigan cities after Detroit.

Connie wasn't some babe he locked eyes with across a bar. They were colleagues in Gary, and she was a serious newswoman, his intellectual equal as a journalist. He respected her and their connection grew over time. She had not had a steady boyfriend before him. He would be the love of her life and she his.

Llewellyn King said that compared to the other women in MacLeese's life, Connie was plain. King said she put up with a lot. "She was loyal, loyal, loyal. Nothing upset her. She would rescue him ... and was determined to hang onto him."

As their relationship progressed, MacLeese was having problems playing well with certain others.

And by the time he and Connie decided to get married, MacLeese had been barred from the National Press Club. "I had bickered overmuch with people (generally lobbyists) and didn't belong to the club to begin with. (As Joe E. Lewis said: 'I would never belong to a club that would have me.')"

They were first married Sept. 8, 1967, in a civil ceremony in Arlington, Virginia, just outside of Washington. (Two years earlier, the same magistrate had married actress Lana Turner to her sixth husband. Within the next decade, he would marry actor Richard Burton to wife number four and then-Secretary of State Henry Kissinger to his second wife, Nancy.)

Shortly after that first ceremony, they held a more formal one, with a reception, as a show for Connie's mother, Hilda Reed, who was unaware that her only child was already married.

For the second wedding, Connie sought the aid of U.S. Rep. Guy Vander Jagt and his wife Carol. The Vander Jagts put them in touch with the minister who married them despite MacLeese's timid "admission" that he had no "proper religion."

In addition to Connie's mother, among those attending that ceremony were Alan's mother, Alan's sister Deborah and the Vander Jagts.

The Michigan congressional delegation gave them wedding presents, MacLeese said.

Then-congressman Gerald R. Ford's "agents dispatched some fancy drinking glasses" bearing the seal of the House of Representatives. Years later, after Ford became president, those glasses assumed a position of more prominence in their china cabinet, along with unsolicited explanations about the presidential connection.

The next year, after being soured on Washington by the race riots in April 1968, both were working in Michigan at different Booth papers.

When they left Washington, she had a job lined up at the Saginaw News as outdoor editor. He was between engagements again. He applied for a sportscaster job at a Flint-area TV station and as a copy editor at the Flint Journal, where he was hired for the second time in three years. At the time, Booth prohibited spouses from working in the same newsroom.

MacLeese said he "wrote headlines the very same day" he was hired. No two-week indoctrination in the morgue.

How was he able to get hired again after his previous disappearance? The likely reason is that the news editor that hired him the first time had retired, leaving no institutional record of that short-lived employment.

A month after he started working the second time at the Journal, he and Connie went golfing near Harbor Springs and he hit a hole-in-one with a nine iron on a 115-yard par three. "After the shock wore off," Connie said, "we looked around for other witnesses. You never saw a more deserted golf course."

Connie suggested he preserve the ball. "I will," he said, "after the next hole." He drove it into deep water off the next tee.

In 1969, MacLeese wrote a column for the Journal that ended up on the national Associated Press wire and in many other papers. He told about fishing with Connie on Crooked Lake, near Petoskey. Connie's mother had a cottage on the lake's Oden Island.

Before his marriage to Connie, he wrote, he was wont to tell tales to feminine ears about "a danger-fraught mission" into the fishing wild, where a "six-inch captive bluegill would be wondrously transformed into something as big as a wash pail and as surly as a wounded rhinoceros."

But that was before. And his hole-in-one history counted for naught in their boat.

"Follow us as we sally into our 16-foot runabout diligently churning away from shore," he wrote. "Is your hairy-chested correspondent at the helm? Well, no.

"Seems the wife has 'lines' on all the good beds – lines being triangulation markings using fixed shore points as references. I don't seem to be able to fix these lines in my head, thus am I relegated to

212

the bow (part that goes through the water first) to stand by alertly ready to drop the anchor.

"The wife, once achieving captaincy, runs an exceedingly taut ship.... Docile and feminine during shore duty, she becomes a bit of a militant afloat. With this crew, I suspect, she has to.

"The anchor has possibly descended nine-and-a-half feet and already the spouse has impaled an inoffensive minnow upon hook and whizzed a cast some 30 feet outward. Your reporter, at this stage, is attempting to extricate his hook from the fleshiest part of the left palm.

"Her minnow immediately goes to work – I suspect he's been told he is on a commission rate – while mine lackadaisically begins to plumb the depths, possibly debating on whether to call in sick....

"The masculine ego isn't only deflated on the field of action, however. The good wife has been fishing this particular lake since, roughly, the repeal of the Volstead Act and all the local outdoor types know her. Now they all know me. I'm 'Connie's husband.' Sort of like being married to Liz Taylor, if your name is Eddie Fisher."

Once, MacLeese thought he was the winner in one area of outdoor endeavors. "I'd always fancied myself a crack shot, a belief falsely imprinted the day I nailed a running squirrel in the head at 200 yards with a .22-caliber rifle.

"Modestly, in my unassuming fashion, I spun this little gem of a tale before my rapt audience of one – Connie. Shortly after this I discovered she had shot her first duck with a .410 gauge shotgun at the age of 7 and had been mentioned in Michigan newspapers as 'one of the state's best young trapshooters' when she was only 9."

Connie was also a rock hound, and during summer vacations, they "busily scratched about" the stony beaches near Copper Harbor in the Upper Peninsula.

"Now I've always thought," MacLeese wrote, "a rock is just a rock but I never doubted that I would excel at spotting a valuable one if the occasion arose. This, needless to say, did not prove out. Connie had collared about 15 agates during a period in which my major find was something left by a seagull."

Besides being relegated to the front of the boat, how had his life changed with Connie? He was seriously working on quitting drinking full-time. Working on it, yet never quite succeeding.

It didn't take his family long to recognize that things were going to be different with Connie as his wife. There was a sense of relief.

After their father died, his sister Deborah said, "I remember mother being worried [about Alan] much of the time and I don't think there was a sense of peace until Alan was with Connie, a blessing for both Alan and his family."

In a progress report more than a dozen years into the marriage, he said his credit had "bounded from zilch to improbable, probably because I only carry one check at a time and turn the paycheck into the wife as soon as is decent while also maintaining my manly image. Connie then does mysterious things with a checkbook while I go out and play in the yard."

He would be at the Journal far longer than at any other paper, and he credited Connie with helping him settle down and with smoothing out many of his rough edges. She was a calming influence for his normally roiling mindset. His chief vice hovered in the background, though, during periods when he was a "dry alkie" and still struggling to stay off booze.

He hadn't been jailed since their marriage, where before he had been arrested more than 30 times, "generally as a common drunk or disorderly person or vagrant," in a dozen states.

(As an aside, he said he had "never once been mistreated by a cop. And I assure you that often the circumstances of my apprehension were not good."

(MacLeese said he liked to think "my attitude toward the cops that arrested me directly affected the treatment I got. Thing was, I could never persuade myself that the cop arresting me for being drunk and broke and in disarray on a Miami skid row was to blame for my current misfortune. A bit of residual smarts made me know that it was I alone who had put myself at risk.... There is police misconduct, but it is rarely as prevalent as a cop's routine competence and, yes, heroics.")

He drew a Before and After Connie contrast at Christmastime, too. He remembered one Christmas Day, Before Connie, when he was lodged in the Hollywood (Florida) City Jail.

"Poor sod, I had been rounded up twice for public intoxication and finally the chief of police, a friend, decided I could be a guest of the city until I could get funds to flee Florida for Connecticut. Christmas arrived and the funds didn't. There I sat with various felons and fellow lushes. The chief took pity on me Christmas morning. Said I could leave for Christmas [if I was] back at midnight.

"Great idea, chief, but where do you go for Christmas in South Florida with 50 cents in your knickers? Bummed a ride to Miami, strolled around skid road a bit, then bummed a ride back to Hollywood and the sanctuary of jail."

A gay man picked him up. "He inquired of my circumstances," MacLeese said. "I told him I was on leave" from the Hollywood jail.

"Isn't that stinky," the other man said.

MacLeese's response: "My thoughts exactly."

Fast-forward 15 years to a Christmas after a decade of marriage to Connie. "I am soberly employed, have a family, a home, two cars and a leisure suit. I can have goose for Christmas dinner if I desire. Perhaps this is enough. Maybe joy is a fillip that accrues only to those more deserving. Those, as a wise alcoholic friend told me, who have permitted themselves to be happy."

For him, driblets of happiness came "fleetingly, without premonition or cheerleaders." Such as "after opening the presents on Christmas Day, when you espy the cats entangled in the wrappings and feel, suddenly, secure."

Through Connie and his column, he had found as much ease, contentment and satisfaction that one with his restless nature could eke out. He had become mainly a homebody, with a wife and a family of cats.

It may be a good thing that cats do not require references for their owners. Cat lover MacLeese likely would have been blackballed for once collaborating on a friend's idea to parachute cats down from a Key Biscayne high-rise.

Drinking, of course, was involved. After calling animal agencies, they had lined up eight cats within an hour, and they drove around Dade County picking them up. Returning to their high rise, they smuggled the cats "up to the skatey-eighth floor, not forgetting sewing materials. Sheets were fashioned into cute parachutes. All eight cats made the jump, and I am happy to report all made it to the ground safely."

The real joy was "in watching startled heads poke out of windows as cats on gentle sea breezes wafted down."

Any investigative report would have been balanced, from the cat perspective, by MacLeese's bird-attracting gimmick in Connecticut.

"It was winter and the birds were hungry, though no fault of mine. I attached a piece of pork to a string and chucked it into the yard. By slowly drawing the pork ... I enticed sparrows toward the house. And, not incidentally, toward our cats, which lurked everywhere. I witnessed no execution-by-cat but am confident the sparrow population ... must have suffered significant setbacks."

MacLeese said he wrote the local paper, the Ansonia Sentinel, about his technique. "Several readers responded angrily, but by then I had fled to San Francisco and was not concerned about regional New England problems."

It is doubtful, though, that he told Connie about drowning and shotgunning litters of kittens when he was a mere lad, at his father's behest. Not one of his life's prouder moments, even if he was following orders.

Life in a MacLeese household could be assumed to be complicated, and even a simple matter of retiring for the night had issues. Connie once wrote a column about a time when they had three cats, Spike, Spook and Sarah. One can only imagine what it was like with their second family of cats, the F-Troop, which at one time enlisted eight in its ranks. All had names that began with the letter F.

"The first step," Connie wrote, "is finding the bed, the second is excavating it and the third is sweeping it out. Usually these three steps consume the better part of seven minutes, three husbandly 'Don't lose thats,' four swipes of various cat's paws, one 'What are you doing with those papers I haven't read' and looks from four pairs of eyes, ranging from tolerant amusement to feline indignation."

Here's the picture Connie drew:

"One adult male stretched out on the west half of the bed, munching on his nightly snacks and surrounded by six magazines, four tattered John D. MacDonald adventure books, 11 sections of at least three newspapers, a topless box of Ritz crackers, its contents trailing across the bed's east side; one empty ice cream dish, from which the sticky spoon has escaped onto the sheet I had changed the night before; two books of matches, each containing but one firestick; one crumpled cigarette package; one half-full cigarette package; two demolished cigarettes – the male person has rolled over on them, ruptured them and inadvertently glued their tobacco to the sticky place where the ice cream spoon landed...."

All that was before the bedcover rollback, which on a typical night revealed "such diverse objects as a dish of juicy peaches, much of the juice soaked up by the top sheet; four scrapbooks of newspaper clippings; two chocolate candies, only slightly crushed, one with a bite out of it; a disposable cigarette lighter; three more cigarettes, each bleeding tobacco; one sock; two black and two red felt pens, sans caps, which have scrawled hieroglyphics of their own on the sheet; an empty root beer glass (well, it's empty now – its former contents are being thirstily slurped up by the mattress) and Page 99 of 'Black Marble.'''

But, wait, there's more. Connie said "the job really isn't finished until the male person trudges off to brush his teeth…. Think for a moment. With all that debris everywhere else on the bed, can you be so naïve as to believe there is none under HIM?

"By the time his teeth are brushed and his face washed, I have removed from the west side three piles of cookie crumbs, another empty cigarette package, a T-shirt and the other sock, and have scraped three melted chocolate squares from the recently clean sheet. When he returns from the brush-wash operation, I scrape the rest of the melted chocolate off a spot just above his left kidney."

Then and only then, Connie settles in, sharing her pillow with Sarah.

Scraping his clutter out of their bed barely touched what Connie did for her husband, the polar opposite of self-reliant.

Each morning, she laid out his clothes for him, so he wouldn't look mismatched. She not only served as maid and butler but also as cook and bottlewasher.

She served his evening meal in a large rectangular cake pan, which he used much like a TV tray, except he placed the pan in his lap while sitting in his recliner and watching TV. This way, Connie had a reasonable shot at keeping the food groups from escaping to his pants, the chair or the floor.

Out in the world, she either handled, or held his hand through, the complexities and minutia of daily living that were so frustrating to him.

His sister Deborah said there once was a little handbell next to the bed so he could summon Connie when he was hung over or otherwise sick. "I'm not sure what percentage of that bell ringing was in jest."

For a man who might make a bet on such matters, it was a sure thing that most outsiders viewed him as her dependent.

While he was at the Flint Journal, MacLeese did continue to be a betting man, ranging from small wagers to a trip to Las Vegas, where his gambling was draining, cash-wise.

Lou Giampetroni said he made a bet with MacLeese on the Detroit Tigers one year.

"At the start of a Tigers baseball season, I bet him $1 a game that the Tigers would lose. It was their 1984 season, I believe." That was the year the Tigers started out 35-5 and won the World Series. "He would smile his little grin as he collected the dollar bills."

On his jaunt to Vegas, Bob DeLand said, "Mac took what he thought would be enough cash but quickly lost it all. He called Connie and she sent him some more, which he also lost. He called me at home and said he didn't dare call Connie again but if I could wire him some he was sure he could win back some of his losses.

"I think I sent him $500 and I seem to remember him saying he won some back on the slots at the airport before they flew home. He paid me back over a few weeks and nothing more was ever said about it."

MacLeese went on that trip to Vegas with Bill Eastham, a colleague at the Journal. DeLand said they were taking a break from the gaming floor and resting in their room, when Eastham, who was lying on his bed reading, looked over at MacLeese, "who was lying on his side with some dark liquid running out of his mouth.

"Eastham jumped up and shook him awake." DeLand said Eastham thought he had a medical emergency on his hands. Actually it was chocolate overload. "Mac had put a chocolate candy kiss the maids had left on the beds in his mouth and fell asleep before he swallowed it."

MacLeese also was notorious for screwing up, as he put it, "one-car funerals."

Don Dahlstrom, a fellow copy editor at the time, remembers when MacLeese put together a pool for the Kentucky Derby, and he managed to include the name of a jockey in the list of horses. Dahlstrom drew the jockey, and as he recalls it, MacLeese drew Secretariat. MacLeese gave Dahlstrom his winnings.

MacLeese once told DeLand about a scam he perpetrated at some papers when he ran short of drinking money before payday. "He would concoct a bogus horse race and collect bets then return the money to his co-workers when he got paid."

Dahlstrom said MacLeese pulled that one on him and Jesse Hatcher when the three of them were putting out a holiday paper.

"I suspected it was phony, but didn't realize he would leave for lunch and never return and go off on a toot. Jess and I worked our asses off to get all the copy edited and out for the paper.... I think I was too busy getting everything out to be upset and dwell on it. Mac did apologize to each of us the next work day."

[July 30, 2007]

Second Christ visits, seeks intro to Mike Moore

Dutchers,

UNLEASHED

I was sitting around reading when there came a knock on the door; and it was [a friend and her male pal], who I had never met.... [She] declared, "We're gonna smoke you up!" So ... we proceeded to puff, puff and pass, just like we were normal people under ordinary circumstances....

[My friend says her pal] is so brilliant hardly anyone understands what he is going on about. [He] said he'd unraveled the DaVinci-Dan Brown code and quickly realized it connects all events in the history of the universe: a Ted Williams homer, Men in Black, Superbowl scores, the arc-Radians of Nibiru, the Uranian God of the Middle Way ... video games, wars ... the whole ball of wax sits bare and naked in [his] mind....

[She], it developed, had told [him] I'd written about Michael Moore and even knew that portly visionary. So [he] pulled out his script and jottings.... As I scanned the script ... [he] revealed he was the Second Christ. Calmly came right out with it, and I'd had no clue. I looked over to [her], and she nodded, indicating, yes, this is unusual, but it is what it is, what can you do? If not [him], who? Or whom.

[He] acknowledged being the Second Christ is, initially, unsettling, but contended he could "handle it." But now, he said, he needed help in persuading Mr. Moore to make a movie about him and his revelations, the whole true skinny. [He], I thought later, seemed to think Mr. Moore would snap up this concept like a pedophile homing in on the younger Shirley Temple.

Dutchers, I told [him] that, Him being who He is, He didn't need any help from the likes of me in getting Moore on board. By this time we were all pretty high, and [he] good-naturedly said he would carry on by himself....

Later, Alan (I Found Christ) MacLeese

[Harlingen TX; Aug. 14]

Lost in the horse latitudes

Hey Mac –

We are reviving after driving for four days [in an RV bought after selling Gulf Shores condo] through triple-digit heat in the nation's midsection to reach the tip of Texas, where my mother is ensconced in a nursing home after breaking her hip....

The good news is my mom recognized Jessica and me when we walked in the lunchroom while she was eating, so it's been a worthwhile trip from that respect. She has some good periods mixed in with the unusual gibberish. She consorts with a lot of old friends who aren't here and dead relatives who have been long since gone, but she seems content in creating her own environment, so we don't dispute her any more in an attempt to straighten out her fictions with facts.

The bad news is the dementia probably won't allow her to comprehend how to walk again, so we wait for pneumonia or some other illness to set in....

While dozing, or attempting to doze down here, I've been thinking about my erstwhile novel, "Fighting City Hall".... Since I've been able to create zero interest in it as is, I'm seriously considering turning it into something that sells nowadays, and that something would be a romance novel. Maybe "Sex in the City Hall," or "Whores and Hounds."

The latter seems to fit any genre. My market research shows that there are men who write romance novels, but they do it under a female or sexually vague nom de plume. I'm thinking Alana MacLeese....

So that's my plan, unless you can come up with a better alternative. It's all in your hands.

RJ

[Aug. 20]

Dutchers,

Are you still in Texas, and if so, in path of Hurricane Dean? And after Dean, are Frank and Sammy in the wings? (This is my own joke, and I just went to a computer chat room in which posters were worried over how fierce Dean was, how he might wipe out Jamaica, which would not be a bad start. So I posted my Dean gem, but nobody responded — probably because such a sparkling defies any rejoinders.)

UNLEASHED

Glad to hear mother having fits of lucidity, and guess that alone might make the trip worthwhile. And it is good to hear you are not discussing the finer points of logic with Mom. When the Second Christ visited me recently, I wholeheartedly accepted his divinity and he appreciated adding a follower....

I don't know what to say about "Fighting City Hall." You know, I just read the NYT's bestseller list for fiction, and there were more than a score of books listed by the Nora Robertses and James Pattersons and Sidney Sheldons and, oh, a dozen more, and I realized I hadn't read a one of them, and hadn't read them on purpose.

These bestsellers sell because of the established names ... Robert Ludlum has been dead six years and sells more books than ever. Ditto others. Popular hacks hire their own hacks so they can turn out four books a year rather than only three.

So there is no point in changing your name to Alana Von Christ. Screw it, that's my take. Besides, it is wrong to try to make money and become famous from words, Roger, and also immoral and elitist. We should give freely of our words, what did Socrates ever write, huh? Nothing, Socrates wrote nothing. He would go down to the park and aggravate the shit out of people, make fools of them for flawed thinking, and all for free.

You should go down to a bar every night, Rog, and converse with fellow patrons, exercise your creativity in that good-hearted manner. Buy everybody drinks and tell them when you leave each night you're not going to charge them for any of your words; tell them you're going to be like your friend Al, be as free and easy as he with the Dean snapper....

Later, Mac

[Grand Blanc; Aug. 23]

Hey Mac,

Yes, we are finally back home, having avoided much of the rain from storm/depression Erin during our drive. We did, however, have a few anxious moments getting through

Houston, which seems to be a sister to New Orleans, in that a sprinkle there causes a flood of problems.

Houston had more than a sprinkle, though, from 4-8 inches of rain from Erin, and many of the freeways and their exits were under water. So we took a new tollway around the city, and had to pay $3.75 every few hundred feet. But it was worth it just to get out of harm's way.

Not all of us can count Jesus Christ as an intimate friend, so we are pretty much on our own, paying as we go....

[Oct. 6]

News happens

Hey Mac –

Well, after 65 years and two marriages, I've finally become a grandparent, plus Jess can finally add a form of parent to her list of credits, and my mother has become a great-grandparent for the first time. Let's hope she can fathom that concept....

In other news, you might already know this, but Boothies are being offered massive buyouts, to take effect at end of month. Sound like about 30 people in editorial will be taking the offer at the Journal alone.... Journal has been looking more and more like a Podunk weekly lately. I think we got out of the business at the right time.

The Grand RJs

[Oct. 6]

Dutchers,

I did not know you had become grandparents. How could I? I never hear from you people! You don't write, you don't call? For god's sake, I am out here in this remote outpost on the Kennebec? Up where Moses lost his jockstrap. What do I know?

Congratulations to Ryan and Jamie....

Haven't heard from you people in a coon's age. Whenever I don't hear from a far-flung correspondent, I suspect I must

222

have offended that party. It seldom occurs to me that correspondents have lives of their own and their activities, trivial as they seem to me, sometimes become paramount in their concerns.

So when I didn't hear from you folks in a reasonable length of time ... I figured something untoward had occurred: a collision with a grizzly bear in a national park, an argument with a psychotic ranger or birder, something of that nature....

Roger, I knew nothing about this stuff regarding the Booth people. I don't know how to put this delicately, but I don't give a rat's ass for Booth Newspapers and 97.5 percent of its current or former enablers. I was a lousy employee, but never woulda left if more of their people qualified as people.

Later, Almac

[Oct. 16]

Roger,

You wanna talk porn writing? Here's an idea for a work we could do, sort of like those Ellery Queen mysteries written by two guys in different states. Here's a "rough concept" for our first porn epic. This concept involves guy in seventies living in rigid clime, but is in no way autobiographical. This gem comes from the whole cloth, and is a work of the imaginative mind.

Anyhow, this hypothetical gaffer, let's put him in straight-laced northern New England hamlet, is widowed yet sort of interested in copping a feel (at least) now and again with a member of opposite sex. So our gaffer hits the bars and bean suppers and finds, after repeated rebuffs, that twenty-year-old chicks are not into getting it on with men with brown age spots splotching backs of hands, orifices that may spring leaks at any given moment.

So gaffer decides to forgo sex with others and please himself, if I may express masturbation in that manner, and things go along okay for a while but soon gaffer's limited stock of fantasies (Gardner, Hayworth, Turner, the early Monroe on a sewer grate) do not suffice to arouse his interests.

Disconsolate and no longer able to even satisfy himself, the poor gaffer turns to the Internet to do crossword puzzles, read science and philosophy and self-improvement blogs, come to a better understanding of the universe. Our gaffer resolves to dedicate himself to the life of the mind.

And then, wholly by accident, the well-meaning gaffer, seeking a porridge recipe on Google, mistakenly calls up "porn," stumbles on pictures of humans having all manner of sex, one with the other, or in groups. Gaffer had never sought out porn because he had always been fearful that somehow someway someone would find out he was seeking out porn.

Once, in San Francisco, our imaginary and merely prototype gaffer had been sorely tempted to enter a porn shop but did not, fearful that a friend from Flint, Michigan, might be passing by as he entered or exited.

Our fanciful gaffer, who might be referred to as a naive narrator, never watched porn during his married years, was too shy to inquire as to whether his mate might want to watch a little porn and we could even, Rog, manufacture a situation in which the gaffer was in Toronto and could not watch "Fiona on Fire" because of a feeling it would somehow be wrong to watch sex on the screen with his life companion.

Anyhow, and I hesitate to go into all the details here, Rog, our narrator discovers porn on the Internet, and learns much more about sex and its infinite possibilities than he had ever imagined in his most fevered youthful moments.

Our gaffer, our hero finds there are many many porn sites, and that the main thing a porno buff must avoid is paying these filthy porno distributors for their wares. Gaffer learns he can get enough porn for his incipient needs WITHOUT PAYING by dodging around, checking up on all the sites, getting the free samples before they ask for your credit card, then quickly exiting the site....

So here's the snapper. Soon enough, our gaffer has a staggering epiphany, an aha moment that causes him to clap his brow in wonderment.... This creature of our imagination, says to himself, hey, why don't I start a porn site strictly for old folks. Septuagenarians, octogenarians, the sky's the limit. Old wrinkled people having sex, creeping up on each other, the possibilities boggle the mind.

Shortly, our gaffer has the first porn site for older Americans and is being featured in People magazine, the AARP publication.... there may be a new career, even a new genre, for those fortunate enough to be in on the ground floor.

Of course, it might be 5:51 a.m. on a Tuesday morning in Hallowell and I may have stayed up too late.

Later, Almac

[Jan. 8, 2008, snail mail]

Dutchers,

... In a startling and quite gratifying occurrence, sisters Deborah and Sharon came to Hallowell on my birthday. They took me to lunch and brought me gifts. People sang Happy Birthday, got a slice of cake. The split or schism or, if you wish to understate, the rift, is truly over. I had seen Sharon only once in six years, so now am cool with both Debbie and Sherry....

Sherry and Debbie reported, dishearteningly, that GGAG (Grating Great Aunt Gert) remains sound as a dollar ... old people both suck and blow....

Friend Almac*

*MacLeese is a Journal humorist.

(When I first started writing a column for Journal, [an editor] thot it would be good to have a tagline that said the writer was a "humorist." So then readers would understand that the above material was funny.)

P.S.: D & S discussed at length at lunch as to whether they had what both called "The Gene." D & S feel that I have "The Gene" ... but D & S ... do not believe they can yet tell whether they have it.

"The Gene," I learned, was the one GGAG has. D & S say I got it, but humorously wonder whether I am properly nurturing it.

A storyteller's odyssey

[March 25, snail mail]

Dutchers,

... Am enclosing, as even senior citizens can tell, a copy of a recent article about my celebrity great-aunt. This article has been tacked to one of my walls ... and a friend came by and stood there reading the freaking thing. Like all my friends — and some mere acquaintances — he knows about GAG. And, commenting on the headline "Milford woman, 108, keeps on going" — he said, "That headline really rubs it in, Al." And he actually chuckled.

... I am in lousy shape, having done hardly any walking during these long winter months. Was walking miles a day, but now an amble to the free library, two blocks away, has me tuckered. And of course I keep on smoking, check the papers every day for the report declaring smoking is good for you....

Later, stay well, Almac

Roger: You asked me about my kicking the computer, did I miss the Internet access? Strangely, I haven't missed it much at all. I am reading more and watching more cable crap than is good for you.

Plain fact was the Internet and the computer offer a lot, but with my increasing inability to deftly move about on the computer, not a lot to me. I did not understand and would not learn so there was more frustration than anything else. And I found email about the only thing enjoyable, and emails, as we all know, can lead to even more frustrations.

Still, I was getting addicted to scuttling and lurking around the various sites. I don't think that, at age 77 for crissakes, I should be saddled with another addiction. But don't get me started. Mac

[Aug. 13, snail mail]

Dutchers,

... I feel like a piker when I say that the best I have been able to come up with, in re physical problems, is that I ... am prone to hematomas. I have had two hematomas, one

226

on the back of my right hand and one, for the sake of symmetry, on the back of my left hand. Now, I cannot say, like many writers say folks do, that I know this or that place like "the back of my hand." I no longer know the back of my hands. But then, in all honesty, I never really knew backs of my hands....

I am getting bald, but am not as bald as Roger. Perhaps it would be more precise to say that my hair is "thinning." ... It happens that I am becoming older; now, instead of relative strangers telling me I look ten years younger than my age, they say I look five years younger, damning me with faint praise. (GAG is homing in on 110, and if she keeps going for three more years, she will be the oldest fucking person in the world. I shit you not, this is irony beyond compare!!!! I can't bear it.)

... It is hard for me to admit this, but I have managed to infiltrate the community here, and feel at home as I have never felt — even when at "home." I have many friends here and know scores of people, mostly younger persons, and have been able to help a number of young people. Some even allege I am a "mentor." So, despite all my earlier fuck-ups, I feel as if I were atoning — and enjoying it, which I suppose is not the right mode for an atoner....

Love, Almac ...

[Dec. 19, snail mail]

Dutchers,

... Great Aunt Gert continues to grace us with her presence. On Election Day, Nov. 4, 2008, she was featured in several Connecticut papers, eagerly endorsing Sarah Palin and her running mate. Gertrude is now, as I understand it, 110. She is now a "supercentenarian." Last year, the papers billed Gert as the "oldest woman in Connecticut," but this year she is touted as the "second oldest." ... Do old people emigrate??

... An interesting facet of the GAG story is that I have not been reticent about what I consider the supreme irony of my situation vis-à-vis the venerable Gertrude Noone. In brief, why me?? ... I have often bemoaned the circumstances that are denying me my rightful heritage, my, well, my legacy.

So it is not uncommon for me, as I trudge these chartered streets to be greeted by townfolk who ask, in dry Mainer fashion: "Hey, Al, how's Great Aunt Gert doing?" My favorite response, of late, is: "She's still on the right side of the grass...."

Friend Almac

[Feb. 25, 2009, snail mail]

Dear Dutchers,

... I've been wringing my hands over the fate of our beloved news biz. Just today I learned that the S.F. Chronicle is on the brink of an El Foldo, and the New Haven Register is in the throes of bankruptcy.

I worry that the fact that I worked for both may have been a factor in their failings. I owed both papers advance money before flitting out of their respective towns. (A "moonlit flit" is what they called it in Baltimore.)

... Here's a rare victory for Joe the Consumer. When I called Time-Warner to cancel cable, I got to chatting with the T-W guy, poor-mouthed about the plight of old folks. He was sympathetic. So T-W stopped billing me four months ago but, I'm guessing, the guy who was supposed to kill cable didn't. So I'm getting free cable!!!

Great Aunt Gert Noone is well past her 110th birthday now, and a panel of gerontologists convened in Hartford last week and concluded, unanimously, that Great Aunt Gert will never ever die....

I don't know if you folks are in Michigan or Monte Carlo, but I'm figuring Grand Blanc is still your home base. I hope you guys are in good fettle. Fine fettle OK, too. I'm doing OK, in reasonable decent fettle. Took a fall on the ice last week — we are surrounded on five sides by snow — and garnered bruises, sprains and cracks, and my knees are not as dependable as of yore.

Oh, Arthur Itis has made appearances in and around my knuckles. But since I avoided athletic activity while young, I am probably in much better shape than 42-year-old NFL retirees. Am doing so well, in fact, that I recently let my doctor go. You feel bad when you let your doctor go, but, hey, this is a recession....

What is a fettle anyhow? I just looked it up, first definition is a "proper and sound condition." So a fettle is being sane, healthy and in good spirits. And two out of three probably is good enuf. I certainly hope so.

Later, Love, Almac

[May 20, snail mail]

Dutchers,

It's good to be old, Dutchers, and let me tick off some of the ways.... I was able to default on my credit cards and a piddling bank loan without fear of reprisals because I am old.... Dutchers, our greatest fear of deadbeating the predatory lenders, is that we will lose our credit. So what? I reasoned. I don't need credit cards at my stage and state of life. I have local credit, have never missed the rent for the penthouse or the tab in my restaurant across the street or my grocery store downstairs.

... the longer relatively minor ($14,000) unsecured debts go uncollected, the less chance there is they will ever be collected. So yes it is good to be old, and ... I am not only old but also alcoholic ... and a Korean War veteran who suffered a fractured skull in Boston during the height of the hostilities and am both a widower and an orphan....

I am saving money in all kinds of ways now that I am older. I saved about $1,000 by not filing income taxes. I "forget" to file because as [one even older person] advised, "They don't even check if you're over 75.... They think you are dead."

I am aware, Dutchers, that banker Jess in particular may feel that [this] advice could backfire. But ... I have come to think that snap judgments, gut feelings, are often superior to hemming and hawing. And I don't want to hear a lot of "I-told-you-so's" if I should call from federal court someday....

Good old Al

A storyteller's odyssey

[Sept. 20, snail mail]

Eagle Defecates

Dutchers,

It has been a coon's age, but I trust you all have been making it through with your usual aplomb. As for me, well, my story is both instructional and inspirational!

When I came here to Maine in Ought One, my prospects might have seemed limited, I was the new septuagenarian in town, had an income fixed by an idiot, and was further hampered by various character flaws. And I kept breaking things, an elbow here, a shoulder there, an ankle cruelly fucked with. (Yes, I know we should not end our sentences with prepositions — unless we have read Winston Churchill.)

I had one job and lost it, and got another and lost it as well, and when one considers my engagement to a Canuck nurse was aborted owing to her refusal to socialize at community bars, it faltered and then foundered, well, one might think my move to Maine might turn out badly.

But, because of my winning nature, my Great Aunt Gertrude E. Noone has seen fit to die at 110 years and 10 months and leave me a hundred large. As an ex-banker, Jessica may recognize that expression as connoting $100,000. Beaucoup scoots. Large coarse bills. I was informed of this by sister Deborah last week and will get the geedus next month. An October surprise....

Deborah, who is visiting Bailey Island this week, was here in Hallowell last week, and sought my assurance that I would not rush off to Vegas. I told her I was going to buy some CDs, do volunteer work. So, because of my ability to ingratiate and persevere, my venture to Maine has paid off, and I have yet another chance at realizing the American Dream.

I was laid up this summer with a broken shoulder, a smashed [rotator cuff], and it does not seem as if I will ever again be able to paint ceilings with my left arm, throw spiral passes or get in bar shoving matches. But I can drive, wave to passers-by.

230

As you can see from the enclosed obit, Gertrude apparently was the "world's oldest living veteran" when she passed over the shoals. Also, just three years behind the world's oldest person, a geezer of 114 from New Hampshire....

What do you do, R & J, after you have stumbled on a hundred large? Do you tell your friends? Ah, you should keep it to yourself. Of course, I could not keep it to myself, I am now a person of substance. And all because I had the courage to strike out for northern climes, even though I hate the godamned snow.

So howze by youze?

... I got a cell phone, mainly to dodge the credit-card people. Now, maybe I can settle with [them] for not much on the dollar. Not much or very little.

Later, Love, Al

[Sept. 25, snail mail]

Hey Mac,

Cutting to the chase, Jessica says the prudent thing to do is to send her the money and she will put it in CDs, etc., and dole it out to you when you can prove to her that you have a legitimate need....

We were sorry to hear of GAG's passing. We were hoping that she could make it to be the oldest. Period. She seemed like a spunky sort. I'm sure you had more mixed feelings, some of them involving aid to your younger generation.

Four days after GAG died, we got the news that my mom died in her nursing home in Texas.... At the end she seemed content and was convinced all her dead relatives and friends were staying with her in her "hotel." She didn't recognize me the first two days we visited her in February and she didn't recognize Jessica at all. Then about two weeks later, she called [my sister] Jessica. Such is life with dementia....

We had her body flown north for burial in Dutchland on the west side of the state. Services were last Saturday....

Good to hear from you, my friend,

Roger

[Sept. 30, snail mail]

Embarrassment of Riches

Dutchers:

Chastened by Jessica's admonitions about CDs, I met with sister Deborah in Hallowell today, and we progressed to the Savings Bank of Maine on Winthrop Street. There, Deborah and I purchased two CDs worth 50 large each. CDs for me!!

And then, with an insouciance born of my long unrecognized nobility, I told this banker, a French-American, that I would put the other $25,000 into my checking account — just in case I needed walking-around money.

I can hear the Dutchers now declaiming, "He said he only got a hundred thousand scoots." Well, yes, I did. But then I got a telephone call from my beloved sister Deborah, in which I was informed that my share of the loot (or swag or booty) was $125,000 rather than a less satisfying $100,000.

... earlier I had been told that I had a hundred thousand coming, and in less than a week I accumulated $25,000 more and that perhaps wonders never would cease.

One of my CDs, Jess, is for a year and the other one is for nine months. The usual rate of return applies: a mere 1.2 or 1.05, but we are more concerned here with keeping this money out of immediate reach.

After Deborah and I left the bank, we had lunch at Hattie's restaurant on Water Street. Deborah and I discussed this and that, and then she confided that in a few months, [I would get] "about ten thousand more." Something to do with closing out the trust....

Anyhow, today, it would appear that I have made $10,000 more to add on to the $125,000 I skillfully raked in earlier. I am thinking about opening up shop as a financial consultant – that I could improve my lot in such a short time and in such dramatic fashion must mean my future lies in an area in which my financial acumen can be used to help others. I need to give something back.

More later, but, as a former newsperson, I felt constrained to update this running story on my financial comeback, a story with legs.

Later, Mac

[Nov. 11]

Hey Mac —

Just making sure I have your right [email] address. I'm attaching two pictures of an Oden Island cottage that we had occasion to visit (prowl about outside, really) last month and commiserate about, because we didn't have enough money to buy when it was put up for sale by some couple about 30 years ago. Hope you still recognize it.

Roger

[Nov. 13]

Hi, there,

And yes I got the pics of the horrible rundown condition of my beloved cottage on Oden Island. Believe you me, when I was ramrodding things out there on the island, the cottage was appropriately ramshackle, truly shabby but inoffensive, with none of those artsy-fartsy obscenely clean, even Nordic, fine sharp lines.

Once I tried to fix a faulty faucet at my beloved retreat, and cut my hand, bled copiously, and never thereafter did anything to disturb the natural beauty all around me. But this note is more in the nature of a test — can I possibly finish an email without somehow either losing the copy through awkward numbness of my left hand, or, perhaps, sending this block of words to a warehouse in Walla Walla, Wash.

Have written several emails to the vandutchers and sister Deborah, and one or two got through, you know, like hardy sperm. By the way, you should not think, R. and J., that this admitted ineptness, is entirely due to incipient dementia ... a purposeful mind-alterer never knows whether his declining faculties are due to normal aging or abnormal using. Well, I think I am pushing the envelope, although the more I type without untoward incident, the more confident I get. Guess it's like riding a bicycle.

Later, Almac

[Dec. 18, snail mail]

Dutchers.

This is my yule card, the only one Finley and I are sending out this year. Did I tell you Faraday died two months ago at 18? So Finley is the last of the F-Troop.

Yes, [Jeff] Daniels played a Noone. I read "Blood Work" long before movie came out. It was a mystery by Michael Connelly, an Irisher just like the Noones. Saw movie on reruns. I figured Connelly's family was outsmarted by Noones over the years in the Auld Sod and used this means to get even. (No Noone has ever committed a crime as far as is known.)

Sounds bad about your brother, Roger, but I must say R2J2 [family] looked pretty good in that pic you sent. I am sending a pic of me in a bathtub (deep background) and Finley is the cat in black standing by the terlet bowl while Faraday is fleeing the scene in the foreground....

Regarding the loot flowing northward subsequent to the demise in the family: As I boasted earlier, [I already] got 125 large [and was] advised there would be more, a few thou perhaps, but it turned out [I] have $18,000 more coming....

I mention this because there always has been a possibility that I might retain Jessica in some kind of (minor) advisory capacity as I try to control this flood of cash. But the hoard is growing too large to entrust any of it in the hands of someone living in the state of Michigan with its high unemployment, rising crime and poverty on all sides, shoppers for newspapers, Detroit disappearing.

The necessity of adding twenty grand to my funds is onerous, and I must abashedly deposit another twenty. You will notice I have upgraded the latest unsolicited bundle to twenty grand rather than something less resounding. Unfortunately, this chunk is capital gains and taxable, unlike the first batch.

So, I spent three days at the IRS in Augusta this week. Paid taxes for the four years I forgot to file — '05, '06, '07, '08. My bill: $735. That's pretty cheap but I got discounts and break on penalties because of my earnest desire to set things aright, but also owing to the fact that I brought my attorney along. Oh, you didn't know I had an attorney? Don't all thousandaires have attorneys?

… Hope you guys have a good year and many more to follow.

Later, Al

[Grand Blanc; Jan. 10, 2010]

Hey Mac,

… We are still up north waiting for [brother] Ted to get an operation for the melanoma on his back….

Jessica says she still hasn't seen any of that money you allege you have acquired. She's saving a lot of coffee cans, so she can bury them in the spring. Just needs something to put in them.

RJ

[Jan. 16]

I, too, can own a friggin condo

Dutchers:

I have purchased a condominium just off Second Street in Hallowell. This condo, that I picked up for 72.5, is smack under the condo in which I resided when first I fetched up in Hallowell…. And it was [sisters] Deborah and Sharon who directed me to this condo vacancy.

Deborah and Sharon and I were observing the historic occasion of my 79th birthday at Hattie's Chowder House on Water Street, when Sharon declaimed I should get a condo at ground-level else I would soon break more bones climbing two flights of stairs several times daily, stairs that daunt even youngish Mainers.

A storyteller's odyssey

Long story short: Sharon unilaterally contacted realty office, found a condo downtown that suited the needs of a gimpy oldster....

Jess, of course, has never realized the true fiscal craftiness that I possess, so artfully do I pretend to not understand matters dealing with money. This condo that I got for 72.5 was first marketed 18 months ago for $150,000. Cannily, like a good old Scot, I bided my time, then acted. After, of course, being notified by a smart sister.

Jess, this is just another example of how ... you can thrive even in these recessionary times. Now I am both a thousandaire and a condo owner. Yet I do not feel my friends should truckle and kneel, scrape and bow.

On serious note, hope the situation with Ted is as easeful as can possibly be.

Later, almac

[Kalamazoo MI; Feb. 6]

Heading south, finally

... Ted had his operation(s) on Wednesday and, good news, the preliminary biopsy on his armpit lymph node was negative. Surgeon said 90 percent of the time the preliminary result turns out to be the final. So we are happy....

Roger

[May 25]

Dutchers,

... am back on the email circuit; I have been absent for reasons that would both baffle and bemuse normal humans such as yourselves.

Suffice to say I now have my very own recreational room in my upscale condo in central Hallowell, far removed from the seamy underbelly of this hardscrabble rivertown.

So I now have my laptop on a desk, and an ergonomic chair on a mat that stops me from rolling around the hardwood floor on these godamned casters and a lighting situation that allows me to read the keys on the fricking computer. Heretofore, I could not operate this machine for reasons you would not find plausible.

... as I venture further and further into my dotage, all of a sudden I get a UTI. I did not know what a UTI was until I got one, and it reminded me of the saying we had aboard the USS Allagash regarding those of us who were loose enough in our conduct to contract what was then, in medical terminology, referred to as a dose of the clap. We the afflicted would chant: "Break off a leg, don't hurt; break off an arm, don't hurt; but when I pee, ooo-ooo-ooo."

Hope it's all good with the Dutchers, and all is reasonably OK here although Finley is getting to be a pain in the ass, making unreasonable meows. Sometimes I think Finley and me are in a race toward dementia, but, then we're both fairly hardy....

[Grand Blanc; June 6]

A big oil slick of bad news

Hey Mac,

... we have booked a couple beachy places in which to camp [RV] in Florida this winter, and were also planning to stay at the state park in Gulf Shores, but the tentacles of Big Oil have already reached Gulf Shores and they are nearing two of our Florida sites near Apalachicola. BP says not to worry, they'll have everything cleaned up by this weekend, or some such blather....

The bad news closer to home is that we had to put Pumpkin to sleep a few days ago. She was crying like a baby at night ... and acting strange.... Like standing with her nose in a corner. Like walking around in circles endlessly. The vet now says she probably had a brain tumor.... she almost made it to 14, which is the usual lifespan for Welsh terriers.... So we are still hearing her bark to be let out at night and remembering better times, when she was seemingly always ready to play and eat the leavings of whatever salad Jess was preparing.

So how is your last holdout from the F-troop ... ? How old is he/she? ...

RJ minus P

[June 13]

Dutchers,

Yes, I really know what you feel about Pumpkin, few humans, I suspect, engender the kind of love we can share with "lesser" beings. After Connie died, I had eight cat companions. Now, what with one thing and another, it's down to Finley, who, I will have you know is a male and named for a town in Wales. Why Wales? Because the town's name started with an F.... I think, but am not sure, that Finley is coming up on nineteen. Or, at least eighteen.

He is in remarkably good shape except he cannot leap up to the bathroom sink anymore to drink from the tap — which I keep open at a seep for him, because he will yowl until I lift him up to swill from the tap. [He] has water on the floor, of course, but four or five times a day he needs a drink and I can relate to that. Anyhow, he'll commence to yowl and I must lift him up.

Also, he hogs the right arm of my recliner, making it difficult for me to read, do crosswords or eat from my bowl. Finley eats from my bowl, obsessively licks the pages of whatever I am reading, and also licks the outsides of the cans or bottles from which I may be trying to drink from. Also, when I am feeling down he knows it and comforts me although cynics would say I am misguided to believe that.

Held off on responding to your most recent post because of an awareness that the oil spill seems to have asked itself, "Hey, where do you want to ooze ashore first on the Redneck Riviera? Orange Beach? Gulf Shores? ... Or maybe the Florida Panhandle, where the peripatetic Dutchers reputedly are heading.

Feel like the spill is too bad for me to make light of or lip off about.... it's bigger than the Gulf, which has become an abyss....

Later, Al

UNLEASHED

[Aug. 29]

Dutchers,

... Had been off the sauce and the bud and the nicotine for a spell, but fell off three wagons on the same day, and it proved to be so inspiriting that when I got your email I resolved to respond though incapacitated. What the hell, besottedness never stopped 98 percent of those who scrawl from so doing....

In the Navy, me and a couple of other improvident tars used to go around bumming loose change to go on liberties because we were always broke about eight hours after payday. Six or seven bucks in loose change went a long way when your only purchases on the beach were dime drafts....

... I haven't gotten out of Maine for years, but have been to Bar Harbor, Fort Kent, Bangor, Portland, Boothbay and Skowhegan, and thirty-some towns I disremember because I was traveling with the then-state poet laureate.

And a couple of weeks ago I traveled to Moosehead Lake, 150 miles northwest of Hallowell, with a local group. We stayed at historic Maine hunting camp.... Original camp was shipped to a world's fair in Chicago back when. Saw otters, beavers, loons and one lousy moose. But platoons of loons.

We went motoring for moose at night along the lake, and all I found was if I asked ... to stop so I could go micturate ... I would then fall and sprain and strain my right wrist and forearm, which is already sick and tired of breaking falls....

Mac

[Oct. 10]

Dutchers,

... Finley ... 19 years old on our time and 92 on his clock ... is remarkably spry, a glossy black and white tuxedo, and acts as if he thinks I am Mohammed.

Non cat people are unaware of this, but the story goes that the founder of Islam was a cat person. One day Mohammed was sitting around in the sixth century ... with his best feline

239

friend (BFF) when he had the urge to urinate. His BFF was sitting on the sleeve of his pricey robe so, as not to disturb the ... cat, Mohammed used his knife to cut his sleeve and hied off to relieve himself....

Later, Almac

[Oct. 31]

Dutchers,

I have been misrepresenting myself for these many years, just learned my surname is McAleese, not MacLeese, as I've been spelling it, or as McLeese, as my old man spelled it, and that I am some sort of a jackleg relative to the president of Ireland, Mary McAleese, who is not a true McAleese, but a lass named Lenaghan who married a dentist-accountant name of Martin McAleese.

(The fierce McAleese clan used to include scribes, war correspondents, back in the day, but now numbers accountants and dentists. And failed columnists.) Also, McAleese is the monicker my predecessors ... used when they sidled ashore in Maine and New Brunswick.

Key thing here, Dutchers and Scotchers, is my previous belief I was a bit of a Scot seems largely untrue, although those barbarians did seem to mix a lot. And it is my own belief the only differences between peoples on the British Isles is their accents and preferences for sporting. Still, as it now stands, I may be all Irish, and that does not bode well.

In one swell foop, then, I have learned that both my ancestries are other than I had assumed. The confusion is understandable. My parents never discussed ancestry, and professed to be English. This was back when NINA was in help-wanted ads: No Irish Need Apply.

You'd think it would have occurred to me when I was a kid to inquire as to the significance of the Mac in front of Leese. You'd think that, ... but you would be wrong. My feeling was akin to today's catchword: "Whatever." We eschewed ethnic pride. We didn't have much to be proud of....

Later, McAleese

I think

[Nov. 6]

Hey Mac, or should I say, Mick?

I've been thinking about it, and ... we can put up with an Ir-shm-n. I might have to ask for that anatomically correct Scot doll back, though. And why did we go to Toronto to eat haggis? The world is all upside down....

In the wake of Drudge's disclosure that Obama is spending $200 mil a day for his trip, more than the war in Afghanistan is costing, I feel I should ask the source of your discovery. You didn't say how ... you learned this McAleese allegation....

From the Flemish RJs

[Nov. 9]

Dutchers,

It was inexcusable, not citing my sources on McAleese shocker, although understandable, me being a former newspaper writer. Still, I seem to have a relatively good source — a relative, one of my sister Joan's children [Pam, who] has spent a lot of time researching and writing about the McLeese and Noone families. I saw her reports, all well sourced....

I have recovered from my initial shock of losing my Scotchness. It was good being a person of both Scot and Irish heritage: I could go on a lot of cheap drunks, and rationalize it on grounds that I was reflecting my Scot (cheap fuckers) and Irish (irresponsible sots) descent, and was only human anyway.

In truth, the seeming shocker that I am a McAleese rather than a McLeese or a MacLeese, is small beer. Have always known about variants in spelling of my surname, but [Pam's] research was first to establish the utter Irishness of my situation, which was already fragile, owing to aging and drinking and smoking ... and dithering....

Finley and I have just gone through a hellish week. Several months ago I started letting him go outside after years of being housebound. He enjoyed freedom, didn't run off, and all was well until it became apparent he had picked up fleas, and pretty soon the whole place was infested, and Finley's flea collar was only sending the fleas to me. So I bought a fogger kit and set "fog bombs" off and we had to leave for several hours. Now, two days later, it appears that all fleas ... have been wiped out....

Later, Paddy

[Nov. 11]

Dutchers,

Roger suggested I should surrender the anatomically correct Scot I got in Toronto [since] I've discovered the brute truth about my true heritage. This is not going to happen. As I laboriously peck away at this machine, the Scot, who has a schnozz bigger than his organ, is peering over the top of my laptop, perched on a stack of paperbacks.

We have been together for quite a spell.

Several years ago a young woman was in my residence. She was in her twenties, as a matter of fact, and lissome and quite attractive. A singer, a performer, at local venues. I, and that's just me, would categorize her as a hottie. Me, being an older party, was, I guess, in her estimation, just a nice gaffer....

In any case, as she was leaving, she noticed the little Scot, and said: "Aw, isn't he cute." She tousled his tam.

"Yeah," I said. "and check under his kilt."

She did, and said "Aw" again and kissed his member and flounced out the door.

This was one of my closest brushes with sex since right after 9-11.

So, no, you cannot reclaim the Scot just because I've disowned him and his ilk.

Samuel Johnson said a Scot child, if caught early, probably could be domesticated. I'm glad that now I am Irish, and it looks like soft winds at my back from here on.

Paddy

Part 8: 'Santa killer'

In 1974, with printer jobs being phased out as the lead-type era at the Flint Journal ended, Bob DeLand transferred from composing room to copy desk on a trial basis.

It was a foreign environment for DeLand; he said he "didn't have a clue" about copy editing and headline writing, and he turned to MacLeese, the copy desk chief and a part-time columnist at the time.

"I asked Mac to jot down a few pointers that might help me," DeLand said.

MacLeese went far beyond a few tips. A man without mentors in his own life, he embraced the challenge of mentoring DeLand and others.

During a weekend at the cottage on Oden Island, MacLeese wrote what DeLand called an extensive two-part manual for editing stories and writing heads. DeLand showed it to the managing editor, who proclaimed it "the best damned thing he ever saw." He gave MacLeese a $50 bonus before distributing copies to the editorial staff.

Instead of facing the loss of his job in the paper's shift to computer-generated type, DeLand saw his six-month trial turn into a new career that lasted 24 years. "I owe it all to Al MacLeese. Mac was my salvation."

The following year, MacLeese wrote a column that propelled him into a career shift of his own and created a national stir. His Santa column helped gain him the job of full-time columnist at the Journal.

The column, "The truth about Santa that doesn't hurt," was skylined on the front page a week before Christmas. It was a response to a letter received by the newspaper from two 9-year-old girls named Gretchen and Stacy. The letter, asking if there really is a Santa Claus, made its way to MacLeese's desk.

"Dear Gretchen and Stacy," the column began. "It would be very easy for me to start this letter to you by simply saying, 'Yes, Gretchen and Stacy, there is a Santa Claus.' But I am not going to do that.

"I probably would do that if you were 'little kids' and weren't beginning to understand things. But you have shown that you are not 'little kids' by writing that letter to the Journal. Your letter shows you have taken the first step toward being 'grown-ups' or adults.... A lot of people just believe anything that is told to them and don't bother to ask questions. People like that aren't grown-ups, not really....

"Because you are acting like adults, I am going to treat you like adults and answer in the way I would any grown-up....

"Let's go back in history, 1,000 years ago, to a man – a real man – named Nicholas.... This man, this real man, did many good things for people. He didn't give Christmas presents to children, but he was so loved by the people that, after his death, they made him a 'saint.' ...The people began observing Saint Nicholas' birthday by doing the kind of things he did. Making other persons happy, especially their children.

"In one place in Europe, people began giving their children gifts on this saint's birthday and telling the children the gifts were from Saint Nicholas. Now that was both true and untrue.... It was true because the exchanging of gifts can be traced to Saint Nicholas. It was untrue because the real Saint Nicholas was dead.

"As the years passed, Saint Nicholas was given many names in many countries. In our country, as you know, he is called Santa Claus....

"Question: Is there a real man named Santa Claus who lives at the North Pole and visits children on Christmas Eve with a sleigh full of toys?

"No, Gretchen and Stacy, there is no such man.

"Does that answer hurt? Make you angry at those who have told you this is true? Make you feel that Christmas is spoiled? If it does, maybe you had better stop and think. The way you did when you wrote the Journal. Ask yourselves why would anybody – your parents, perhaps – tell you that such a man was real and coming this Christmas if it weren't true?

"Could it be that this was their way of showing their love for you by telling you a beautiful story and making it come true? Of showing you the joy of giving? Could it be that they wanted to share a wonderful world of 'make-believe'? Could it be that they remember when they lived, ever so briefly, in that world? Before they, too, started asking questions and going about the business of growing up?

"Now, let's ask your question again. Is there a Santa Claus?

"Yes, Gretchen and Stacy, there is, at least for the more fortunate children in our world. This Santa has a lot of names. Mother. Father. Uncle. Friend. Grandmother. Grandfather. And fortunate children can prove this Santa is real. They can just reach out and touch.

"Oh, one more thing, Gretchen and Stacy. Pretty soon there should be two more Santas around. Real ones. Their names are Gretchen and Stacy."

The Associated Press sent MacLeese's column to its more than 1,200 subscribing newspapers, and many printed it in full, sparking an enormous reaction, both pro and con.

Many parents read the column to their children. Some congratulated MacLeese for the way he handled a delicate problem. Others cut it out and put it away for when their children were older.

There also were protests, both written and by phone, that the column hurt children and ruined Christmas. He was called "that idiot" and Scrooge. One suggestive message came in the form of photo of a bare male exterior topped by a sprig of mistletoe. Others told him he had no conscience. "There were some 'drop dead' letters, too," he said. One woman wanted him fired.

One paper that printed the column was the Stars and Stripes, the paper aimed at military readers around the globe. MacLeese's niece, Joan's daughter Pamela, saw the column when she was living in Germany.

245

"I picked up a copy [and on the] front page, I read, Alan MacLeese. Too cool, living 5,000 miles from home and right there in front of me ... Alan's literary talents."

On "NBC Nightly News," however, anchorman John Chancellor reported on the column but didn't give the whole story.

Chancellor contrasted the column with a famous 1897 editorial in the New York Sun that said: "Yes, Virginia, there is a Santa Claus." MacLeese, Chancellor said, concluded that "No, Gretchen and Stacy, there is no such man."

MacLeese drafted a telegram to send to Chancellor:

"Dear John, Scrooge is not alive and well in Flint, Mich. ... Your brief commentary – which I concede may have been hard to resist – indicated that nobody around NBC read the [entire column].... In short, I did not club the kiddies. But there are plenty of folks evidencing a desire to club me after your, shall we say, succinct commentary. Merry Christmas, Alan N. MacLeese."

Chancellor later revisited his commentary on the air.

In his Journal story about the brouhaha created by the column, Daniel L. Dolan wrote this about the author: "MacLeese is no ogre, eager to destroy children's dreams. He is even-tempered and kindly, for a copy desk chief, and generous enough to give one the shirt from his back, if he could handle the buttons."

The last was an allusion to MacLeese being a fumble-fingers with an earned reputation for ineptitude in matters of daily living. He expanded that reputation in his column, writing about being confounded by the simplest of tasks, such as finding his way to work or locating the gas cap on a car.

He also had difficulty drinking coffee sans spillage, a problem made more noticeable amid a trend toward a new order in newsrooms.

By the time he arrived at the Journal, MacLeese said, "a ghastly and highly perceptible change came over newspaper editorial departments. People began getting concerned with neatness.... Stamping out cigarettes on the floor near your desk – or just tossing the butts over your shoulder – was no longer an acceptable practice.

"Still, life-long habits die slowly, particularly when you have no driving desire to change them. I continued my cruddy behavior and this inspired comments [ranging] from blunt warnings such as 'Stop throwing cigarette butts and paper and coffee cups and matchbooks and other stuff on the floor, MacLeese,' to snide comments, archly made, 'Do you do this sort of thing at home?'"

MacLeese described Flint as "determinedly macho" and "a shot-and-beer town where a drink with foliage in it might provoke a manly shot to the chops."

But in the Flint Journal, as in newspapers nationwide, a severe change was in the offing in the 1970s, a change that turned him into a vestige of another era. And yet, many of his same qualities made him treasured as a survivor, an enduring newsroom character.

"Editorial departments," he wrote, "became clean places with rugs. The rugs totally defeated me, along with a number of other dedicated slobs. You cannot grind out a butt with the heel of your shoe, no matter how base your instincts, on a rug.

"Somewhere in the vastness of the Flint Journal, there must be a shabby, ill-favored, rug-less room. Isolated and craving a workman able to match its lack of class. Perhaps someday they will lead me off to this room. To work, I hope."

Four months after the Santa column appeared, MacLeese won a first-place award from the Michigan Associated Press, besting columnists from the other larger state papers including those in Detroit. One of the three columns he submitted was the Santa column.

In June of 1976, he became a full-time columnist for the Journal, writing three columns a week under the title "MacLeese Unleashed."

Aside from writing about Santa and other issues, he often told stories, writing frankly about his life and his demons, with a highly personal style. Using wry, self-deprecating humor, he translated his experiences into entertaining columns.

Two months later, he wrote another column that was nationally distributed by the Associated Press in which he satirically suggested that Ohio State football coach Woody Hayes be enclosed in a cage on wheels before, during and after that team's football games. "It was my tongue-in-cheek reasoning that this would curb Hayes's penchant for striking out at reporters, sideline markers, etc."

The column struck a nerve, especially in the state of Ohio. One letter writer from that state suggested MacLeese was a "yellow, yellow journalist." Another said he was cruel.

MacLeese responded: "There is a fine line in humorous writing, or, if you prefer, allegedly humorous writing, and most writers can sense where that line is. You do not make fun of the weak, the vulnerable, the troubled. A phrase that is apt tells it all: You don't shoot fish in a barrel. Woody the arrogant is not a fish and he is not in a barrel. For heaven's sake, I can't even get him in a cage!"

In an early 1977 "New Year's" column, he made one "little resolution." Noting that a man once said a newspaperman should comfort the afflicted and afflict the comfortable, he added: "If through the use of this space, I can in a small way do something along those lines, so be it hereby resolved."

As for his personal habits, he said "people keep telling me that my body is a temple and I should take better care of it. Exercise, jog, join a cross-country wolf-killing club, etc. Bosh. I became 46 years old (on Jan 5) and, since I didn't figure to make it this far, am content to kind of mosey along without advice."

MacLeese took note of nonsmokers who were on the muscle about that nasty habit, and a Time magazine article in 1976 quoted a portion of one of his columns about the topic.

In his column he said nonsmokers "could get so powerful that one day they'd have us all up before firing squads. And not allow the traditional courtesy of a last cigarette on grounds that it is harmful to our health."

In February of 1978, however, he did resolve to quit smoking for the first time since high school graduation, after months of finding himself "gasping in the manner of a beached whale after trudging up a mere flight of stairs."

He shredded his ever-present pack of Benson & Hedges, and he reported he had made it seven days without smoking. "And even as I write these words – the first words I have ever written for a newspaper without a cigarette smoldering close to hand – my weak and traitorous right hand darts toward the shirt pocket. The empty shirt pocket. It's empty, wretched talon, let it be."

The pocket didn't remain empty long. He reintroduced himself to Benson and to Hedges.

As a newspaperman and a columnist, he didn't just comment on the likes of Santa Claus and Woody Hayes from afar. He had introductions to the famous.

He recounted the time he one-upped Milton Berle during the old jokester's stopover in Flint for a series of Vegas-style shows.

MacLeese was interviewing Uncle Miltie when Berle reached forward to finger the lapel of a Journal photographer's suitcoat.

"That's a nice suit you've got there," Berle said, "Who shines it for you?"

MacLeese said he could not be stifled, and he said to Berle: "That's a nice suit YOU'VE got there. Does it come in your size?"

MacLeese wrote: "Berle didn't even laugh, looked upon me as Dean Martin may have squinted at Jerry Lewis. The man is without humor."

He had other tenuous ties to stars. He recalled "painful leg cramps from interviewing Sophia Loren while crouched at her feet" and how an associate of Phyllis Diller "invited me to go home with him. (It could have been worse. Phyllis Diller could have invited me to go home with her.)"

On his own homefront, his relationship with his devoted wife was severely tested in the late 1970s.

Connie considered filing for divorce after learning he had an affair with a waitress in Flint. "She was hurt and she asked him to leave," according to Betty Hansen, then a columnist for the Saginaw News. Connie was her best friend.

They separated for several months, with him living in a walk-up apartment near the Journal. As was often true after one of his monumental screw-ups, he was filled with remorse. He realized how much he had lost. He desperately wanted back with Connie, and she eventually decided to let him return.

They were "very much in love" in spite of his flaws, Betty said.

Betty first met Connie on a slow Saturday at The News. They sat and talked. Connie said her husband was an alcoholic, and Betty said hers was, too, adding, "mine's a sleepy drunk." Connie said: "So is Al."

They talked every day after that from 1968 to 1981, when Betty left for California, and they kept in touch on a regular basis during her 12 years there.

Betty said that she "really liked Al," even when he was drinking, and that when her husband, Herb, died from cirrhosis of the liver in 1976, MacLeese said the right things to her and was more helpful at that time than Connie.

"I was angry, he calmed me down."

MacLeese told her alcoholism is an addiction, and he said Herb was lucky because he was a well-functioning alcoholic who never got arrested, just came home and got drunk and fell asleep.

Betty said she was not aware of Connie ever crying about Al's alcoholism. "She'd just take care of him. It did get her down and she worried about him all the time." Betty described Connie as a rock and a very nurturing person for him.

Back home with Connie and the cats, MacLeese came up with the idea to sponsor a Flint Journal Fat Cat Contest in a downtown park. He said the idea came to him while he was watching their huge cat

Spike, a 23-pounder, lounging on top of the television set. (He probably was aware, too, that Miami Herald humor columnist Larry Thompson sponsored one in 1965.)

A Journal article describing the event said: "What began as something of a put-on evidently caught the spirit of the community, an exhausted but pleased MacLeese said.... About 800 people attended, along with more than 140 cats."

Along with his cats, words were precious to him, and he handled them with care in his columns, down to the last line.

One of his better columns and most memorable closers was written in 1980 about Cookie Wascha and her car, a 1968 Ford Galaxie convertible, the car Laura "Cookie" Holt drove north from Kentucky to her first job, at the Flint Journal, where she and MacLeese became colleagues.

Cookie married Don Wascha in 1970. By 1975, the convertible had become decidedly less snazzy; it even had mushrooms growing under the back seat, a result of the top being down during a heavy rain. That year, Don came home and told his wife that he had sold the clunker for $50.

Cookie immediately said: "OK, where's the $50?"

The sale of the car became a bone of contention as the months passed, to the point where it became an open secret that Don was getting the car restored as a surprise. But still no car. There were problems with the restoration, and Don finally told Cookie that he had been offered $3,000 for the car as is, and he had taken the money and ran. Cookie thought: "Well, shoot, where's the $3,000?" That was in 1978.

Don now is promising her a mysterious, wonderful gift, which never comes. In June of 1980, five years after the car disappeared from Cookie's life, Don asks the family to go to the front lawn so he can take pictures for their daughter Amy's birthday.

Someone then drives up to the house in a restored Ford Galaxie, the one that was sold 12 years earlier, MacLeese wrote, "to a young woman named Laura Holt, who standing on the lawn, screams and screams again. And blurts:

"Thaa-aa-tt's m-m-my car.... Th-aaa-aat's my car."

"It was," MacLeese concluded, "and it was from Wascha, with love."

His column was on a roll. But on Oct. 16, 1981, a change in editors at the Journal had a devastating impact on the column and long-range consequences for MacLeese personally.

MacLeese went from working for a simpatico editor, Ray Stephens, who enjoyed "MacLeese Unleashed" and its free-wheeling style, to an editor, Alfred L. Peloquin, who put a leash on it.

Like MacLeese, Stephens often poked a stick in the eye of the establishment, and this was considered to be one reason he was pushed aside, ostensibly "to pursue a business opportunity."

Dan Gearino was hired as a reporter under Stephens, and after his arrival, he "settled into something pretty close to surrogate son status."

Gearino said he and Stephens talked a lot about the people in the newsroom, and "Ray loved Al MacLeese. Al was the perfect columnist for Ray: an unpolished, fearless guy with a knack for piercing hypocrisy and being funny while he did it.

"But however great Al was for Ray, it worked the other way around, too. I think Al stayed sober for a long time because he knew Ray didn't tolerate fuck-ups."

Gearino said he thinks MacLeese was doomed when Stephens was forced out and Peloquin came in. "A lot of old scores were settled in that time. Peloquin knew MacLeese was one of Ray's favorites, so he maneuvered him out of the columnist spot – not by outright reassignment, but instead by placing restrictions on the column that he knew MacLeese wouldn't accept. So it was off to the copy desk for Al."

As for Peloquin, he soon gained a reputation for cultivating the powers-that-be in Flint. He re-established relationships that had frayed in the Stephens regime.

Dave Vizard, a Journal reporter and editor during the Peloquin era, said Peloquin was determined "to set a new tone and style for the paper after Stephens left. He wanted Mac to be more positive and uplifting in his approach to column writing in general and in regard to Flint in particular."

For a columnist whose best work often was about grittier details of his life – a suicide attempt, a bizarre escapade or dealing with the reality of alcoholism – the new commandments were crushing. They seemed aimed at stilling his voice. He didn't feel free to write about the essence of his being.

Before the arrival of Peloquin, who was once a seminarian, MacLeese could tweak the local establishment and write about non-local experiences, such as spending time at Brighton Hospital, "where alcoholics go to try to stop drinking."

He could write about the idiosyncrasies of the hospital, where, he said, patients were urged "by some counselors to 'make some eye contact' while strolling through the hall or heading for the pool table, where the latest (and shakiest) arrivals could be hustled for laundry change.

"Try to picture, if you will, about 55 alkies skipping about one asylum trying to make eye contact. For a day or so, the place was the most open, most sincere, most concerned building in Michigan, with the possible exception of the state Capitol. This activity continued until everybody involved was getting ... quite suspicious of this eye contact on demand...."

Peloquin also was production-oriented, and he may have thought a full-time columnist, no matter how popular, was a luxury the Journal couldn't afford. The sequence of events lends weight to this.

"MacLeese Unleashed" was running three days a week, usually Monday-Wednesday-Friday, anchored at the bottom of the Back Page, when Peloquin took over. Two weeks later, on Nov. 2, an Editor's Note on the Back Page said "Al MacLeese has been granted, at his request, a temporary leave from his duties as columnist."

A month later, on Nov. 29, in his "Letter from the Editor" column, Peloquin noted that "readers have written in to inquire about why the MacLeese column has not appeared in recent weeks.

"The author, Al MacLeese, has ... asked to have a short leave while he recharged his batteries, as it were. So he is now working on the Journal's copy desk. But come Jan. 1, 1982, you'll be seeing his columns again, if perhaps not as often as in the past."

The month of January came and went with no "MacLeese Unleashed." February passed. No column.

This was a turbulent period for MacLeese psychologically. He later referred to an "alcoholic slip" around February. One coworker remembered more than a mere slip. Kim Crawford recalled MacLeese having at least a couple "spectacular falls off the wagon" during his "period of extreme unhappiness, anger, depression."

(On a brighter note during this period, MacLeese reconnected with his son. A few months after Doug's 18th birthday in 1981, he came to Michigan to spend time with the MacLeeses over the Christmas holiday. There is a photo of Al and Doug enjoying an Atari game. The next year, Doug would join them on a trip to Miami.

(In 1995, Al and Connie attended Doug's marriage, and two years later the couples exchanged visits that included a successful salmon fishing trip out of Tawas City on Lake Huron. Al and Connie expressed delight that they were "becoming closer to Doug after many years of estrangement.")

UNLEASHED

On Friday, March 26, 1982, a short paragraph on Page One announced that "Mac is back" and said: "After an extended hiatus, the Journal's Al MacLeese will again be writing a column. It will appear on Saturday's Back Page...."

On Saturday, his column appeared with a logo that said "Al MacLeese." The headline was "Some disjointed mutterings from unchained scribe."

"As I was saying," MacLeese wrote, "life is difficult or at best not a bowl of cherries; leastwise that's my recollection of what I was saying when last I columnized for the Journal in Autumn '81 of the Instantly Egregious Eighties.

"Now I need to again attain the fine anger or awed appreciation or smug satisfaction or humorous indignation or clever disdain or resigned exasperation of those in the columnizing dodge. Idea is that I'll write a column on the Back Page every Saturday....

"Thought is that I'll write about people, places and things in Genesee County. But today I merely disjointedly mutter because lately I haven't been around and about and have no notes from which to incorrectly translate misperceptions....

"Thing is, I've been chained to a writing machine on the Flint Journal copy desk, where stories are edited and headlines written.... Yes, the copy desk, the best of all so-so worlds.

"I hope occasionally to complain on Saturdays, maybe squeeze in a column attacking mimes before I perish. I have never heard of anyone attacking mimes and never done so myself and heaven knows where I found the restraint."

If he sounds peevish in the column, the likely cause is that he felt Peloquin breathing down his neck, restricting his column to Genesee County when he enjoyed relating events to his adventures around the state, the country and the world.

In his memos to the staff, Peloquin usually signed with his initials, alp. In a reflection of MacLeese's attitude toward Peloquin, he later referred to alp as the "lowest mountain in all of North America."

Although Mac was back writing a column, it was not "MacLeese Unleashed" and it was only once a week, on, horror of horrors, Saturday.

As MacLeese wrote, "Saturday's newspaper has always been 'Saturday's child,' poor neglected little shaver. Far too few people read the paper on Saturday. Most citizens are out deftly dismembering teeny panfish or tearing up the landscape in recreational vehicles or puttering around the cistern...."

A storyteller's odyssey

Looking at his weekly columns, they are definitely less inspired, with less of the creative flash and edgy brashness that attracted readers when he was a full-time columnist.

While "chained" to the copy desk as his primary job , MacLeese found time to be a mentor. Doug Sanders remembers him for a pep talk and a handful of words of advice.

Sanders said he was "swimming in some pretty deep water" when he was hired as a reporter at the Flint Journal. He said he had no background in journalism "and little confidence that I'd ever find a fit in that world."

One day, MacLeese was editing a Sanders story when he called Sanders over to the copy desk. "(He) told me he'd seen better from me than the crap that had just come to him."

MacLeese's advice: "Do your thing and don't listen to people whose only purpose in life is to drag everyone else back to their level of mediocrity. He told me I had talent few others had been given and to just let it flow."

"I was seriously dumbstruck. I'm trying to hide in the newsroom and just be accepted and Al notices me," Sanders said. "He made me believe in me."

Less than 10 months after resuming his column on a weekly basis, MacLeese wrote his last column for the Flint Journal on Jan. 1, 1983. A three-year period of purgatory followed.

During those three years, he was working as a copy editor while writing occasional features, such as about men's rights, a shop bar, the smallest city in Michigan and Alfred Packer cannibalism. He also wrote about his experience with prostate problems.

"My prostate gland's enlargement was found to be non-cancerous after it was, er, fingered ... when the doctor who cares for our family ... performed a digital rectal examination.... It occurred after I'd belatedly told [the doctor] my tale of woe.

"My urine stream had grown hesitant and weak, pressure was poor, erratic. I was dribbling time away, staring at bathroom walls. Increased frequency of urination occurred at night, though, along with fears of losing bladder control."

His stories, about the prostate surgery he underwent to correct the problem and about prostate cancer, won a statewide award for feature writing.

Giving up his column, though, was hard on him, and he was easily bumped off stride. What's worse, his darker moods often held him captive for long stretches.

Crawford remembers "a dramatic change in his personality ... he was much gruffer and more unhappy. I remember one of the young people who was hired, I think a copy clerk, talking about the mean grumpy old guy who edited copy, and I was surprised to figure out she was talking about Al."

This was about a man who, when a full-time columnist, could be seen smiling as he typed, perhaps at a particularly clever turn of phrase or a stretch of sparkling prose.

MacLeese once told a friend that after his "alcoholic slip," he was off booze for 10 years and counting. As a substitute, he was smoking pot. With pot, he didn't have to deal with hangovers. "I did try to get addicted to marijuana, but it didn't take, I failed. But you must pick up the pieces and carry on."

By 1985, Vizard was Tempo editor, and he had "rescued" MacLeese from the newsroom to become a feature writer and copy editor.

"His features were actually pretty good and his copy editing was fine with lots of good headlines," Vizard said. "But he could not do layouts, even simple inside pages with ads on them baffled him. Al was eager to help me, but I definitely thought he was in a malaise of sorts...."

"I remember during one visit to [the MacLeese home in] Bridgeport that Al had run out of pot and his mailroom connection had failed him. When I found him in the kitchen, he was attempting to dry up and roll some catnip into a joint. When I left, he took a big, long, puff and said, "Hey, this is not bad, want some?"

The end of MacLeese's career at the Journal came after a reunion of MacLeese and Michael Moore.

In the fall of 1985, Moore wrote an article in the Columbia Journalism Review about the Journal's relationship with General Motors and civic organizations, which had changed dramatically after Peloquin came on board. Moore was then editor of the Michigan Voice (the statewide successor to the Flint Voice), along with being a commentator on National Public Radio's "All Things Considered."

The only Journal staffer who allowed Moore to use his name in making a comment critical of Journal management was MacLeese. He didn't flinch: "The Journal is in bed with the very institutions it should be covering." The paper, he said, "has begun to resemble a community newsletter."

In the article's concluding paragraph, MacLeese said he had decided to leave the newspaper in the next year. "If this is what it means to be a journalist in Flint, Michigan, then I don't want to be a part of it."

Predictably, Peloquin was not happy to see the CJR piece.

"He felt he had been a good, solid foot soldier in the day-to-day grind of putting out a newspaper in Bay City and Saginaw," Vizard said. And in Peloquin's view, "that reputation and hard work [were] smeared by Michael Moore and CJR" at the height of his newspaper career.

Vizard remembers "Al and ALP did not speak to each other after that – even if they happened to bump into each other in the men's room."

True to his word, MacLeese officially left the Journal five days into 1986, taking early retirement on his 55th birthday.

His retirement plan was to "rise to the occasion" and finally write a book. For that, he took his final Journal check and bought a computer and a printer. Would the book be the one friends wanted him to write, the story of his life? The question turned out to be immaterial.

After a few weeks of being sequestered south of Saginaw in his "Bridgeport bungalow near the pickle factory," he had serious doubts about his goal, saying he hadn't written anything except a few letters. Wife Connie was making encouraging noises, but he was down and admitted he was suffering from a lack of focus.

"Indeed, last night I had a dream in which I was looking for a town named Nowhere. Seriously! Now is that fraught with meaning or what?"

Fast forward six years, to 1992, and MacLeese was working Friday and Saturday nights for the Saginaw News as a copy editor "under the lash" of Connie, the news editor there. Tongue-in-cheek, he claimed two good headlines in the first month of the year. "Mexican bus plunge kills 38" and "Malaysian ferry sinks, drowning 215."

Then he switched to working a couple of weekday shifts. "Why should a gaffer work weekends? At night, no less."

He didn't sound happy, calling his health only fair, with two ulcers and "a little band of pain creeping across my left foot, killing as it goes."

At one point he wrote that although his stomach had been fine for a couple weeks, in a way he missed his morning vomiting.

"I have a theory that I don't mind vomiting too much because it is punishment I richly deserve."

MacLeese was not feeling kindly toward his profession.

256

"I am glad I am not much in the media business anymore. I think the media get worse as they go along, and I am not proud of the way newspapers do their business. Most newspapers today – far, far more than when I got into the business in 1953 – overwhelm their readers with trivia and simple-minded presentations of complex issues."

Perhaps because of the nurturing support, not the 'lash," of Connie, he was approaching the 10th anniversary of his last alcoholic "slip." All without Alcoholics Anonymous.

"Difficulty I had with AA – and I earnestly attended meetings over many years before throwing in the towel – is that it wants you to forever primarily identify yourself as an alcoholic and, not incidentally, forever attend meetings.

"I feel this is harmful overkill. The addict must be encouraged to confront his problem by investigating why, get clean, and then put the matter aside, go on to other things. Make it small, not big." The question about his logic was whether he was ever able to consistently make his problem small.

His niece Pamela said that whenever she saw him, "he was either under the influence [or] wishing he was there."

He was spending most of his time reading, plus working the New York Times daily crossword puzzles. "In pen in 20 minutes, the insufferable ass said."

His reading focused on Updike, Cheever, Roth, Pynchon, Bellow, Freud, Bertrand Russell, Samuel Johnson and the like. He apparently was disdainful of women writers. He told at least two people that he wouldn't read anything written by a woman.

To him, of the modern writers, Updike was the most impressive. "I can't think of anyone as good." Updike, he said, "has a mind that I marvel at, and the bastard makes me realize how limited I am." In general, he wrote, "good writers depress me." He said it would be "much more intelligent for the likes of myself not to compare themselves with certified geniuses such as Updike."

He also was reading mysteries and thrillers and true crime and science fiction, plus magazines and newspapers.

"I don't mind spending time home alone with the cats. Amend that: I prefer spending time alone with the cats." They were living with their second group of cats, the F-Troop, all four with names starting with F – Fiona, Farquarhar, Fogarty and Faversham. Previously, there had been a set of three cats, all with names beginning with S.

By the end of 1994, the only member of the original F-Troop on the scene was Fogarty but the ranks had expanded to six with newcomers Finley, Fenwick, Faroon, Firth and Faraday. Within two years, with the addition of Faith and Fergus, the F-Troop numbered eight indoor cats and one that stayed outdoors, Blackie-Farnsworth.

"Occasionally I try to write something but lack fire in the belly," he wrote in a letter. "Unless you count the ulcers, I am more content than ever, though that's still gloomy by accepted standards.

"It feels good not to have to go to work, although sometimes I miss calling in sick. In my working days I seldom minded the work, often minded some people. You know, the fuckers who gave me ulcers."

He would have stomach surgery, and a whole new world of eating opened for him. He was down to 155 pounds when he left the hospital, and he gained 30 pounds.

Connie, a photographer, nature lover, and rock hound, retired at the end of 1992, after 40 years in journalism. In her 25 years at the News, she was outdoor editor, assistant city editor, city editor and news editor.

Alan kept his hand in, still working 40 hours a month at the News, and submitting occasional columns, primarily about their cats.

Six months later, Connie had surgery for breast cancer, followed by a course of chemotherapy. In addition to his concern for Connie, he showed the inner strength to change his stripes. He not only cared for her but also did work around the house and ran errands – a big step by a man for whom Connie had done everything. Coddled may be too weak a word.

MacLeese was learning how to write poems, and he never did anything halfway. He took the plunge by collecting anthologies, handbooks on the basics, biographies of poets, critiques and books on meter, stress, tone and form.

"The thing I like about it is there are no expectations. I don't expect to sell any poems or make any money and there are no deadlines. Just the satisfaction of trying to do something right."

Or wrong. If he couldn't write good poetry, he could at least have fun writing poetry that ranged from bad to worse, and in May of 1994, he took second place in a bad-poetry contest, the Julia A. Moore Poetry Festival at the Flint Public Library. As MacLeese said, Moore is less.

His poem, "The Premature Demise of Melissa McDrew," told of the death of a woman who lived a grand and long life on inherited money. He wrote it, though, as if she had died as a baby. And he threw in the "required redundancies and stupidities and understated overstatements and grammatical atrocities. It seemed to come easy."

UNLEASHED

Missy, he wrote, "Fled to Palm Beach once 70s came longg; Shuffling to eterne in grip of mah jongg."

A year later, Connie had "rebounded magnificently" from her cancer operation, he reported. Her hair had grown back curly after the chemo and no sign of cancer was found in her checkups. "She's slimmed down and more active than any time in recent memory."

MacLeese cut a deal to delay his pension so he could work longer hours and become a part-timer, 20 to 29 hours a week. "This is a big deal to me because I really didn't want to retire when I did."

He also was "reading like a cramming sophomore." Not only poetry but also non-fiction on culture, history and philosophy and books on the brain.

In mid-1996, MacLeese reported he was suffering from a disorder involving his private parts that was called Peyronie's disease, or "bent spike syndrome." With Peyronie's, "when you get an erection, your member curves" up or down or to the right or left. "A hideous sight, even disconcerting. It might bring a John Wayne to his knees, sobbing girlishly."

In December, the problem still hadn't straightened out.

"As long as it doesn't hurt I'm not having anything done about it; indeed there isn't much to be safely done.... So, for now, I am using the thing for a corkscrew."

He was still working part-time and writing a column, which appeared every third week on the Pet Page. And writing good headlines. James J. Kilpatrick lauded MacLeese in his syndicated national column for two heads, one on a story from Dublin: "Irish ayes smile on legal divorce," and the other, a twist on his good old summertime standard, "The economy's fine but the living is queasy."

After Princess Diana's death on Aug. 31, 1997, and what he called the "wallowing" that followed, MacLeese wrote one of his few non-cat-related columns for the Saginaw News.

He said he could not "grieve over irrelevant deaths. Yet the world bites its lower lip and tousles my hair, claims I must be distraught over the bizarre passing of a ritzy spendthrift who had it soft and called it hard. But how can I deal myself in on a faraway and pseudohistoric happening involving a dodo dubbed royalty?

"And how many of the globe's public mourners of [Diana], I wonder, preoccupy themselves with a 'princess' while kith and kin waste away in dark rooms and have no flowers?"

A high school freshman responded by calling him selfish, uncaring, greedy, ignorant, and starved for attention.

"I was going to write her an angry letter until I realized that, at one time or another, I've been all of the above."

Connie had congestive heart failure by 1998 and used a cane and a walker to compensate for severe back problems and arthritis. He continued to step up and help out, especially with the housework.

Many with her heart condition died within five years. She was three years into the five on Dec. 22, 1999, when she had a heart attack and a seizure or a stroke.

Alan came home after a shift of copy editing, found her lying on the floor next to their bed. She spent the next week in a coma before dying on Dec. 29.

Connie, who had been married to him for 32 years, was eulogized as a mother hen and an unbelievably supportive wife. She was a kind and sensitive woman, yet strong enough to make her way in a man's world.

As a woman journalist, she was a pioneer. Not only was she the first female correspondent for the Booth Washington Bureau, she also was the first woman to serve as city editor and news editor in the chain.

A little more than a year after her death, MacLeese had retired again and was getting ready to move to Maine when he had a break-in at his home. Stolen were a recliner, a computer, a printer, and other items.

"They even stole a pizza out of the freezer and a full bottle of vodka," he said.

MacLeese said he was better off getting an insurance check than carting the items east. He said he had been giving away items, ranging from tons of books to collectibles, for 18 months. By nature, he was generous, and he gave away sets of fine china, silverware, antique furniture, and Connie's rock collection.

"This house was just full of stuff, and I gave things to dozens of people. I didn't want to sell [certain items] because I didn't acquire [them] through any of my own effort. It was all through the efforts of my wife and her mother, and I didn't want to profit from their deaths. I never really attached any value to it. It was just stuff."

[Jan. 31, 2011]

Once again I am a Scot

[With this subject line, MacLeese forwards an explanatory email from his niece Pamela, in which she informs him that a Scotsman is found to be his great, great, great, great

260

grandfather. The man, Neil MacNichol, fought with the 42nd Royal Highlanders (later known as the Black Watch) in the Battle of the Plains of Abraham near Quebec City in 1759 when he was 19 and in New York seeking to put down the American Revolution. One of MacNichol's descendants was the mother of one of MacLeese's grandfathers and one of his grandmothers, making him the son of first cousins and giving him Scottish blood on both sides of his family.]

[Port St. Joe FL; Feb. 10]

Hey Mac,

Good to hear you again can claim Scottish heritage. Never liked those shifty Irish, never will. A man of battle in your background and a Black Watchman, no less. Of course, I have to question whether you consider fighting against the rebellion a claim to fame....

RJ

[Feb. 16]

Dutchers,

I apologize for being out of pocket, but am in midst of break from the family ... over the leavings of three women who died....

It has been revealed ... a [then] 108-year-old woman [lopped] me from her will, depriving your earnest correspondent of more thousands of dollars than I like to think about....

All this has thrown me way off stride and I have been walking the floor and talking to Finley and the spider plant on top of the icebox....

Almac

A storyteller's odyssey

[Micanopy FL; Feb. 16]

Hey Mac,

... If you have time, explain to us how many GAG's you have out there that are wanting to give you money. Maybe we can put some money in MacLeese futures.

RJ

[Feb. 21]

Dutchers,

Yes, previous post was ill-tempered rant and poorly outlined. The long and short of it was I had just learned that I had [share] in an unknown but large amount of money but was scotched, if I may use the opprobrious term, because I had not been sending postcards and sucking up in various and sundry ways to a series of ancient Noone females who had never tousled my curly locks from tadhood to j.d. status.

So I had no due, Dutchers, and was only able to collect the relative crumbs from another dead Noone name of Essie who had expired way before GAG but the foul loot could not be scooped up until GAG had exited into the ether (which was proved not to exist about a hundred years ago, I think, but you take my point).

In any case, I had been besieged for many a day by communications from [siblings] and finally after confronting them, in my essentially passive-aggressive manner, I decreed that ... I was, in the fashion of Samuel Goldwyn, including myself out.

So now, Dutchers, I am isolated from all members of my clan and I think that this gr.gr.gr.gr. granddad MacNichol would be hugely ashamed. But, Dutchers, I have an ace down in the hole that this dead Scot did not. I haven't told you this, Dutchers, but a while back I joined this secret society of friends who will help each other through thick and thin. It is called Facebook. I already have more than eighty friends.

You would not believe this, Dutchers, but in a scant few months I have people, bars, singers, weavers, potters, even some politicians. You must understand, Dutchers, I did not seek these people and concerned concerns out, they sought me.

Aside to Jessica: I can get you into this outfit ... because Roger might resist. These Dutch people are not born sharers and empathetic supporters like those of us from the good honest bogs and highlands and moors and other desolate places in the British Isles.

Later, Almac

[Several months earlier, he wrote sister Deborah that he had Facebook friends, many of whom he actually knew. "Am not sure I like this, must I now keep up with and interact with these people every day? ... Suppose a lot of these people decide to unfriend me on some trumped-up charges?"

[He said he didn't join Facebook himself; two friends did that for him.

[In May, he told his niece Pamela, he saw a Facebook message to poke her and he did, "although I wasn't sure whether that was proper given our kinship. It seemed that the poke was delivered but maybe something clogged the Internet tubes or pipes?"]

[Grand Blanc; April 1]

Hey Mac —

While waiting on Ford to complete an oil change operation on the Beast [our RV] yesterday, I started reading a novel intriguingly called "The Guernsey Literary and Potato Peel Pie Society" and am hooked. It's set (so far) in the British Isles during the immediate aftermath of the war and consists entirely of short, chatty letters to and from the various characters surrounding a young female author.

During the reading I had an epiphany. Said epiphany involves an exchange of emails between yours truly and a certain Maine expatriate. They [include], intriguingly enough, an introduction to Great Aunt Gert.... Anyway, I find I have saved most of our Internet correspondence....

Why did I save the emails? ... They gave me enjoyment. I have reread many of them, some several times, like a collection of old columns. I also had a feeling that I didn't want the unique personality expressed in the emails to die....

At one point, I had a vision of you finally writing your autobiography, which, of course, became wildly successful, and after our deaths these emails eventually became fodder for future scholars analyzing each and every artifact to try to discern what made you tick. The flaw in this thinking is that, as we know by now, the Noones never die.

Until they get bored at 114 or thereabouts.

Back to Potato Peel Pie. This gave me the idea, seductive in its simplicity, yet fraught with any manner of pitfalls. My first thought was that we could write a section of your biography, with flashbacks, through our actual email exchange....

Then I thought, maybe we could take my idea but turn it into a Potato Peel novel, with fresh characters. Maybe the Great Aunt Gert Chronicles. No real answers here yet, just a tantalizing possibility from my perspective. What do you think? It's your life and your emails....

We are back home.... During your travels, have you spent any time in Savannah? We stopped in Charleston on the way home last year, and this year we spent a week in Savannah area. In our brief exploration of Charleston, it seemed a bit standoffish but attractive. Savannah seemed as easy on the eyes in an antebellum sort of way but much more approachable....

So how fares it with your body? I turn 70 this year....

RJ

[April 2]

Dutchers,

Can't express my pleasure at hearing from you. You were the last folks I have emailed to, pretty much out of pocket lately but have spotted light at end of this tunnel after

264

hectic time ... [drafting a complaint alleging that he was disinherited] to the tune of about $300,000.

... we haven't talked in so long, figured you guys were put off my last bitter rant, in which I gratuitously railed against any innocent in range. [Provides phone number]

Later, Mac

[April 10]

Dutchers:

You asked about the state of my body. Have not seen "my" doctor, who I can sometimes unofficially see out my window, in about three years, but have physical on 19th of this instant. Now weigh 165 pounds, which is just about what I weighed when I became a squid in 1948.

I have broken three bones since fetching up in Hallowell (but found a real homeplace), and been earnestly advised, lungwise, that I may score a hat trick — emphysema, bronchitis, and that other one that I can never think of. I have occasional "episodes" of hypoglycemia, but generally they only occur at home....

Also the neurologist told me several years ago she had good and bad news. The good tidings were that it seemed as if I might make it pretty far into my eighties, but the left foot won't, owing to peripheral nerve damage caused by a combination of alcoholism and — this is so ironic it is funny — the long-term taking of the drug Antabuse, which makes [drinking] impossible as long as it is in the system.

Still and all, I must say there are upsides. My alcoholism — ever notice how we can get so proprietary over our "conditions" — seems to be easing up, mostly because I lack the vigor of yore, and do not hit the 13 (count 'em) night spots in the seamy underbelly of this hardscrabble river town.

But, Dutchers, I cannot in all candor say the same [about] my use of the marijuana. it seems to me, and other trained observers, that, as the cannabis intake surges, the ethyl alcohol intake [declines], although sometimes slightly. And my eyesight is failing, of course, ditto hearing; am still able to achieve an erection, a woody of a sort, and would like to try it on another person....

Joan and I have reconciled [after seven years].... Drove hundred miles to [her home] and back and am tuckered but, healthwise, no sign of heart mutter, no cancer seems in offing and the liver is not being liverish.

Go figure.

Mac

[April 11]

Dutchers,

Yes, as a matter of fact, I have been to Savannah; and it was on the occasion, which I may have mentioned [when I was] deported from Miami, Florida ... on a Greyhound to New York City....

[After the stop in Jacksonville, I] hitchhiked as far as Savannah and fell in with a group of youngish vagabonds and woke up a couple days later sleeping on a warehouse floor with about fifteen of that ilk. Was lying on my side and felt a poke in rear. Looked around and there was a seedy looking fucker with an erection which fortunately was still in his dungarees.

I've been in Savannah since but just passing through, avoiding warehouses....

Later, Mac

[April 14]

Dutchers,

... [niece] Pam, in her gene-tracking, reported yesterday that I am strongly related to a group of Polish people who somehow made it to the British Isles way back in the day. If I am now Polish, you can have that redheaded ragdoll back....

Later, Mac

[April 22]

Dutchers,

... I had a physical day before yesterday and found that my alleged hypoglycemic episodes are really manifestations of an irregular heartbeat — arrhythmia — although I haven't had this disorder long enough to know how to spell it....

[Switching subjects to finances in less flush times, he writes:] My mother once sent me fifteen bucks when I was in Navy. When I confessed the money was used so me and two buddies could go get drunk, she vowed never to send money and didn't, although she took me in when I had no home. My father once, unbidden, sent me three one-dollar bills when I was going to U-Miami. Three bucks bought a lot of draft beer at ten-cents a glass.

Later,

I am all worn out and it's only 9 a.m. of a morning, and it looks like spring may finally kick into gear.

Mac

[April 24]

(Email from MacLeese to niece Pamela)

... This Neurontin [drug he started taking that can be used to treat peripheral neuropathy] can make you, I mean me, woozy and tired....

[April 24]

Dutchers:

Yes, April is the cruelest month, Dutchers. After a series of disconcerting events, I have been struck a body blow.

It develops, and I know not how to say this but.... I, er, well ... well, Dutchers, it has been revealed to me, on this wet and gray Easter Day that ... I am a Dutcher.... as [niece Pamela], my ace researcher shows, my people may have been lowlanders before your kind, or ilk, even showed up.

VanLeese

[MacLeese forwards email from his niece that talks about his haplogroup, "a permanent marker that is handed down on the male Y chromosome from father to son, father to son. Your haplogroup has an interesting past. Once your distant but direct ancestors hunted the forests and fished the coast of Doggerland. Doggerland is now under the southern part of the North Sea, east of Great Britain, once attached to Holland and Germany."]

[He also forwards his response: "... the dope on my ancestors' time in the Holland area turned out to be especially helpful in my decades-long squabble with Roger. In emails and even in newspaper columns I have pointed out the many failings of the Dutch people. So you can imagine my chagrin when I tell Roger that I may be more Dutch than a Van Noord...."]

[April 24]

Doggerland??? Say it ain't so.

(To MacLeese)

Even one of my early wives never thought you were part of that ilk that she called the no-necks.... Send recent picture, so I can compare necks. I thought you always said yours was longer than mine....

RJ

... just to be clear, no one is as Dutch as I am. So dream on, ol' MacDuff. But it's nice to have you in our neighborhood....

[April 24]

Dutchers,

... It dawned that I had five plastic bags of ephemera and suchlike stored in a closet; during the four years I lived over Boynton's Market on Water Street, I tacked or pasted or otherwise affixed all the stuff that made it up to the third floor.

Coincidentally, I had decided to throw all this crap out — the bags had been languishing in the closet for more than a year — and it struck me as I prepared to carry them out to the trash cans that it might be good to check, see what ... was in there.... In bags of stuff ... was one of four paintings of Persians on horseback. These paintings were given Connie and me by [Iranian family] in appreciation for us putting [their son] up during those parlous Iranian hostage times when, fortunately, our president was unaware of what was transpiring.

In any case, I found the last of these four paintings in the bag, all curled up with blotches and stains and a tiny rip or tear or two.

Sister Joan knew of this painting and I think wondered what happened to the set of four.... (I was giving everything away save for my dentures, which they will have to pry from my cold dead gums.) So a week or so ago I got the pic restored and framed at a place in Hallowell called Occasional Framers, and presented it to Joan.... It felt good to give Joan the pic, a sign that I had made peace with the person I had known all my life, the only one like that around and about.

Later, Almac

[Stories also surfaced about his generosity in Hallowell, giving one person who was arrears in mortgage payments a big check and another seed money to start a grass farm, perhaps hoping for a pot dividend later.]

[June 1]

Dutchers,

... I see the doctor Friday about the heart murmur and will leave for Jonesport Saturday morning. Going way down east, commune with mussel and squid. Which would be all well and good but, from [what] I've gleaned from Pam's messages, there may not be any bars or taverns or liquor stores within miles and miles....

... didya hear N.Y. Congressman Weiner's weiner allegedly was on twitter? Can't make this stuff up.

Later, Almac

[June 2]

(To Mac)

... we have decided that, after a year, it's time to get another dog, so we are trying to adopt a puppy mill survivor from Missouri. It's an involved process; we have to fill out a long application, and they check references, etc. Dog is an Irish terrier with name of McKenna but we are thinking of changing name to that of the Irish prime minister, I think her name is MacLeese. Nobody around here by that name so should be unique.....

RJ

Headline about Weiner today in NY rag: Battle of the Bulge.

[June 2]

R and J:

Gotham's other rag's hed wasn't bad: WEINER'S PICKLE.

[June 12]

Dutchers,

... I should warn you, Dutchers, if you name this unoffending adoptee McAleese, there will always be some wiseasses in the nabe that will call puppy "MacAlush" — particularly if this canine displays any signs of his Irishness in whatever workplace he's thrown into. But McAleese works for me.

I just returned from Jonesport ... [niece Pamela and I] rode around Jport (we Mainers refer to Jonesport as Jport).... We visited a number of cemeteries looking for dead relatives, but found none — did find an appalling number of Kelleys, Alleys and Beals.

I went into place where lobster hunters gathered at four ayem before venturing out into the vasty deep. I eavesdropped on their conversations but could understand only about every fifth word.

Everybody in these parts waves to everyone they encounter on the highways and byways even though this city of 2,000 has no police force and, worse luck, no mayor. Courtesy and politeness run rampant. Scenery wonderful, Jport is quaint and we [drove] to Eastport, sixty miles more downeast than Jport, where my grandfather reputedly sailed from in 1906 or thereabouts. (In Eastport in colonial days, lobsters were so highly thought of that they were mostly fed to prisoners. One group held in durance vile petitioned authorities to for crissakes only serve us lobster three times a week.)

Spent six days without cellphone, TV, radio, computer or newspapers, should be a better person after all that, but now am back reading about Weiner, Gingrich ... and feel soiled and, well, violated.

Dutchers, feel free to use me as a reference in the paperwork involving the former McKenna. Finley will vouch for me....

Later, Almac

[June 21]

Hey Mac,

Sorry about the slow response. We've had a lot going on the last couple weeks.

My brother Ted, the one who had the melanoma removed from his back about 16 months ago, had a spell where he thought he blacked out while he was home alone one day [in Kalamazoo]. He finally told me about it a few days later, and I ordered him to go to ER, where a CT scan found some spots on his brain.

Doctors suggested he not drive because he might have had a seizure. So we've been driving back and forth to Kalamazoo area to get him to doctor's appointments and tests. Long story short, so far it seems to be a replay of what Sharon had. Melanoma spreads to brain, causing a seizure....

Regret to inform you that we have decided not to call dog McAleese or any iteration. Jess says this is no reflection on you, just that it was recommended we keep her name similar to McKenna for training purposes. I decided we should at least be able to name our own dog, so I picked Kilkenny, a town we loved in Ireland, and we'll call her Kenny for short....

RJ

[July 1]

Hello from Hallowell

Dutchers,

Sorry to hear about Ted's troubles, and hope you all can work it out. Downside of not being dead is all the unbearable stuff you have to deal with. (Is that the most cheerful face I can put on things? No, just give me a little time to think on it.)

In a development only slightly related to Ted's problems, I was operated on earlier this week for a suspicious (to the doctor) brown spot on the left side of my nose. This minor procedure was done in the doctor's office, and after the deed was done, I asked the doctor if I would still be able to play the piano. He heartedly said yes, and I zinged him with, "That's funny, I couldn't play it before."

The good doctor will inform me Tuesday about the biopsy result but I have had these spots scraped off before and, besides, I have better genes than 89 percent of the U.S. population, so cancer will not be the answer.

Meantime, I leave Hallowell tomorrow for Moosehead Lake to attend ... party for friend Juliette Guilmette.... Moosehead Lake is about 170 miles deep into the piney woods, and friend Aaron Green will do the driving. Gotta stop all this gallivanting around....

Later, Almac

[July 13]

Hey Mac,

Ted has finished his radiation on brain and spine, and we have returned to Grand Blanc and he has moved in with us, pretty much permanently, to await possible treatment at

UM in Ann Arbor. His biopsy came back as metastatic melanoma, which reading online I guess gives him a 50 percent chance to live eight months. No one's talked about those odds.

Kalamazoo doctor said they have done all they can for him there. Now his only real hope is that he has right gene mutation or whatever to get in a treatment protocol (formerly called clinical trials, I understand) that has had some success, not for a cure but at slowing things down....

So what's up with your operation? ... What did your biopsy show? ...

RJ

[July 15]

Dutchers:

Got me one of them melanomas, must be a lot of that shit going on around the nation.

Gather this cutter will operate a week or so after my first visit. Hallowell doc says [we won't] know how serious this thing is until the surgeon goes deeper than he did in biopsy. Downside of his assessment was that I have had the splotch on left side of my nose for quite a while, there was a two-year stretch that I did not bother to visit the doctor, his office being almost a half-block from my abode.

Hope Ted gets a break on the odds.

Later, Mac

[July 15]

Hey Mac,

Wow! Hope I didn't stick my foot in it by giving you TMI about Ted's situation.

When are you scheduled to see the surgeon? Melanoma can be scary stuff, but you got some great genes. Hopefully, they will win out....

RJ

A storyteller's odyssey

[July 26]

Courageous battle against the dread big C

Dutchers,

The surgeon's nurse in Waterville called me early Monday and, after assuring herself I was who she thought I was, said that the test had returned from Boston and that I had no cancer.

So what do I have on my nose? I [asked]. Some crusted dead skin, she said. (As you have doubtless discovered, Dutchers, not all medical practitioners lack humor.) ... my chances of becoming a heroic survivor have been dashed.

Meantime, my place has been up for grabs since a Friday showing, and nothing since, I think that's because the first visitors are the ones who have already sewed it up.... Dunno, it's too complicated to go into now. Anyroad, am pretty well packed up and ready to go.

Where I am going is another question. I was thinking about Jonesport, but friends say the winters are wicked and rentals seldom have car shelters. Maybe Jonesport, maybe anywhere, feel like what they used to say (and probably still do) in naval servitude: Do something, even if it's wrong....

Regards, Almac

[Aug. 2]

Downeastward Ho

Dutchers,

... Today I qualified for a one-room apartment at the senior citizens and family rentals building ... in downtown Jport. The confirming letter ... notes that "your credit could be a little better" but assures me [their] staff can live and work with that.

So I am on the very short list and, in good order, if all goes well, and the Kennebec don't rise, and this place sells with dispatch, I will soon enough be gaping out my window at the harbor in the Moosabec Reach. If you people don't know what a reach is, I am not at all surprised.

Just the other day I told a woman in a bar I was from Michigan, sort of, and she sniffed and said "The Midwest is so eighties." Still puzzling over that, but my reach exceeds my grasp....

Later, Almac

[He forwards two emails to a neighbor in which he says he is leaving for Jonesport on Sept. 1 and whatever can be done to rid the condo building of Finley's fleas, he will "pay the freight."]

[Aug. 28]

Hey Mac,

... We have been very busy with Ted lately. After a week in the hospital at the Karmanos Cancer Center in Detroit to explore treatment options, Ted was transported to a hospice in the Flint area Thursday night ... no good treatment options are available for the cancer around his spine or in his brain. He will, however, be among the first to get the new melanoma drug after its general release.... We are hoping that the pills, while not a cure-all, will give him some relief....

Have you moved already? Not even sure you will get this if you don't have an email connection....

RJ

[Aug. 29]

Waydowneastward ho-ho-ho

Dutchers,

Need it be said that I feel like an asshole transmitting my quotidian concerns — Jess, you may have to look that up for the other Dutcher — while you folks are dealing with hard things, but I did so want to let you to know that I

275

survived Hurricane Irene, although I really don't wish to talk too much about it.

I was in my bedroom with Finley ... and the wind was gusting to about 17 miles-an-hour, and slamming leaflets and twigs against our windows and this frightening madness kept up for almost a minute or so....

I leave out of Hallowell in a two-vehicle convoy Sept. 4; have not sold condo yet, but closed it down.... Have already paid first month and deposit on two-bedroom apartment [in Jonesport]. So by this time next week I should be lodged [there]....

I have been able to maintain my Time-Warner account despite moving into what many folks in these parts liken to a gulag in remotest Siberia. But Jonesport has a downtown library, coffee places that open for the seafarers at four ayem, an IGA, and no police or mayor, and, oh, yeah, no bars.

This is a ploy that may allow me to live a little in a manner [up with] some ... would not put. Also Jonesport is in the poorest county in Maine and has a veteran's hospital in case one needs some coddling.

Later, Almac

[Sept. 16]

Hey Mac,

I'm assuming you are indeed now ensconced in Jonesport. How goes it in the Gulag?

We are carrying on. We thought brother Ted was fixing to die about a week ago ... then after a couple days he made this huge comeback. I think it was because he was not taking his cancer drugs, which can cause some major side effects.

Now we can talk to him, he's eating, drinking and he's mainly coherent....

RJ

[Jonesport ME; Oct. 15]

Jonesport in the upeast

R & J Industries Inc:

I am writing from the top floor of a big red building [on Main Street] that once was Jonesport High School. It was built in 1933 and converted to the Thomas Kelley apartments in 1989. My two-bedroom flat [with a view from five big windows looking down and out at a working wharf] once housed the English classes, and a good job it was for me that it wasn't the place for math students.

The rosy fingers of dawn have just worked their magic; the pink and gray and blue skies are filled with birds of various feather, the working wharf is just a couple of football fields away, and out in the Moosabec Reach are the lobster boats and trawlers that haven't already ventured out to the open sea.

To my right is the bridge to Beals Island; there is a smaller island between Jonesport and Beals Island, and it is called Mystery Island, although why it is called that is a mystery to me, but you must keep in mind that I have graced Jport with my presence for about seven weeks, and met a mere handful of people, most notably Mona the postmistress who identifies herself as "Mona as in Lisa" and Heidi the librarian. (The library and the post office are close to hand, as is the IGA and two churches, which are irrelevant to my purposes.)

Niece [Pam] ... has been invaluable in introducing me to upeast, which for centuries has been mislabeled "downeast." We have motored ... to Lubec, Eastport, Machias, Beals Island and Great Wass Island and other less notable places, and you can't get more upeast than in Lubec, which has a historic lighthouse, and Machias is the site of the U.S. Navy's very first battle (against, of course, the scurvy limejuicers).

Pam has been good enough to do all the work in buying for me a 32-inch on the diagonal Samsung TV, land a landline, LL Bean winter coat, boots fit for an upeaster lobsterperson, gloves and hats, and all kinds of stuff for larders and pantries, including so much toilet paper that I fear I will not

A storyteller's odyssey

live long enough to have sufficient bowel movements to exhaust the supply....

Jport does not have any bars, or restaurants, but you can get breakfast in nearby Columbia Falls, which also has a giant blueberry, a Shop and Save, a gas station and a hardware store. The lack of bars has aided me immeasurably in abstaining from booze, [am] off the buds as well, and nicotine patches have kept me from the butts, so I have been cleaner than the Rover Boys since arriving upeast.....

So, in sum, it begins to appear that I may have accidentally made a good move by relocating upeast. Dutchers, you have no idea how much money you can save by the simple act of not smoking, not drinking alcohol and not purchasing the weed, which grows more expensive every year. [He occasionally used this pre-rolled method for smoking pot: He would gently knock all of the tobacco out of a cigarette, then fill the paper tube with weed.]

This is one of the few emails I've sent in recent weeks and so I hope you will pardon me for confining this letter to my mundane activities, and not inquiring how R and J are doing, good I hope.

Later, Mac

[Oct. 15]

Hey Mac,

Not sure I still have your right email address but here goes....

Ted died Sunday afternoon. He was 54, as they say in obits. We called him Rocky because everytime he took a major body blow, he kept getting up for more.

Finally, though, the melanoma got the best of him....

RJ

[Oct. 15]

Roger:

The email I wrote you was sent — I thought — at around quarter to nine, and the email you wrote telling about Ted was read by me, well, after I had written you — just got Time-Warner deal combining the TV-laptop-telephone , and ever since my laptop and phone have been screwed up.

So if it seemed that I was ignoring Ted's death, it was because I sent your email three times starting at about 8:30 a.m. ... Just wanted you to know I was not ignoring the import of Ted's death. Sometimes I suspect I am losing it. In_any case, so sorry about Ted.

Later, Al

[On Nov. 9, MacLeese wrote an email to a friend in Hallowell about his situation in Jonesport.]

... Like Hallowell, only more so, the folks here are friendly as all get-out.... Main Street has sidewalks, although only on one side and you trudge along the sidewalk-less side at your peril....

In sum, I miss my friends in Hallowell but, after two months of watching the lobster hunters chug out to the open sea, I kinda like where I've fetched up.

[Nov. 19]

RJ Enterprises:

It is not commonly known, but the far reaches of coastal Maine are known as the Bold Coast. Leastwise that's what the signs along U.S. 1 proclaim. Florida has the Gold Coast, we-uns have the Bold Coast.

Mainahs driving the Bold Coast are indeed bold, they tailgate and pass you on curves and doublelines, confident in the knowledge that no cops, staties or county mounties are seen. Even in downtown Jport you can't trudge the one sidewalk without casting nervous peeks over your shoulder, though it must be noted that that sidewalk is rolled up at 4 p.m.

A storyteller's odyssey

Do I sound querulous and out-of-sorts after only 11 weeks at the Thomas Kelley apartments? No, I always tend to accentuate the negative. I spend most of my time in solitude, save for the great company of Finley who seems to think I am his companion rather than the other way around. And I watch a lot of cable, which is always raising Cain, and this seems to feed the inner racism that most white boys must restrain.

And keeping company with Gingrich, Perry, Bachmann, Santorum, Romney (who Connie knew when he was a mere stripling) and the egregious libertarian pipsqueak whatshisname from Texas offers no relief.

I should be in a better mood today, having closed yesterday on the sale of my condo, and I didn't even have to be present at the event in Hallowell. So even now a check is winging its way to the upeast. It is for 57 large, and I have 29 gees in the bank, so am probably in better shape financially than most of the folks I will run into tomorrow save for those hardy souls that venture to the open sea daily to hunt and kill the wily lobsters that scuttle around on the ocean floor, all of them [the lobsters] having somehow fallen off the ugly tree and hit every branch on the way down....

And last week I bought a bed for my second bedroom from an outfit in Machias, which delivered it free and put it together but still wanted $800. The bed is for any putative guests, although no one but myself has been in the former English department save for ... the guy who fixes problems like faulty toilets and light fixtures.

I am a [frequent patron of] the Peabody Memorial Library, and a steady customer at the IGA, both of which are in easy hobbling distances. Next week I motor to Ellsworth, sixty miles farther down the upeast from Jport, to get some braces for my feet, required because of the nerve damage. My neuropath (probably you didn't know I have my own neurologist and keep him in an office in Ellsworth) says I need the braces, not so much now but down the line for sure....

Am on the outs ... with sisters [Sharon and Deborah] but also Joan ... with whom I briefly reconciled but un-reconciled.... Meantime, up here in the upeast, my plan to

280

stay alive by moving to a place with fewer attractions for drunk/stoners seems to be working. Have had no vodka, my drug of choice, and no grass, my alternative to legal pacifiers, since arrival.

Instead am taking a non-addictive drug for foot pain, and powerful prescription vitamin B, and have only succumbed to occasional canned beer, and I don't like beer.

So I am doing OK, reading a lot and getting ferociously difficult crossword puzzles from Amazon....

How are you folks? ... And, oh, sorry to hear about alp's demise. That man was a yachtsman's yachtsman.

[Nov. 19]

Hey Mac,

Good to read about some human events in the Bold Coast. I've been lost in the horse latitudes of estate matters for the last month....

J-port sounds idyllic if it weren't for the intrusion of that dastardly 24/7 cable and the 24/7 stupidity of those ersatz presidential candidates on the Repug side. I've been too busy to watch much cable but I have been following the major daily gaffes online....

[Nov. 21]

Dutchers,

Salted my swag from Great Aunt Essie's estate, which bought my condo, in bank in Machias today....

I haven't been on the computer much of late and type like old people fornicate, and I also send stuff off as soon as possible, and without really editing said stuff cause am always fearful that I will lose what I have wrought through fumble-fingeredness. Have written several messages to you folks and lost them, they vanished, but have just figured out that the reason is that my left hand's small finger keeps hitting the key right above the caps lock key on the left side of the ferking keyboard.

Have little or no feeling in several digits on the left hand and this often makes me feel sorry for myself but soon this piteous reaction segues into a blinding rage and I begin expostulating and asking the supreme being the ultimate question: why me you rotten inept creator of all of us creatures, even sparrows.

And then I tell myself to kwitchurbellaching, and, all atremble, retire to my bed of nails, providing Finley will give me some space....

Later, Almac

[Nov. 30]

Bracing for braces

Dutchers,

Am guessing you plutocrats are on the Redneck Riviera, and am properly envious. Myself I have not been outside the state of Maine for six years or more, and those forays have been to Vermont, which is just a mini-Maine although neater and easier to figure out how to get from one quaint town to another.

Reason for the three Vermont forays was to visit an elderly woman who was two years younger than me.... She could not play Scrabble or gin rummy as well as I or me, and was not interested in sex, at least with me, and now that I look back on it, it would not have been pretty, a geezer and a geezeress fumbling about in the dark.

Am writing now because I realized that I had not covered your query about the distasteful subject of canes and braces. I had been using a cane in Hallowell but since I came to the Bold Coast here in the upeast I have not used a cane, though niece [Pam], commissioned to buy me gear ... took it upon herself to include TWO, count 'em, 2 canes, on the theory that anybody that needed one cane probably would need another somewhere along the way.

... Pam did a lot to see to it that I settled in in the upeast, and saw to it that I had all the necessaries while I sat idly by, exaggerating my helplessness, which I have played to good effect on several occasions on Pam and a few others.

I figured out the reason I haven't found canes necessary for the past three months is that I no longer use vodka and weed to help me get through this part of the golden years. But my doctor, who is not yet a certified doctor but a PA, which is what most doctors at the medical center on Snare Road outside Jport are, realized that my left leg is not reliable, even when I am not doing V and W (vodka and weed) so arranged for braces for both feet, even though the right foot is not as advanced in the nerve problem [that] affects all the extremities, but so far those to the left side much more so than the right.

Good news is that I am taking medication and vitamins designed to slow the inevitable damage. I was falling down a lot in Hallowell but am a great deal more steady on the ground, to borrow a phrase from a Willie Nelson song....

[A few years earlier, MacLeese wrote that he had "heard that Willie Nelson, a wonderful artist and person as well, had repeatedly stated that marijuana 'saved me from alcoholism.' This seems to be a clear-eyed way of looking at things...."]

Tomorrow is Dec. 1. Winter has not really arrived in the upeast, just one minor snow event. When it does show up my game plan is the same one that served me well elsewhere: Travel with all due speed from one warm place to another warm place and my place at this former high school includes heat with the rent. This is major.

Later, Almac

[Dec. 23 email to niece Pamela]

Footicapper makes it to Ellsworth and back in same day

Hi Pam,

Your excellent instructions enabled me to arrive at the hand, read foot, therapy place without misadventure.... hit it off OK with Greg whatshisname because I was wearing my USS Allagash cap and his opening salvo was "Hi shipmate" since he was a chief engineer in the Navy and retired after twenty years....

He measured my feet while finding the left foot much inferior to the right and said the braces would differ in flexibility owing to that. He said he would send away to Massachusetts for them and they should reach Ellsworth between Xmas and New Year's Day.

... It has taken until today to overcome the side effects from the trip and the double-whammy of side-effects from both Cymbalta [an antidepressant] and Neurontin. Didn't — or couldn't — leave apartment since then, but feel OK enough to venture outside today. Slept most of the time but, curiously enough, had pleasant dreams, none of the usual unpleasant ones. Today am beginning to feel flashes of well-being, which I guess means the Cymbalta might be kicking in....

Later, Alan

[Goodland FL; Jan. 4, 2012]

Hey Mac,

After a four-day-long commute, we have arrived in the southern tip of Florida and are camped in a state park/mangrove swamp just east of Naples.... Kilkenny traveled well....

RJ

[Estero FL; Jan. 28]

Looking for Mr. Alan Mac

Hi Pam,

I don't know if Al ever mentioned me to you, but I am a longtime friend of his and since I haven't heard from him in a couple months, I was wondering what might be going on with him up there in the frozen tundra. Absent any information, the mind races ahead with possibilities, slip and fall on his bad legs, a deep funk ... tossed his computer in the dumpster, the possibilities are so endless I thought I could put my mind at rest through an email to you, the only possible contact I know up there.

My wife and I are down south and I don't have his phone number, can't remember if I ever got one from him in Jonesport, since we usually communicate by email.

If you could give me some information, I'd appreciate it....

Roger Van Noord

[Feb. 1]

Hi Roger,

As far as I know all is well at Moosabec Reach. But I know he has not been online. I think his computer acts up and he seems to rather not care to deal with it. Your guess of Uncle Vanya throwing the computer in the dumpster is most likely the correct answer....

Roger, it is good to finally "meet" you. I would suggest you give him a phone call. But I will tell him I heard from you.... [Provides phone number]

Pam

[Feb. 1]

Hi Pam,

Thanks for the number. I just called him, and he seems in relatively good spirits now that he is taking his new medicine....

Good to hear he's getting some help for his pain although his reports of eye problems are a concern, especially for someone who gets so much enjoyment from the written word....

I appreciate you helping to connect me with him. Now I can call if he doesn't get online for weeks at a time.

Roger

[April 2, snail mail]

Dutchers, For quite a spell I didn't even fire my laptop up, but last week I decided to email the VNs, and found I could not even access the miserable device. So it's snail mail. I truly wish to divorce myself from as many appliances as possible: Electronics are not my friends.

Might as well get this part of missive over with: Finley died last week. He was [20] ... a cat-lover's friend. He was with Connie and me and then just me all that time, and, despite five moves, he never made a wrong move. He died in my arms while I slept.

I talked to niece Pam and she suggested I bury him in the garden at her cottage, and I did. I keep thinking I see flashes of movement on the floor in different parts of the apartment but the alerts are false.

It's one o'clock on a Monday, and I just made a 100-mile roundtrip to Eastport, from where you can't get any more east and still be in the contiguous forty-eight. I was going to ask at the town's library if there was any way to find out the name of a ship.

My grandfather, Albion McLeese ... shipped out of Eastport in 1900. The ship sank in Chesapeake Bay and crewmembers swam to Tangier Island, where gramps met and married my grandmother, name of Vigolia Dize.

But I had not reckoned on the brute fact that Eastport is closed on Mondays. This true of many hamlets here on the Bold Coast, and I should have known. The library was closed and there is no shoe store.

The closest places, I found, that have a shoe store are Ellsworth and Calais, and both are about 60 miles away — Calais to the north, Ellsworth to the [west]. Have been to Ellsworth several times and been tempted to gawk at the tall structures.

Will be going to Ellsworth more often, since it has one of the state's six medical marijuana dispensaries. They peddle a variety of strains and my current strain is called AK-47. I found the brand name unsettling, and asked ... the "retailer" about the choice of AK-47 and discovered she didn't realize what AK-47 stood for.

A doctor — a Jport PA — is the one who put me in touch with the state on getting certified ($300 "entry fee"). He marveled over one statistic in recent check-up. The first five months downeast I did not smoke any marijuana and was not drinking either. My blood pressure (high end) climbed to

177; it had never in memory been over 135. Six weeks after resuming marijuana, my high reading was back to the 130s.

Have given little thought to rejection of my [complaint] after initial depression....

I think the Dutchers would like Eastport. What I particularly liked about Eastport is that the trees are just the right height. And the little [bays].... I love the little [bays].

Hope all well, am not even sure whether you all are in Alabama or Michigan. I am in Jport and it is snowing but not scaring anyone.

Regards, Almac

[May 4, 2012]

Alan MacLeese

Hello:

This is Deborah, Alan's youngest sister.... Alan died some time in late April (perhaps a fall, I am not sure — I learned of his death in a roundabout way....

Alan estranged himself from me and my sister Sharon a few years ago so I have no specifics about his death but I do know that he was living in Jonesport, Maine, with plans to move back to Hallowell when his Jonesport lease expired. His last F-Troop cat, I think Finley, had died and he had just gotten a new kitty from the humane society and I understand that it is the kitty's meowing that alerted his neighbors that all was not well.

Here is a link to an obituary that some of his Hallowell friends wrote. It is a great community and he fit in perfectly. They loved him.

Alan was nothing if not an interesting guy. He was smart, intellectually curious, generous and entertaining. He was many other things, as well — being his sister was not always an easy path — but I am not going to focus on them. I'll inter the bad with his bones. I never got to say goodbye to him and that makes me sad.

287

A storyteller's odyssey

My best regards to you. I know you were a good friend to Alan and, if I remember correctly, Connie as well. She was a very special lady and a wonderful wife and partner to a complex man....

HALLOWELL — Alan MacLeese, 81, a longtime resident of Hallowell, died suddenly at his home in Jonesport. Al, as he was affectionately known by his friends, led a full life of adventure and charm; he always had a twinkle in his eye....

Al was a born social progressive and an accomplished writer. His columns were full of wit, intellect and insight.

Al moved to Hallowell after the death of his beloved wife, Connie.... He brought along his cats: Fogerty, Faraday and Finley. Al was at home in Hallowell and was embraced by the community, a community that quickly became his family. Al could often be seen walking along the river in the early morning.

He was a sharp dresser and a gentleman, with a generous and gracious heart. He was truly a "Hallowellian" — an honorary townie. Al was a voracious reader who could read a book a day. He enjoyed a competitive game of Scrabble and could finish the Saturday New York Times crossword puzzle in no time at all. Al was a walking dictionary and his stories were vivid and alive.

Al supported his values and his community by supporting the Hubbard Free Library. He was also a great enthusiast of local artists and could be counted on to buy an original painting or photograph at various art shows. Al loved the music in Hallowell, too — although his first choice might have been Frank Sinatra, Dean Martin or Willie Nelson. Or maybe even Lucille Ball up on the big screen.

Always adventurous, Al enjoyed travelling and exploring with members of his Hallowell family — from Moosehead Lake, to Bar Harbor to Las Vegas. Al enjoyed seeing the world and could strike up a conversation with anyone. Al was a great man who had many friends; he was timeless. He will be missed by his Hallowell family. His absence will be felt on holidays, for excursions, walks, talks and afternoon cocktails with friends. Until we meet again, Al, "Over the falls!"

UNLEASHED

A celebration of life will be held from 2 to 5 p.m. Sunday, May 6, at Joyce's restaurant in Hallowell....

[Published by the Kennebec Journal on May 3. This obit was written by Hallowell friend Juliette Guilmette, with an assist from Aaron Green and Bruce Mayo.]

[May 5]

Hi Roger,

With heavy heart I must tell you Alan has passed on. A neighbor in his apt. building notified me that it appeared something might be wrong with Alan. They heard no TV and his cat was at the door crying. Thus the police were notified and that was when Alan was found in the bathroom [by a sheriff's deputy]. It appears he died while getting out of the shower; Alan might have fallen, hitting his head badly on the corner of the sink and thus died.

The sheriff had Alan's body picked up by a Machias funeral home. My mother and I arrived shortly thereafter and stayed in Jonesport for a week, packing his things and clearing out his apartment, returning his books to the library and donating whatever we could to the two churches for their rummage sales and such.

I am still stunned, he was rather healthy regardless of his foot problem, but I bet between getting out of the shower, lifting his foot over the tub and maybe that bad foot gave-way, thus he fell.

I am sorry it took me so long to write to inform you of Alan's passing. We just got back late Thursday pm from Jonesport.

We have spoken with Doug, Alan's son....

Pamela

[Pamela later said Fiona was returned to the Cherryfield animal shelter.]

289

A storyteller's odyssey

[A ready-to-be mailed letter from MacLeese to the shelter, dated April 19, was found in his apartment after he died. In it he said that "Mystic asked that her name be changed to Fiona. This was done." He also offered to do a couple of five-hour shifts a week as a volunteer. "I lack a certain amount of spryness — at 81 I'm no spring chicken — but can do light stuff and am willing for my car to be used if needed."]

[May 5]

(Portions of return email to niece Pamela)

... I last talked to him on April 7, the day I received a letter from him saying Finley had died... By that time, he told me on the phone, he had gotten another cat and named her Fiona. The name was an inside joke between us and our wives during a trip to Toronto eons ago. ["Fiona on Fire" was an X-rated movie advertised on the TVs in our hotel rooms there.]

... in our last conversation, he sounded more comfortable with his lot than he had in a long time. The medical marijuana helped with his foot pain but he didn't sound high, and I have heard his voice often when he was plastered. He said he was off the booze but still drinking beer. He sounded good, and I had been prepared for the worst because of the death of Finley....

Epilogue

Why did Al MacLeese leave his many friends in Hallowell for the remote outpost of Jonesport? No definitive answers from him, but there were indications he was frustrated by elements of his situation in Hallowell. As he said, he wanted to "do something, even if it's wrong."

One source of irritation in Hallowell was the condo he bought. Ownership, he learned, bore a different level of responsibility than that of tenant. In addition to dealing with repairs, his condo-related frustrations included a barking dog upstairs and complaints about his smoking and about Finley spreading fleas.

Perhaps a main reason for the move involved his drinking. MacLeese said there were 13 bars in Hallowell, none in Jonesport. "He definitely thought moving out of Hallowell – to Jonesport – would help with his drinking due to the lack of opportunity," said Juliette Guilmette, one of his friends in Hallowell.

If he cut back on his drinking, he could focus more clearly on his writing. And that was another facet of his Jonesport plan – to begin creating an account of his life.

"I was to take dictation as he went through various stories and things he hoped to put into a book," his niece Pamela said. "He was not wanting to type himself."

Or he couldn't. A big complaint about typing involved his left hand. He couldn't make it perform his will, similar to his problems with his left foot.

Relocating to Jonesport was his third big move apparently related to writing his life story. He took early retirement in 1986 to write, and he also mentioned writing a book as part of his reasons for moving to Maine in 2001.

His first attempt at serious writing ended because of a lack of focus, which also may have been the fate of his second. His last attempt was foreclosed by his death.

According to his death certificate, MacLeese died on April 25.

His sister Joan and her daughter Pamela however, believe there was evidence that he died days earlier after a fall, probably as early as April 20, the day a neighbor heard a cat mewing but no other sounds, such as a TV, from inside his apartment.

On April 24, the cat was still mewing, and the neighbor set off a chain of phone calls that resulted in a sheriff's deputy checking the apartment. The deputy called Pamela with the news: His body had been found on the bathroom floor.

Pamela and Joan believe he fell while stepping out of the tub after taking a shower.

When Joan and Pamela arrived two days later, they found the apartment "in its usual sloppy, disorderly style," with half-eaten pizza on an end table and dried coffee spills everywhere. The cat, Fiona, had already been picked up by the animal shelter.

On his counter were a small stack of books, ready to be returned to the Jonesport library, and the aforementioned April 19 letter to the Ark, the animal shelter in Cherryfield.

Joan took the books across the street to the Peabody Memorial Library, where he was a regular patron, usually taking out four or five books a couple of times a week. That would mean he was maintaining his usual reading pace, as many as two hundred books during his eight months in Jonesport.

Other than basic furniture and a few trinkets, there was not much in his apartment.

"He really hardly kept anything, especially anything of value," Pamela said.

MacLeese's body was cremated, and in October a portion of his ashes was taken to Back Bay's Crow Island Cemetery in Charlotte

County, New Brunswick, where they were buried next to his great great grandfather.

Pamela called him Uncle Vanya, a character in a Chekhov play by that name, and in early January, she invited "Uncle Vanya" to her home, a two-hour-plus drive west of Jonesport, to celebrate their early January birthdays. That was the last time she saw him.

The face of the man she saw had not aged well, with decades of smoking likely taking a toll, evolving from the chiseled "Gregory Peck" of his early manhood to the baggy-faced Walter Matthau of "Grumpy Old Men" in Jonesport.

When he left, Pamela said, "I told him I would see him the first of May" in Jonesport.

Shortly after that trip, he made an unannounced visit to Hallowell in mid-January, the last time his friends there saw him.

Some of those friends were excited that MacLeese was talking about moving back to Hallowell when his Jonesport lease was up in September.

Even though MacLeese talked about moving back to Hallowell, Guilmette said, "I think he knew it would be the same for him regarding drinking if he moved back ... the tension, it seemed, was between having his friends around who loved him dearly, and being in a drinking environment."

His sister Joan said she thought the talk of moving back to Hallowell was a momentary thing, for a week or two, in the depths of winter. She said he talked more seriously of moving to Eastport, about 60 miles east of Jonesport. In a letter three weeks before his death, he wrote complimentarily about Eastport and added: "You can't get any more east and still be in the contiguous forty-eight."

After a life often on the edge, he would be literally on the edge, the edge of U.S. territory.

For MacLeese, a big attraction in Jonesport was the atmosphere; he loved being close to the water and the activity on the waterfront, watching the "lobster hunters chug out to the open sea." And yet, because it had no bars, no restaurants, not even a place to have breakfast, Jonesport offered no obvious venue to socialize, to tell stories.

His emails and letters became less frequent in Jonesport, maybe because there was so little going on to tell about, no activities involving friends. He mentioned only two people in town by name, the librarian and the postmistress.

"Even though I think Al liked it in Jonesport, I got the feeling that he missed us – and may have felt isolated," Guilmette said. "Even though he felt that getting away would be good for him, he liked talking and meeting people."

She remembers when she first met Al, he was "sitting at the bar in a button-down shirt, a red windbreaker, and a fedora, elbow on the bar, hand waving in the air conducting his own story – a screwdriver in front of him, his eyes twinkling with the joke he'd just told or in anticipation of the one he would tell in a moment."

Guilmette said MacLeese "always listened to people, but he also always had stories to tell. He was a wonderful storyteller – intelligent and funny – and everyone wanted to listen to him talk. There was a lot of laughter involved – Al had such an interesting mix of 'old school' properness, dry wit and grit to his stories, and the way he told them."

On his last visit to Hallowell, Guilmette got a call from a friend. "He said that Al was in town and sitting at Joyce's bar. I had no idea he was coming....

"When I walked in, he had a whole crowd around him," which was not uncommon. He was "telling the outlandish adventure of getting his 'green' card [for medical marijuana] and making his first legal purchase of marijuana at a 'wellness' facility. He was making everyone laugh...."

Another day in the life of Al MacLeese, storyteller to the end.

UNLEASHED

Acknowledgements

This book would not exist without the assistance of many people.

I owe a major debt to MacLeese's oldest sister, Joan, whom he once described as the only person he had known his entire life. She patiently suffered my intrusive and repetitive questions, especially about his early years, and connected me with others who knew him during his grade-school days.

Our first conversation didn't take place until after he died and after I had broached the idea of writing a book in an email to her daughter, Pamela. Pamela and I had exchanged emails starting a few months before MacLeese died. When his emails stopped, she helped me reconnect with him by phone and graciously continued to provide answers to my questions about sundry topics, including the circumstances of his death, his genetic background and her conversations with him.

Joan, who would become the executor of his estate, loaned me numerous family photos that helped fill in blanks in his history. She also gave me permission to use his correspondence.

His sister Deborah also gave great assistance. An expressive writer in her own right, she helped immensely in describing his relationship with his family during the years before he married Connie. His longtime friend Bob Hardin, who knew him well during MacLeese's drifter years, helped clear up confusion during that same period when MacLeese was changing jobs more than three times a year. Hardin also was generous in sharing his insight into MacLeese's personality.

Special mention must be given to my wife, Jessica, and three former colleagues of mine and MacLeese at the Flint Journal, Don Dahlstrom, Dennis Herrick and Bob DeLand. They read versions of the manuscript and made valuable suggestions.

Grateful acknowledgement is made for permission to quote numerous excerpts from MacLeese's columns and other material referring to him that appeared in two newspapers:

–The Flint Journal, copyright for various years from 1969-2012. All rights reserved. Reprinted with permission.

–The Saginaw News. Copyright 1997 and 2001. All rights reserved. Reprinted with permission.

I also want to thank the numerous other people who were interviewed by me, exchanged emails in providing recollections about MacLeese, or made other contributions. Many are quoted directly in this work.

Special thanks go to Peter C. Cavanaugh, Lou Giampetroni, Juliette Guilmette, Betty Hansen, Jim Houck and MacLeese's third wife, Laurie. Their help was greatly appreciated.

28106245R00181

Made in the USA
Lexington, KY
05 December 2013